"From the second I learned about Hands-math conference, I couldn't wait to try tl this beautiful, inspiring book that allows us to dive in and imagine the possibilities of engaging our students meaningfully and critically in listening to one another and building theories to understand and improve our world.

There is so much to love about this book that I hardly know where to begin. For elementary teachers, to consider how to plan for, navigate, and reflect on discussions across the school day and across disciplinary contexts is a gift because it is so often overlooked in professional materials. Kassia and Christy have forged a powerful collaboration in bringing to life what students are capable of accomplishing through Hands-Down Conversations.

This book challenged me to think about facilitating discussions in a whole new way. Shifting authority to our students to discuss in-process ideas is a goal many of us hold and involves incredibly complex work, not the least of which is selecting discussion-worthy tasks, listening ever so carefully to who participates and how and to what ends, and lifting out important social topics that students need to reflect on in order to grow.

Hands Down, Speak Out will guide you to take the leap and be there with you as you encounter your first questions about how to navigate the nuances and complexities of listening and supporting students to "speak into the silence." The rich examples for how to use micro-lessons, Conversation Clubs, Turn and Talks, and Hands-Down Conversations bring to life ways of engaging children in the work of critical mathematics and literacy. No doubt this book will help you consider with your colleagues the goals you have for advancing equity and justice in our educational systems and the liberatory possibilities of engaging critically with mathematics and literacy. So I urge you to gather a few colleagues, read this book together, and waste no time in growing and deepening your practice.

—Elham Kazemi, coauthor of *Intentional Talk: How to Structure and Lead Productive Mathematical Discussions* and coeditor of *Choral Counting & Counting Collections: Transforming the PreK–5 Math Classroom*

" Imagine this: joyous classrooms brimming with curious children earnestly exploring ideas through the interconnected work of talking and listening. What do these classrooms sound like? What do they look like? And, how do we all create these environments for our children? Chapter by chapter, *Hands Down, Speak Out* offers a clear progression of lessons for teaching into the often-messy dynamic of talk in ways that support teachers and students alike. This work has the potential to transform learning communities and lift all individuals within the community. Today is the perfect day to get started!

—Maria Nichols, author of *Comprehension Through Conversation* and *Building Bigger Ideas*

" *Hands Down, Speak Out: Listening and Talking Across Literacy and Math* by Kassia Omohundro Wedekind and Christy Hermann Thompson is both a timely book and a timeless book. It is timely given the complex and challenging sociopolitical climate in which we find ourselves and timeless given its underlying message of the importance of creating spaces where children are able to speak out and take on the challenges of today's world, in order to participate in ways that contribute to making the world a better, more equitable place for all. This is the kind of book that I believe will inform teaching and learning for years to come.

The book is written in a way that readily transports its readers into classrooms where teachers and students intentionally, and powerfully, engage in real life issues, drawn organically from the interests and passions of children. Through beautifully told stories of life in classrooms, Kassia and Christy guide their reader to an understanding of different discourses at play including a discourse that fully supports students as readers, writers, and mathematicians as well as discourses that create spaces for students to participate powerfully in the world in and out of school. Following each story are suggestions and/or strategies for engaging in such discursive practices that can be used with diverse texts including picture books, advertisements, websites and social networking texts, for taking up sociopolitical issues such as gender, race, and consumerism.

As I savor each page of the book, a theme that stands out is, at its core, this book is also about how to be together as a community, and the discourses that inform that being together, as well as the building of a classroom where all students are valued as competent thinkers and doers with experiences that matter, and that can inform the thinking of the group as a whole, in the classroom and beyond."

—Vivian Maria Vasquez, author of *Negotiating Critical Literacies with Young Children* and *Getting Beyond "I Like the Book": Creating Space for Critical Literacy in K-6 Classrooms*

Hands Down
Speak Out

Hands Down
Speak Out

Listening and Talking Across
LITERACY and MATH K-5

Kassia Omohundro Wedekind & Christy Hermann Thompson

Stenhouse
PUBLISHERS

www.stenhouse.com

PORTSMOUTH, NEW HAMPSHIRE

Stenhouse Publishers
www.stenhouse.com

Figure 7.4: © 2019 Faith Ringgold / Artists Rights Society (ARS), New York, Courtesy ACA Galleries, New York

Figure 8.4 is from *Chameleon, Chameleon* by Joy Cowley, photographs by Nic Bishop. Text copyright © 2005 by Joy Cowley. Photographs copyright © 2005 by Nic Bishop. Reprinted by permission of Scholastic, Inc.

Figure 4.1 is from Science World, February 12, 2012. Copyright © 2012 by Scholastic, Inc. Reprinted by permission of Scholastic Inc.

Library of Congress Cataloging-in-Publication Data
Names: Wedekind, Kassia Omohundro, author. | Hermann Thompson, Christy, author.
Title: Hands down, speak out : listening and talking across literacy and math / Kassia
    Omohundro Wedekind and Christy Hermann Thompson.
Description: Portsmouth, New Hampshire : Stenhouse Publishers, 2020. | Includes
    bibliographical references and index. |
Identifiers: LCCN 2019057556 | ISBN 9781625312693 (paperback)
    | ISBN 9781625312709 (ebook)
Subjects: LCSH: Thought and thinking--Study and teaching (Elementary) | Listening--Study
    and teaching (Elementary) | Oral communication—Study and teaching (Elementary) |
    Discussion--Study and teaching (Elementary) | Language arts—Correlation with content
    subjects.
Classification: LCC LB1590.3 .W44 2020 | DDC 371.102/2—dc23
LC record available at https://lccn.loc.gov/2019057556

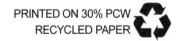

PRINTED ON 30% PCW
RECYCLED PAPER

Cover design and illustration: Natalia Cardona Puerta
Interior design, and typesetting by Gina Poirier, Gina Poirier Design
Author photo on back cover taken by Sanya Chopra

Manufactured in the United States of America

26 25 24 23 22 21 20   9 8 7 6 5 4 3 2 1

To Ella, Frank, Louisa, and Sage

For inspiring us with
the ideas you talk about
and reminding us how much
we still have to learn.

CONTENTS

Foreword by Peter H. Johnston .... *xi*

Acknowledgments .... *xiv*

Section I **A Brief Introduction to Hands-Down Conversations, the Authors, and Coconuts** *1*

Chapter 1 Hands-Down Conversations: The *Why* *7*

Chapter 2 Becoming a Hands-Down Teacher *20*

Chapter 3 Facilitating the Hands-Down Conversation *29*

Section II **Orienting Students to Dialogue: The Micro-lessons** *40*

Chapter 4 Jumping In *50*

Chapter 5 Talking About Our Ideas *78*

Chapter 6 Listening and Linking Ideas *94*

Chapter 7 Growing Ideas Together *112*

Section III **Exploring the Crossover: Conversations in Literacy and Math Classrooms** *132*

Chapter 8 Nurturing Disagreement *136*

Chapter 9 Developing Theories Together *156*

Chapter 10 Engaging with the World *181*

Parting Thoughts *212*

Appendix A If You Notice . . . Try . . . : A Complete List of Dialogue Micro-lessons *213*

Appendix B Conversation Map Template *219*

Appendix C Sample Social and Classroom Community Topics *220*

Professional Resources and References *221*

Children's Literature References *226*

Index *227*

FOREWORD

Hands Down, Speak Out: Teaching to Maximize Development (and Possibly Save the World)

Peter H. Johnston

Knowing how to build ideas together, to disagree civilly and productively, and to collaboratively solve problems is the foundation of civilization. All advanced human accomplishments have been, directly or indirectly, collaborative accomplishments mediated through language: higher mathematics, modern medicine, cell phones, music, theater, and certainly democratic society itself. Multiple minds working well together overcome the limitations of individual minds. When children know how to think together well, they can solve more problems collaboratively than can groups who have not learned how to think together (Mercer, Wegerif, and Dawes 1999). But that's not all. As they become more capable as a group, the individuals in the group become more capable than students who have not learned how to think together. This, alone, should place the ability to think together at the center of school curricula. It would also be sufficient reason to put *Hands Down, Speak Out* at the top of teachers' and administrators' reading lists, though there are many more reasons to do so.

Without knowing it, I have been waiting for this book. Engagingly written, thoroughly practical, and consistent with a large body of research, *Hands Down, Speak Out* is a systematic and responsive approach to maximizing children's ability to think together. I say *systematic* because the authors' practice is organized to strategically build from entry-level skills and understandings to more complex ones. At the same time, it is *responsive* because Christy and Kassia make it clear that the array of well-structured "micro-lessons" they provide should not simply be delivered in sequence. Rather, they recognize that different groups of children have different chemistries, bringing different individual and collective understandings, propensities, and relationships to classroom life. Consequently, they will not encounter the need for particular lessons in the same order. With concrete examples, Christy and Kassia show us how to recognize when particular lessons are appropriate, what those lessons might look like, and how to improvise in the immediate context.

Christy and Kassia make little distinction between thinking together in language arts and in mathematics. As they point out, categorizing knowledge in these ways has its limitations: becoming critically literate requires an understanding of math. Indeed, if they had written a longer book, they could have included other categories of knowledge such as science and social studies and still have been consistent with research. The interleaving of math and language arts examples is particularly useful because it helps us to more easily generalize the principles and practices they offer.

Although advanced human accomplishments depend on the skills, understandings, and propensities described in this book, there are even stronger reasons for teachers to read it. Vygotsky (1978) taught us that individual minds are created in the process of thinking and acting together with others. Indeed, the kind of conversations described in this book result in considerable individual intellectual development, including not only better reading comprehension (Rojas-Drummond et al. 2014) and better understanding in science and math (Mercer and Sams 2008), but also better abstract reasoning and creative thinking (Mercer, Wegerif, and Dawes 1999; Wegerif 2005). Children who experience these conversations also become more persuasive, partly because they are more likely to provide evidence and reasons for their perspective (Latawiec et al. 2016).

Although these intellectual benefits are well documented, it would be a mistake to assume that intellectual activity is merely about academic achievement and reasoning. Children who experience Hands-Down Conversations become more expressive and willing to speak in public (Trickey and Topping 2004) with increased confidence (Trickey and Topping 2006). Intellectual activity is not separate from the emotions and relationships that color, motivate, and enable it. In my own work with colleagues, we find that as children engage in conversations taking different perspectives, they become more understanding, develop better relationships, have stronger moral reasoning, and acquire a better understanding of both themselves and others (Ivey and Johnston 2013, Johnston et al., 2020). Indeed, I often wonder how many future marriages and friendships these teachers save as they teach children how to think and solve problems together, engaging their partners' perspectives.

It is no exaggeration to say that human development, both collective and individual, is made possible by the qualities of our collaborative intellectual practices. In fact, I sometimes wonder how the world will survive if children do not experience the sort of teaching presented in this book.

References

Ivey, Gay, and Peter Johnston. 2013. "Engagement with Young Adult Literature: Outcomes and Processes." *Reading Research Quarterly* 48 (3): 1–21.

Johnston, Peter, Kathy Champeau, Andrea Hartwig, Sarah Helmer, Merry Komar, Tara Krueger, and Laurie McCarthy. 2020. *Engaging Literate Minds: Developing Children's Social, Emotional, and Intellectual Lives, K–3.* Portsmouth, NH: Stenhouse.

Latawiec, Beata M., Richard C. Anderson, Ma Shufeng, and Nguyen-Jahiel Kim. 2016. "Influence of Collaborative Reasoning Discussions on Metadiscourse in Children's Essays." *Text & Talk* 36 (1): 23–46. doi: 10.1515/text-2016-0002.

Mercer, Neil, and Claire Sams. 2008. "Teaching Children How to Use Language to Solve Maths Problems." *Language and Education* 20 (6): 507–528.

Mercer, Neil, Rupert Wegerif, and Lyn Dawes. 1999. "Children's Talk and the Development of Reasoning in the Classroom." *British Educational Research Journal* 25 (1): 95–111.

Rojas-Drummond, Sylvia, Nancy Mazón, Karen Littleton, and Maricela Vélez. 2014. "Developing Reading Comprehension through Collaborative Learning." *Journal of Research in Reading* 37 (2): 138–158. doi: 10.1111 /j.1467-9817.2011.01526.x.

Trickey, S., and K. J. Topping. 2004. "'Philosophy for Children': A Systematic Review." *Research Papers in Education* 19 (3): 365–380.

———. 2006. "Collaborative Philosophical Enquiry for School Children." *School Psychology International* 27 (5): 599–614.

Vygotsky, Lev S. 1978. *Mind in Society: The Development of Higher Psychological Processes.* Cambridge, MA: Harvard University Press.

Wegerif, Rupert. 2005. "Reason and Creativity in Classroom Dialogues." *Language & Education: An International Journal* 19 (3): 223–237.

ACKNOWLEDGMENTS

We must first thank the students of Bailey's and Belvedere Elementary Schools. Listening to you talk is what inspired us to write this book. We're so glad the future of the world is in the hands of kids like you!

We are deeply grateful to the amazing teachers of Belvedere Elementary School—in particular, to Sanya Chopra, Yolanda Corado Cendejas, Mary Beth Dillane, Stephanie Hammel, Emily Jemison, Preshion Lynch, Kathleen Maturan, Janet McHale, Alexa McKenrick, Ellen Rogers, and Margaret Summers, who were part of the Hands-Down Conversation study group. These teachers met with us monthly before school to talk about dialogue, analyze transcripts, and give us incredibly helpful feedback. We are also thankful to Pagan Bragdon, Sanya Chopra, Yolanda Corado Cendejas, Mary Beth Dillane, Kelsey Friend, Allyson Gray, Lisa Gump, Steve Miner, Jess Mundy, Ellen Rogers, Margaret Summers, and Wendy Welch for welcoming us into their classrooms to play with Hands-Down Conversations as we wrote this book, sharing their insightful reflections and ideas with us. We are continually inspired by Belvedere teachers' deep commitment to listening to children and letting their ideas lead the way.

Thank you also to the Mt. Eagle Elementary School kindergarten team—teachers Althea Goldberg, Katie Keier, and Kara Reid and math coach Michelle Gale—for teaching us so much about the brilliance our youngest students bring to school and the ways in which they are already so good at listening to and talking with each other.

There are some teachers who we don't see every day anymore, but whose ideas stay with us and whose advice we continually seek. Kathy Birge, Tricia Brown, Mary Anne Buckley, Kath Fay, Carol Felderman, Melissa Fleischer, Katie Keier, Steve Miner, Lauren Schrum, Melanie Rick, and Suzanne Whaley, our time learning and teaching together at Bailey's Elementary will always be in our hearts and minds no matter where we are.

We are grateful for the professional fuel and friendship Jen Corcoran has given us over dinners with many tiny plates and much laughter. Our train rides back and forth to New York City left our brains full of ideas and questions to pursue.

Sara Kugler, we are equally thankful for the ways you have contributed to our thinking about talk and for the way you taught us to parent at playgrounds. Thank you for being a reflection partner on all the things that matter.

We are lucky to have worked with administrators who have supported our learning and believed in the power of student dialogue. Jay McClain, Cecilia Vanderhye, and Lauren Badini, thank you for making space in your schools for your teachers and students to grow and learn in authentic, meaningful ways.

We are very appreciative of Pat Johnson's input and advice on this project. Pat selflessly gave her time to read every word of this manuscript and share valuable feedback with us. We are so lucky to have a literacy education expert and author who is also our generous friend. There's no one else we'd rather meet for lunch at Panera!

Thank you to Peter Johnston, who first got us thinking about talk across content areas with his book *Choice Words*, and whose work we return to again and again.

Thank you to our wonderful editor, Tracy Zager, for the deep care she took with our book. She encouraged us when we needed it and helped us work through the hard spots. Thank you for supporting us in the moments when we were breathing into paper bags, battling dragons in basements, giving birth to ornery babies, and whatever other odd metaphor of the day we had for our writing and revising process.

Thank you to all the amazing folks at Stenhouse Publishers for their hard work and belief in this book. Shannon St. Peter tracked down permissions and is just generally extraordinary. Amanda Bondi, our amazing production editor, helped us move from plain words on a page to a beautiful book. Natalia Cardona Puerta illustrated and designed the delightful cover. Gina Poirier designed the exquisite interior of the book. Thank you also to the incredible marketing team, Jill Backman, Faye LaCasse, and Lisa Sullivan and the entire production, sales, and operation teams. And thank you to Stenhouse's publisher, Dan Tobin, for his support of us and this book.

From Christy

To my husband, Jeremy: your support for this endeavor has been unwaveringly enthusiastic from the start. Thank you for helping me, without a moment's hesitation, create space in our lives to write this book. You are my best friend, and an excellent cheerleader as well.

To my Hermann and Thompson families: Thank you for your interest and encouragement during this project. I am very lucky to have all of you. A special thank-you to my parents, Pat and Jeff Hermann, for tirelessly listening to me talk for more than four decades and fostering my identity as a writer from a very early age.

To my Belvedere office mates, Yasemin Bayraktar, Mika Burkett, Stephanie Hammel, Emily Jemison, Preshion Lynch, and my other half at work, Alexa McKenrick: Thank you for the encouragement, the laughs, and the hot beverages. You people make any workday brighter.

To Suzanne Whaley, Kathleen Fay, and Sara Kugler: Thank you for guiding the giant cruise ship we call the Fairfax County Public Schools Literacy Department into brave new waters. I have been honored to be on the ride.

To Rosary Lalik and Vivian Vasquez: Both of you taught me that a literacy educator has the power to be a change agent and a rebel, and demonstrated that you believed in my potential to work toward that noble goal. Thank you.

From Kassia

To Aron: When I asked, "Do you think I can write this book?" you responded, "Yes!" without hesitation or doubt. Your support, unwavering belief in me, and humor always keep me going. Now get off my chaise!

To my family—the one I was born into and the one I married into: Thank you for asking how my writing and work were going and also for giving me a wonderful space outside of work and writing.

To coffee—lattes when I can get them, but mostly just regular old java from my coffee pot at home and occasionally a lukewarm cup I've forgotten in the microwave: Let's be honest. I couldn't have written this book without you, friend. I tried to convince Christy of your benefits, but alas, she's still drinking something noncaffeinated called a turmeric latte.

To Toby Gordon (Look! You're right after coffee! I knew you'd understand): Thank you for being my first editor and, even more importantly, my good friend. Your advice on writing and pretty much anything else is always spot on. I hope this is a "good enough" book.

Thank you to my editorial colleagues at Stenhouse—Maureen Barbieri, Jay Kilburn, Terry Thompson, Dan Tobin, Bill Varner, and Tracy Zager. Each week in our editorial meetings you teach me something about bookmaking, writing, and what it means to be a writer.

I'm forever grateful to Chandra Lowe, who made me feel like a "real" Stenhouse author when I was a newbie and became my conference buddy and dear friend.

Thank you to my Fairfax County math coach colleagues, especially Lynne Bursch, Mary Beth Dillane, Mimi Granados, Kelly Halpin, and Wendy Wall. I am so lucky to have taught and coached with colleagues who continually challenge my thinking with their ideas and inspire me to pursue my own questions.

Thank you to my math colleague friends who have contributed immensely to my understanding of what it means to nurture a community of mathematicians. Some of these friends—including Christopher Danielson, Heidi Fessenden, Megan Franke, Allison Hintz, Elham Kazemi, Jenna Laib, and Tracy Zager—especially pushed my thinking around talk and listening.

1

A Brief Introduction to Hands-Down Conversations, the Authors, and Coconuts

One afternoon, years ago, Kassia ducked into Christy's first-grade classroom to borrow some masking tape. As Kassia entered the classroom, she noticed Christy and her first graders sitting together in a circle, with a coconut, a hammer, and a screwdriver in the middle of their meeting area. "So, what are you thinking about this coconut?" asked Christy.

"What's gonna be in there when we cut it open?" called out an eager student.

"Hmm . . . that's an interesting question. Let's ask our Turn and Talk partners that question and see what we're thinking," Christy prompted.

The classroom burst into immediate debate. The coconut would be filled with rainwater. The coconut would be filled with milk, but not cow milk. The coconut would be empty, because it makes a hollow sound when you tap on it. The coconut would be filled with millions and millions of tiny ants.

Kassia's search for the masking tape was forgotten. She stood inside Christy's classroom, totally captivated by the coconut conversation. Christy knelt beside the Turn and Talk partnerships, listening to her students' ideas, jotting a few notes, and gently prompting them on how to engage with and respond to each other's ideas.

"It's the milk inside there," said Angeli, confidently. Carl, her partner, rubbed his shoelaces back and forth across the rug, seeming unsure of what to say or do next.

"You can keep the talk going by asking your partner a question like 'Why do you think that?'" Christy whispered to Carl.

"Oh yeah! Why do you think that?" asked Carl, looking up at his partner, relieved and curious.

"My mom buys coconut milk at the store. So, maybe they do the cutting up the coconut at the store, and then pour it in the bottle for you to buy the milk."

A lot of details surrounding this story have been lost in the subsequent years since Kassia came to borrow masking tape and stayed for the coconut. Namely, what in the world were Christy and her class doing with that coconut in the first place? Did they actually ever get it open? And were there a million ants inside? Neither of us remembers.

But what we do remember is that our shared interest in classroom discourse across literacy, math, and sometimes coconuts grew out of tiny moments like this one, in which we slowed down to really listen deeply to how children talk with and listen to each other. It is through this kind of intentional listening to both the content of children's ideas and the ways in which they communicate these ideas that we began to develop the questions that drive this book:

- How can we create communities in which talk is a vehicle for students to build identities as readers, writers, and mathematicians?
- How do we create talk communities that are accessible to everyone, especially those whose voices have traditionally been left out of classroom discourse?
- How can we make space for students' ideas to lead the conversation and also meet our instructional goals?
- How can we value the interconnected roles of speaker and listener?
- How can we, as teachers, facilitate classroom conversations without taking over the thinking?

This is a book about what it means to live these questions on a daily basis. And while this book focuses on Hands-Down Conversations as a powerful tool for doing this work, it is really a book about transforming classroom communities through discourse and empowering students to transform the world beyond the classroom with their words and their actions.

So, What's a Hands-Down Conversation?

Hands-Down Conversations are, most simply put, conversations that flow among students without the use of hand-raising, and in which the teacher is not the primary speaker. The structure of a Hands-Down Conversation is intentionally simple and predictable so that the real work of the conversation is focused on constructing meaning, not on following a set of complicated rules.

In Hands-Down Conversations students gather in a circle facing one another. The teacher sits just outside the circle, listening deeply, taking notes, and sometimes entering the conversation briefly to facilitate.

There are three basic guidelines for Hands-Down Conversations:

1. No hands. Listen for the space to slide your voice into the conversation.

2. One voice at a time (more or less!).

3. Listen closely to everyone's ideas.

Hands-Down Conversations are designed to deepen the level of classroom discourse by creating conditions in which students take on greater ownership and have more decision-making power in conversation. The students' ideas lead the conversation. And yet, while the teacher's voice is much less present in

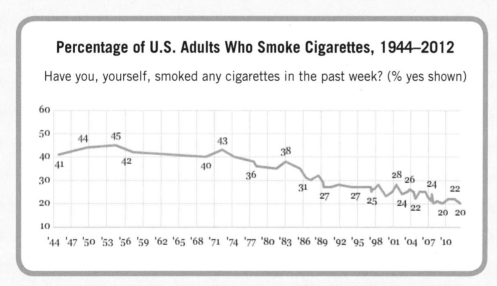

Figure I.1 Fifth-grade students analyze a graph about cigarette smoking.

Hands-Down Conversations than in traditional classroom discourse, the role of the teacher in facilitating the meaning-making remains critical.

Let's take a peek into two classrooms to get a feel for the kind of talk happening in Hands-Down Conversations.

It's November. Students in Yolanda Corado Cendejas's fifth-grade class are gathered in their meeting area, analyzing a line graph about cigarette smoking in the United States. The students spend a few minutes noticing and wondering about the parts of the graph. What do those numbers on the x-axis and y-axis mean? What does that title tell us this graph is about? What does the shape of the line indicate is happening with cigarette smoking over time? There's a pause in the conversation, and then Brandon asks a question.

Brandon: But where did this graph come from?

Marta: Probably from the Internet, right?

Brandon: Yeah, but I mean, like who made it?

Alexa: I think maybe a doctor made it. Like maybe a doctor is trying to show her patients that smoking is really bad for you. It can turn your lungs black and you can die.

Gabriela: Yeah, but we said that smoking is going down. See, that line is bumpy but it goes down from forty-one to twenty. So not that many people are smoking.

Isaac: But it's not zero. Some people are still smoking every week, and maybe the doctor is trying to get that line down to zero. Twenty percent is still some people.

Alison: The doctor is trying to show people this graph he made and tell them that other people are stopping smoking and you should too.

It's March. Christy has just read the book Something Beautiful, *by Sharon Dennis Wyeth (2002), to Steve Miner's second graders. The book tells the story of a little girl who is looking for "something beautiful" in her neighborhood but isn't sure she can find it. She asks several neighbors what is beautiful in their lives, and they show her: a baby's smile, a pair of new shoes, an array of fresh produce, a jump-rope routine. The girl returns home and is told by her mother that she is the beauty in her mother's life.*

After listening to Christy's read-aloud of Something Beautiful, *the students begin to discuss what they think beauty is.*

Byner: I think *beautiful* means like something that you really like and really want and it makes you feel really good.

Lionel: Yeah, 'cause the meaning of *beautiful* is not the way something looks, it's what you make with your heart.

Rechna: I agree with Lionel 'cause it's like a joy. It just makes you feel happy when you think about it.

Lilly: I agree with Lionel and Rechna. Because beauty can be everything.

Charlie: But, well, if something breaks and you try to fix it back and it doesn't look the same, then you start not liking it.

Christy: Can I interrupt for a second? 'Cause I hear something interesting. Some of you are saying, "Anything COULD be beautiful," but I also hear some of you saying, "If a beautiful thing breaks or gets old, it's not beautiful anymore." So there's something to talk about there. Could *anything* be beautiful?

Niles: It could be possible. If something is beautiful to you it is your opinion.

Charlie: But I used to have this necklace that was shiny and then it got this brown stuff on it. I tried to wash the necklace, but it never cleaned up.

Lionel: But it was still beautiful though, wasn't it, Charlie? Anything can be beautiful, 'cause it's in your memory. If you had something beautiful once, then you always still have it in your heart.

In both Yolanda's fifth-grade classroom and Steve's second-grade classroom the students are talking—asking questions, listening to reasoning, nudging each other's ideas along, and constructing new meaning together through talking and listening. This kind of discourse does not develop accidentally, but rather through sustained and intentional opportunities for students to learn about dialogue and engage with each other's ideas.

Understanding the Structure of This Book

This book is a guide to a different kind of classroom discourse, a discourse that nurtures students as readers, writers, and mathematicians, but also a discourse that empowers students to use their voices beyond the classroom walls.

The book is divided into three sections.

In Section I we lay the foundation for becoming a Hands-Down Conversation community. We explore why this tool is so powerful for our learners and describe practical considerations that can serve as your guide as you begin to use and facilitate Hands-Down Conversations in your classroom.

In Section II we introduce the idea of micro-lessons, which are designed to help students develop and exercise their dialogue muscles. While we present the lessons in a progression of complexity, you will learn how to thoughtfully choose from the many micro-lessons within this book, as well as how to develop your own dialogue micro-lessons that are responsive to what you are noticing in your own classroom.

In Section III we dive into developing deep learning in literacy and math using Hands-Down Conversations. We explore three kinds of Hands-Down Conversations that we use across these content areas and support you as you plan these for your own classroom.

Our hope is that this book guides you and your students as you co-construct classroom spaces that inspire and empower. We believe that the development of dialogue is worth the investment of time and energy not only because it has the power to deepen our understanding of literacy and mathematics, but because it has the power to deepen our understanding of ourselves, the people in our community, and the world.

1

Hands-Down Conversations
The *Why*

As educators we are politicians; we engage in politics when we educate. And if we dream about democracy, let us fight, day and night, for a school in which we talk to and with learners so that, hearing them, we can be heard by them as well.

—Paulo Freire, *Teachers as Cultural Workers*

Setting the Stage for a New Kind of Discourse

As mothers of preschoolers, we are deeply familiar with many episodes of *Sesame Street*. As teachers, we are particularly interested in the segments that are designed to orient young children to the norms of school. In one particular musical vignette, entitled "Two Different Worlds," singer Ed Sheeran croons along with *Sesame Street* characters Elmo, Cookie Monster, Grover, and Abby about the differences between our school and home worlds.

> *I live in two different worlds like lots of other boys and girls. One's at home with my family. The other's school where I learn all I can be. I live in two different worlds. At home, I can speak whenever I please. I can talk real loud and shoot the breeze. School I raise my hand in the air when there's something that I want to share.*

A little YouTube research reveals that *Sesame Street* has produced at least five other similar musical vignettes on the topic of hand-raising as a critical norm for school. Norms like hand-raising are clearly a deeply ingrained part of classroom discourse. And that makes sense! Hand-raising *can* be a useful tool for facilitating turn-taking among a large group of people. However, hand-raising can also be part of a kind of classroom discourse that encourages compliance over agency and answer-performing over constructing meaning. Too often, school discourse ignores and devalues the home and community discourse skills all kids bring to school. In order to make a shift to a classroom discourse that is inclusive and empowering, we need some new tools.

Let's take a look at the following exchange from a first-grade class that has just finished reading *A Chair for My Mother*, by Vera B. Williams (1982):

Teacher: So, who has an idea about what Vera Williams was trying to say with this book? What was her message to us?

(Five children raise their hands; teacher chooses Jenice.)

Jenice: I think she was saying you should save your money.

Teacher: Okay, good, so the main character needed to save money over time to buy something big. That's true. But what else is the author trying to say? What about the family? Christof?

Christof: Umm . . . She loved her family. Her mom.

Teacher: Mm-hmm, yes, so what is the author saying about that?

(Three children raise hands; teacher chooses Tomás.)

Tomás: That loving families are important?

Teacher: Yes, families are important. Why was the family important in this book?

(Three children raise hands; teacher looks at Jenice and Tomás, who have already talked, and decides to choose the new hand up, Marcus.)

Marcus: They had to work together.

Teacher: Yes! So we learn from this book that families have to work together. It's like how we've learned in social studies about how communities have to work together. Especially in hard times, right? Just like when the family in this book had a fire.

This conversation probably sounds like pretty typical classroom talk. In fact, it sounds similar to many conversations we have had in our own classrooms and to most of the conversations we had in the classrooms we grew up in as children. However, despite and even because of our familiarity with this kind of conversation, it is important to slow down and recognize some troubling patterns within it.

This conversation, like much of classroom discourse, is characterized by the pattern of Initiate-Respond-Evaluate (IRE), in which the teacher asks the whole class a question (Initiate), a student raises their hand to respond with an answer (Respond), and the teacher evaluates the answer as right or wrong (Evaluate) (Cazden 2001). In this kind of conversation, there is little room for negotiating meaning or lingering over questions to which the teacher does not already have an answer in mind.

Moving Toward Dialogue

The shift from traditional classroom discourse to a more dialogic discourse has been of interest to many teachers and researchers over the years. Ralph Peterson and Maryann Eeds (2007) describe "grand conversations" in which children construct meaning through talk in literature groups. Lucy Calkins (2000) and Jennifer Serravallo (2010) write about "whole-class conversations" as a structure designed to move students' discussions about their reading beyond literal comprehension in order to focus on what a text "is really, really about" (Calkins, 15). With respect to math, Chapin, O'Connor, and Anderson's *Classroom Discussions in Math* (2013) introduces teachers to the idea of "talk moves," a set of talk tools designed to deepen the level of mathematical discussion. Kazemi and Hintz build on this work in *Intentional Talk* (2014) by introducing different conversation structures that support students as they use talk to reason, justify, and figure out why things work in math.

Hands-Down Conversations build on these educators' work to deepen the level of classroom talk. Calkins makes the argument that communities of readers are grounded in rich, authentic talk that happens daily, rather than occasionally. She writes, "If we want children to read with wide-awake minds, then we need to invite them to live this way in the dailiness of our classrooms. Teaching reading, then, is rather like teaching living" (2000, 15). We believe this sentiment is true beyond children's reading lives. When we build talk communities with children, our greatest hope is that what they learn through talking about reading, writing, and math is matched by what they learn about living in the world with others.

Making the Shift

As we work alongside our students to create intentional talking and listening communities, we should continually spend time reflecting on ways our actions empower and disempower student voices. In considering what place Hands-Down Conversations have in your talk community, it is important to take some time to compare characteristics of traditional classroom discourse to the kind of discourse we strive to build in a Hands-Down Conversation community.

Traditional Classroom Discourse	Hands-Down Conversation Communities
The teacher is positioned as the "primary knower" (Boyd and Galda 2011).	All students are positioned as competent members of the community with important ideas.

In his classic book, *Pedagogy of the Oppressed* (2018), Paulo Freire describes the banking model of instruction in which the role of the teacher is to be an expert giver of knowledge who makes regular "deposits" of information in the students' minds. The role of the student is to passively receive and recite this information.

It is tempting, many years after the first publication of Freire's work, to reject the banking model of instruction as archaic. Surely we have moved past these oppressive patterns of teacher-student interaction! And yet, fully breaking with the notion of teacher as "primary knower" has proved difficult. We, as teachers, still do the majority of the talking in classrooms. And even in cases in which the conversation is opened up for student input, as in the example of the discussion around *A Chair for My Mother*, classroom conversations often revolve around a game of "guess what the teacher is thinking," as students work to perform a set of knowledge that the teacher has predetermined as true.

It turns out that it is much easier to *say* we believe all students are competent thinkers with valuable ideas than to actually live this in our classrooms. Kassia recently watched a video of herself leading a number talk in which she asked a class of fourth graders to consider whether the statement $\frac{3}{4} > \frac{7}{8}$ is true or false (Figure 1.1). In planning the number talk, Kassia anticipated that students might talk about the size of the pieces in each fraction. They might reason that eighths

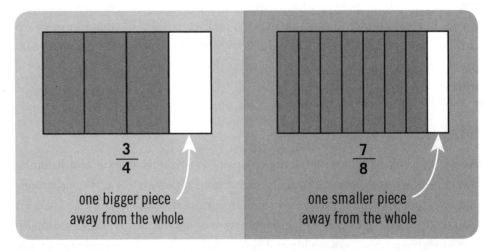

Figure 1.1 One way of reasoning about which fraction is greater

are much smaller than fourths and therefore seven-eighths is greater than three-fourths because it is only one tiny piece away from one whole.

As Kassia watched the video of herself calling on several students with raised hands and listening to each student's reasoning, she realized that she was silently evaluating each response as she waited for someone to bring up the point she had anticipated. In responding this way, she was glossing over some valid and thoughtful reasoning without even registering it in the moment! "Come on!" Kassia thought, watching herself in the video, "You know better than this!"

Unfortunately, knowing is not enough! These IRE behaviors are deeply ingrained in teaching and learning, so breaking with them requires bravery, intention, and lots of practice. Martin Nystrand writes that true dialogue in the classroom "require[s] that teachers abandon the security of their roles as authoritative repositories and referees of unproblematic knowledge in favor of the more subtle and ostensibly risky roles." (1997, 89). Hands-Down Conversations provide a structure that supports us as we take this risk and move toward the dialogue community we envision.

Traditional Classroom Discourse	Hands-Down Conversation Communities
The teacher and a handful of students do most of the talking.	Many different students talk and contribute to the conversation in a variety of ways. The teacher's facilitation supports students in leading the conversation.

Who is doing the talking? This is one of the first questions we should ask about classroom discourse in general and about the specific classrooms in which we work. In order to build an inclusive and empowering discourse community, it is critical to consider research on this topic.

- English learners are frequently asked easier questions than their peers or no questions at all, and thus are offered fewer opportunities for participation in traditional classroom discourse (Guan Eng Ho 2005).

- Prior academic achievement is predictive of participation in classroom discourse (Kelly 2008). Students who have done well in math in the past, for example, tend to be the students who talk more in math class.

- Students in classrooms in which more students live in poverty are given fewer opportunities to engage in academic conversation than students in classrooms in which students come from higher socioeconomic backgrounds (Lingard, Hayes, Mills 2003).

One of the first things that teachers notice as they begin to use Hands-Down Conversations is the inequity of student participation. Some students are silent. Some students dominate the conversations. Some people's ideas are ignored, while others are reverently deferred to. These patterns can be alarming to notice, but it is important to do so. In Chapter 3 we present several strategies for noticing and analyzing patterns of student participation in conversations, and in Chapter 4 we dive into micro-lessons for inviting students to grapple with issues of equitable participation in their conversations and make goals for their talk community.

Teachers new to Hands-Down Conversation also often observe how much they themselves talk in regular classroom conversations as opposed to Hands-Down Conversations. The first few times a class has a Hands-Down Conversation, teachers may notice that students still look to them for confirmation or approval. Their body language expresses messages like "Is this right?" and "What do we talk about now?" In many cases, even young students have received the clear message that the teacher is the expert and should be the most important voice in the classroom.

Therefore, one of the first things a teacher does in a Hands-Down Conversation is to establish some new physical behaviors for herself. Rather than sitting or standing in front of the class, the teacher sits just outside the Hands-Down Conversation circle. If possible, she sits on the floor so that she is at the same physical level as the students. She breaks eye contact with the students for much of the conversation so that students learn to look at each other and respond to each other's words and body language rather than hers. The teacher's focus shifts to listening and understanding students' ideas rather than responding to and evaluating each student's turn.

Figure 1.2 Second-grade teacher Jess Mundy positions herself as a listener, sitting just outside the Hands-Down Conversation circle.

The Hands-Down Conversation structure intentionally de-emphasizes the teachers' voice in order to focus on developing the roles of teacher as listener and of students as meaning-makers. However, the teacher's role as facilitator is still important. We've learned that when we, as teachers, listen more, we can more carefully choose when we *do* want to add our voice to the conversation and what exactly we want to say.

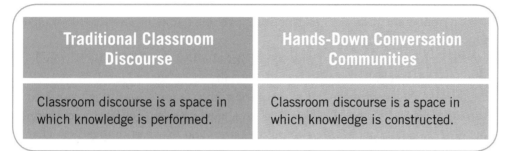

Traditional Classroom Discourse	Hands-Down Conversation Communities
Classroom discourse is a space in which knowledge is performed.	Classroom discourse is a space in which knowledge is constructed.

On the first day of a fraction unit, Kassia and second-grade teacher Mary Beth Dillane gathered with their students on the rug to engage in a Hands-Down Conversation around a set of carefully crafted "Which One Doesn't Belong?" images. The "Which One Doesn't Belong?" routine asks students to consider four images, choose which one they believe does not belong with the others, and justify their choice. The images are purposely designed so that each image could be the one that does not belong (Danielson 2016b). To launch the fraction unit, Kassia and Mary Beth selected images they believed might encourage students to grapple with and extend their understanding around the concept of one-half and around fractions in general.

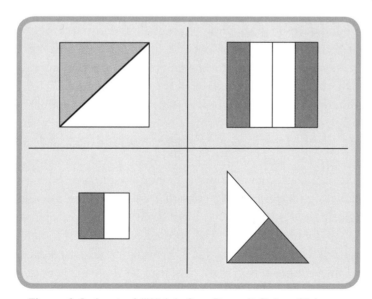

Figure 1.3 A set of "Which One Doesn't Belong?" images designed to open a conversation about fractions

Toward the middle of the conversation, one second grader, Cory, made the claim that the bottom left-hand image was "the only one that was *really* one-half because it's split right down the middle." Most students thought some of the other images *might* be one-half, but the debate quickly turned to focus on the upper right-hand image. Could that image represent one-half?

"No, it's got two purple parts. It can only be one-half if one part is purple and the other is not," offered Amaya.

"It's one-half!" asserted Gladys. "If I move one purple piece over it looks like one-half of a sandwich."

"If I move the parts and shrink it, it looks a lot like that one in the bottom left that you said *was* half, Cory. So it could be half too," claimed Jacob.

Finally, Amber had the last word of the conversation. "No. I don't think you can move pieces like that. Half has to be two equal parts and you have to color one of those parts. You can't have two purple pieces and four parts altogether. That's something else."

Before moving on to the next part of their fraction work for the day, Kassia closed by saying, "You all really have a lot of ideas about one-half. And you don't all agree! Some of you think half has to be one of two parts, and others are thinking half might look different sometimes. You're going to keep thinking about that in the task we'll work on today. I can't wait to hear what your new ideas are at the end of class."

There were many places in this conversation in which Kassia and Mary Beth had to resist the urge to interrupt to correct or "fix up" students' understandings of one-half. There were moments when they wanted to offer an easy path to understanding. But they did not. Kassia and Mary Beth made the conscious (and hard!) decision to use this conversation as a starting point for students to begin to construct a full and deep understanding of one-half and of fractions in general. This meant that this conversation was not neatly wrapped up with a bow at its conclusion. There was no consensus at the end of the conversation on what one-half means or whether all of the images could represent one-half. This Hands-Down Conversation provided Kassia and Mary Beth with critical information about next instructional steps for the unit—which tasks to present to students and which questions to ask in order to nudge students toward deeper and more complete understanding of fractions.

In traditional classroom discourse, the purpose of conversation is to perform existing knowledge rather than to construct understanding through the conversation. Jo Boaler writes that "the problem is with the performance culture in our schools . . . Students believe that the purpose of . . . class is to demonstrate that they can quickly find the answers" (2017). While Boaler writes specifically about the performance culture within math class, this same issue is pervasive throughout the school day.

Hands-Down Conversation communities, on the other hand, are rooted in ideas-in-process. Nystrand writes that "fully dialogic instruction, first of all, involves a conception of knowledge not as previously formatted by someone else but rather as continuously regenerated and co-constructed among teachers and learners and their peers" (1997, 89).

German physicist Martin Wagenschein describes these opposing types of discourse as "the language of trying to understand" versus "the language of having understood" (1970, 162). When students come to the meeting area for a Hands-Down Conversation, the primary goal is for them to engage with one another in the "the language of trying to understand." This, of course, is much messier that "the language of having understood," but it is ultimately more productive and truer to our goal of real dialogue.

Traditional Classroom Discourse	Hands-Down Conversation Communities
Silent students are viewed as unengaged, resistant, shy, or unable to contribute to the conversation.	Silence is viewed as a complex act. The role of listener is valued equally with that of speaker.

"Some kids in my class never talk!" We have said these words, over the years, about various students, often in frustration. When students talk, we have a window into their thinking, but when they are silent, we are filled with uncertainty about their understanding. We often fill in our uncertainties about silent students with negative presumptions such as these:

- Silent students are unengaged. They are thinking about nothing or about unrelated topics. They need to pay more attention!

- Silent students are shy. This is just part of who they are, and it cannot be changed.

- Silence is an act of defiance. Teachers should compel the child to talk by cold calling on them.

A more productive way to view silence is to resist the urge to presume that we know what is happening inside a child's mind and to instead get curious about it. We can shift away from the view of silence as purely negative and the silent child as a problem in need of fixing. We can, instead, seek to understand a child's silence. There are many complex reasons for silence and many possible responses to it:

- Some students are silent because they are listening and thinking. People process information in different ways and at different paces. What opportunities can we provide in our classrooms for students to process new ideas on their own and with a trusted partner in addition to whole-class conversations?

- Some students are silent because they do not feel their ideas are valuable or valued. How can we take a critical look at whose voices are valued in our classrooms? How can we highlight and privilege voices that are left out of our classroom discourse?

- Some students are silent because they're unsure they can translate their ideas into words in a way that makes sense to the group. How can we give students opportunities to rehearse their ideas with a partner or offer them some language that helps them get started with their idea?

- Some students are silent because they feel disconnected from the content. How can we engage students with content in ways that feel meaningful and relevant to their lives?

- Some students are silent as a form of resistance (Kohl 1995). How can we understand students' resistance? How can we understand the structures within and outside of our classrooms that contribute to this resistance?

While it is our goal for everyone's voice to be represented in our classroom, we also acknowledge that talking is not the only way that people learn. At times teachers hold tight to hand-raising because it *seems* like an equitable way of ensuring participation and engagement. And while there is a relationship between a focus on academic talk and students' achievement, the issue appears to be more nuanced at the individual student level.

In their article "The Silent and the Vocal: Participation and Learning in Whole-Class Discussion," Catherine O'Connor, Sarah Michaels, Suzanne Chapin, and Allen G. Harbaugh investigate the question "Is there a significant relationship between what an individual student learns from a discussion, and how much that student verbally contributes to that specific discussion?" (2017, 6). The answer within this study, surprisingly, was no. The authors argue that understanding the particular context of this study is crucial to understanding their findings. All of the classrooms in this study were part of a larger study on academic talk, and thus all of the teachers had participated in significant professional development on fostering academic talk in their classrooms. The students, in turn, had spent between six months and two years as members of classroom discourse communities and thus were experienced both as academic talkers and listeners. The authors hypothesize that being part of an academic talk community benefits all students—those who participate verbally and those who do not. This research demonstrates the transformative power of a strong classroom discourse community—both for students who participate frequently in whole-class conversations and those who do not.

Traditional Classroom Discourse	Hands-Down Conversation Communities
Classroom talk follows a set of norms and procedures that are useful only within the school walls.	Classroom talk mirrors and prepares students for engaging in dialogue beyond the school walls.

A primary goal of Hands-Down Conversation is "natural-sounding talk." But what is natural-sounding talk? We might define natural-sounding talk as the kind of talk that we, as teachers, engage in. But as two white middle-class women, we also have to acknowledge that the way we talk, although it has been elevated as the "norm" in school and society, is not the only kind of valuable talk.

In his book *For White Folks Who Teach in the Hood . . . And the Rest of Y'all Too*, Christopher Emdin warns that, at times, a teacher's efforts to support students in traditional academic language "becomes a process of creating students who look and act like white affluent prep school students . . ." (2016, 177). Instead, Emdin argues for a classroom culture that supports "an authentic code-switching that involves valuing oneself and one's culture while appreciating and understanding the codes of other cultures" (2016, 178).

We must be thoughtful about how and when we support students' language. For example, it is easy to develop a tendency to constantly revoice students' ideas. Without being aware of it, we may revoice and rephrase only the ideas of students whose language sounds different from ours. Therefore, sometimes the practice of revoicing becomes the practice of making student talk sound like ours. At times, revoicing *can* be a useful teacher talk move because we can use it to highlight and clarify a student's idea so that the rest of the class can engage with it. However, when we revoice too frequently or revoice only certain students' ideas, this becomes a problematic practice. Students learn that they do not need to work to understand each other's words because they can wait for us to say the important ideas "better and more clearly." Students get the message that their words are not good enough on their own. It can be tricky to decide when to revoice students' ideas; however, we have found that the listening practice that is central to Hands-Down Conversations allows us to slow down and think, "Do I really need to say that again?"

Sentence frames are another tool that must be used thoughtfully. While we sometimes offer students sentence frames as a scaffold to get their ideas started, we are careful not to allow the scaffold to become the jailer. We remind students that the sentence starter is optional—if they have a different phrasing to express an idea, they should go for it! We also make a point of saying that our conversation may outgrow the sentence starter. "When we're thinking about our reasoning, you might find it helpful to say 'I agree with that idea because . . .' or 'I disagree with that idea because . . .' But as we keep having these kinds of conversations, you're going to figure out other ways of talking about each other's ideas. You're going to come up with your own ways of saying things to each other that are powerful and caring. We'll figure those out together as we go along." With sentence starters, just as with everything in a Hands-Down Conversation community, our goal is to value the students' words and ideas above all else.

Traditional Classroom Discourse	Hands-Down Conversation Communities
Classroom talk values the experience and knowledge of some students, often white, middle- and upper-class students.	Classroom talk values and the experience and knowledge of all students.

Understanding schools as part of a society that historically and currently devalues and dehumanizes the lives and experiences of people of color, poor people, women, and students with disabilities is difficult. We, as teachers, want to create classrooms that value everyone, but in order to do that we must recognize the inequities that exist within school and within society. We must also recognize that our own biases and privilege may make these inequities difficult to see and address.

Pat Thompson writes that all students come to school with "virtual school bags" that contain a wealth of knowledge, experiences, values, and skills (2002). However, not all "virtual school bags" are valued equally by schools and teachers. A student who has "congruence between her school bag and the school setting" is privileged over those who do not (Thompson 2002, 8). The "virtual school bags" of white, middle-class students often contain tools and experiences that are a closer match to those of the teacher and school system. White, middle-class students are explicitly and implicitly encouraged to utilize the tools they have brought with them from home. On the other hand, students of color, poor students, and students with disabilities, whose "virtual school bags" are full of rich but undervalued experiences and tools, tend to learn quickly that it is best to leave their "backpack" at the door. This devaluing of some students often occurs underground, and it can be hard to see it happening, especially for white educators.

We (Kassia and Christy) work in a school in which the majority of students are people of color. However, when we began our work with Hands-Down Conversations, we noticed that white, middle-class students often dominated the conversations and were deferred to in conversation by their peers. This was not something that teachers had purposely or consciously structured, but the inequity was there nonetheless. Hands-Down Conversations often reveal power structures within our classrooms that we may have been unaware of and with which we feel uncomfortable. We encourage you to lean into this discomfort, study who is talking and whose ideas are valued, and work to disrupt inequities you notice. In Section II you will read about using the micro-lessons to support you in this work.

Why Hands-Down Conversations?

Most central to the belief system of a Hands-Down Conversation community is the conviction that all students are competent thinkers with valuable experiences and ideas to draw upon. If we believe that all students are competent thinkers, then we must also believe that all students can participate in and lead meaningful academic conversations. Hands-Down Conversations can aid us in this work as we redefine what it means to be a community of readers, writers, mathematicians, talkers, and listeners.

Traditional Classroom Discourse	Hands-Down Conversation Communities
The teacher is positioned as the "primary knower" (Boyd and Galda 2011).	All students are positioned as competent members of the community with important ideas.
The teacher and a handful of students do most of the talking.	Many different students talk and contribute to the conversation in a variety of ways. The teacher's facilitation supports students in leading the conversation.
Classroom discourse is a space in which knowledge is performed.	Classroom discourse is a space in which knowledge is constructed.
Silent students are viewed as unengaged, resistant, shy, or unable to contribute to the conversation.	Silence is viewed as a complex act. The role of listener is valued equally with that of speaker.
Classroom talk follows a set of norms and procedures that are useful only within the school walls.	Classroom talk mirrors and prepares students for engaging in dialogue beyond the school walls.
Classroom talk values the experience and knowledge of some students, often white, middle- and upper-class students.	Classroom talk values the experience and knowledge of all students.

Chapter

2

Becoming a Hands-Down Teacher

The key is curiosity, and it is curiosity, not answers, that we model. As we seek to learn more about a child, we demonstrate the acts of observing, listening, questioning, and wondering. When we are curious about a child's words . . . the child feels respected. The child is respected.

—Vivian Paley, "On Listening to What the Children Say"

Picture a child with a gallon of milk in her hand. Her cup sits on the counter as the target. She's told you with strong conviction that help is not required. She can, without a doubt, "do it myself." Shakily, she lifts the jug, tipping it slowly. Her brow wrinkles in concentration, tongue sticking out the side of her mouth, as she attempts to control the shifting weight of the liquid sloshing inside. The milk starts flowing—at first just a trickle, then suddenly surging out in a big splash, the flow getting away from the child. Milk splashes into the cup, not completely in her control, but not out of control either. Then, as she sees the cup nearly full, she pulls the jug back upward, dribbling just a bit on the counter as she sets it down. Triumphantly grinning, she looks up at you. "Ha. I did it."

As the adult in one of those moments, we often feel equally in awe of the child's growth and in terror of the imminent mess. It can be hard to resist that urge to step in and offer guidance or even just to take over and "do it right." As teachers, we know deep down that the biggest learning for a child takes place in those moments when the adult has "let go" at just the right time. But sometimes we just don't want to deal with the possibility of cleaning up the sticky floor. This is the tug-of-war that takes place in each teacher's heart as they begin Hands-Down Conversations. Watching our students take on more ownership of our classroom conversation is exhilarating. But it can be a little scary too!

As teachers, we know our decisions hold both great weight and great potential. Peter Johnston writes, "Children offer us opportunities to say something, or not, and the choices we make affect what happens next. Teaching requires constant improvisation. It is jazz" (2012, 4). We also know that even jazz, with all its "in-the-moment" decisions, is based on guidelines and principles that allow the music to hold a shape and create something that is pleasing to the ear. In this chapter, we want to highlight the following teacher moves that we consider essential to orchestrating beautiful "conversational jazz."

- Take a Curious Stance
- Decide When to Put Hands Down
- Balance Conversation and Content
- Lift the Curtain on Dialogue

Take a Curious Stance

We are all familiar with the age-old saying "Do as I say, not as I do." This applies, often tongue-in-cheek, to the parent who has found themselves observing a painfully accurate reflection of their own behavior in that of their child. The irony is, as we all know from our own childhood experiences or as parents ourselves, "Do as I say, not as I do" doesn't work. Our behaviors, not our words, are a child's best teacher. In the classroom we want our children to be curious, inquisitive learners who are willing to struggle through a challenge and take risks. If we want to create a classroom community full of bold, inquisitive learners, then we must visibly be this type of learner ourselves.

Model Curiosity About Your Students

First, we must display genuine curiosity—not just about the world around us, but about the other members in our classroom community. We want to show our students every day that we are intently curious about who they are and what they think. When we model this behavior, we create a learning community in which each student's past experiences and home life are viewed as relevant and important. We make it clear that individual differences and unique ways of looking at the world are an *addition* to our classroom environment, not something to be hidden or forgotten. Of course, we are working against some big obstacles here in building this curious community, namely the outside world, where a culturally appreciative mindset is often not the norm. But as elementary school teachers, we do have the

Figure 2.1 First-grade teacher Kelsey Friend listens with genuine curiosity as her student explains his thinking.

unique opportunity and intense responsibility to create a micro-world in our classrooms—a place where we can nurture young learners as they grow. When we model and foster genuine curiosity in each other, we open the door for productive disagreement and honest sharing of ideas.

Being curious about our students is not something that we do just in certain subject areas or at certain times of the day. It is a deliberate stance, an identity, even, that guides our interactions with students from the time they step through our doorway to the time they depart. We have seen teachers communicate this curiosity about their students in different ways, depending on individual teachers' personalities and styles.

Here are just a few examples we have observed in our own rooms and in others:

- One teacher has a "soft start" during arrival each morning, when students "network," and, importantly, the teacher participates—moving about the room, asking students questions, and fostering conversation about their evening, their soccer games, and their church events.

- Another teacher uses a process for students to lobby and campaign for their choice of next whole-class, chapter-book, read-aloud, listening to several students' book talks and considering various student picks before making her final selection.

- A third teacher makes a commitment to call three of her families each week of the school year with the goal of listening (instead of talking) to the families talk about themselves and their children.

What are some ways you model curiosity about *your* students?

Become Comfortable with Uncertainty

An important attribute of curious people is that, due to their drive to discover, they are comfortable with the unknown. Discovering areas of confusion, uncertainty, and unexpected results are viewed as positive experiences because they drive our learning forward. But again, we must model this behavior if we expect it from our students. It is reasonable to reflect and ask ourselves: Are *we* comfortable not knowing? Are *we* willing to admit our own mistakes and uncertainty in front of our class? Often, in our society, mistakes can feel like debilitating failures rather than part of the natural process of learning—so much so that Stanford University has developed "The Stanford Resilience Project," an opportunity for professors, deans, and students to annually get up and publicly describe their failures and the resulting growth from those failures, in order to shift students' mindset about mistakes.

Besides modeling our own mistakes for our students, we also can make our classrooms into places where we celebrate uncertainty and confusion, rather than trying to hide those feelings or resolve them as quickly as possible. When a student is struggling to figure out a math problem, or two students are disagreeing over how to spell a word, consider the impact we could have if we said to them, "This confusion you're feeling right now is so powerful. You've discovered something here that is really worth thinking about and puzzling over." When you do this regularly, your class will become a safe enough space that you might follow that acknowledgment with an invitation for students to share this part of their learning: "Would you mind sharing the thinking you (two) have done about this with the class?"

The more we are able to cultivate a sense of curiosity about each other's ideas and a place where uncertainty is comfortable, the safer the dialogue environment will be for our students. But it is important to note that you do not need to wait until your classroom community has reached a fully "settled" place before you have your first conversation. Hands-Down Conversations will contribute to your efforts to build a curious community during other parts of the day in a symbiotic relationship. The tighter the community, the more robust the conversations will be. The more robust conversations you have, the tighter your community will feel.

Decide When to Put Hands Down

There are many opportunities for Hands-Down Conversations throughout the day, but that doesn't mean they occur all day long. Hands-Down Conversations are just *one* tool to add to your repertoire of possibilities for exploring content with your students in a whole-group setting. So when is a Hands-Down Conversation a good choice? Hands-Down Conversations support students in exploring ideas that have a variety of possible answers, perspectives, and approaches. We want to plan for conversations in which students really *want* to listen to each other and are not just listening (or pretending to listen) out of compliance. Therefore, both content choice *and* the way we start the conversation are essential.

When planning for a Hands-Down Conversation, we like to use the metric of ambiguity. We often look for topics that are debatable, such as considering how the class should take action on an observed problem in the classroom or digging into the motivations behind a character from a read-aloud. We can also foster this "urgency to listen" by choosing an established fact or known answer and having students spend time in a Hands-Down Conversation digging into the "why" behind that idea. For example, a class may have agreed that the following equation is true: $9 \times 5 = (4 \times 5) + (5 \times 5)$. A Hands-Down Conversation can explore questions like "Why is this true?" "Is this always true?" and "Is this true of other operations?"

Once we have chosen a topic that seems sufficiently ambiguous, we want to make that ambiguity *very* clear to our students so they jump into the conversation with true curiosity about what other individuals might think. Sometimes we emphasize ambiguity by using tentative language. After reading a poem with our students, we could ask, "What was the author's message?" OR we could ask, "What messages *might* the author be trying to send us?" In both cases, the topic is ambiguous (since we do not have the author here in front of us, and we don't know exactly what the author was trying to communicate), but the first question sets up students to anticipate one correct answer. There will be some students in the room who will want to perform that knowledge, and others who will sit back and wait for them to do it. On the other hand, the second question opens up the conversation with the assumption that there will be many different ideas floating about. That word *might* indicates that we value the thinking alongside the answer.

We have found it effective to play around with the way we start a conversation to foster ambiguity, even sometimes starting with a statement or single word instead of a question. You'll want to see what works best for your own community as you get started with Hands-Down Conversations. When a conversation seems to spur a lot of interest and activity, reflect on both the ambiguity of the topic and how you presented the topic to foster your students' desire to talk and listen. In Table 2.1 we introduce several launch moves that teachers have found helpful in fueling robust conversations.

Table 2.1 Ways to Launch a Hands-Down Conversation

Launch Move	In literacy it might sound like . . .	In math it might sound like . . .
Offer a debatable idea Debatable ideas encourage students to develop their ability to disagree productively and articulate clear reasoning for their ideas.	Let's talk about this idea: "Peter was a bad brother." What do you think? *(After reading* Peter's Chair, *by Ezra Jack Keats, 1967.)*	Today *some* of you said that this shape *(from a shape-sort students had previously worked with) could* be a triangle. Others of you said it *could not* be a triangle. Let's talk more about that.

Launch Move	In literacy it might sound like . . .	In math it might sound like . . .
Invite working theories Talking about working theories communicates to students that they should always be looking for patterns and thinking about where they do and do not apply.	We are looking at this word *mad* and we have this word *made*. You've also been recording other words in your books with an *e* on the end. Looking at these words, what are you thinking about how these letters and words might work?	Yesterday when you were playing "Multiplication Five in a Row," some of you noticed a relationship between multiplying by two and multiplying by four. I wrote down a few problems where you noticed it. *(Teacher displays problems on chart paper.)* $2 \times 10 = 20 \quad 4 \times 10 = 40$ $2 \times 3 = 6 \quad 4 \times 3 = 12$ What are you noticing? What are you thinking might be true?
Offer a single word Single-word launches are accessible to many students since there is no specific question to answer. They also allow students to deeply explore the question "What does this really mean?"	We just read the book *Something Beautiful* (2002), by Sharon Dennis Wyeth. Let's talk about *beauty*.	We've started thinking about multiplication and division, but we haven't really figured out as a class exactly what division is. So, what *does division* mean?
Start with a student quote Keeping students' ideas front and center is important. While we always ask permission from a student before presenting their words to the class, we find most students are proud to have their ideas elevated for consideration by the class.	Samantha, when I was conferring with you yesterday, you had a celebration. You said, "I finished my first novel that isn't a graphic novel. It was hard, and I had to read it in a different way, but I did it." Let's have a conversation about that idea. How is reading a graphic novel different from reading a "regular" novel?	Here's something Diego and Marco said yesterday. *(Teacher displays chart paper with the quote.)* "I can count my shells by twos and fives or tens and I still get the same number at the end." Let's talk more about Diego and Marco's idea.

Balance Conversation and Content

Imagine a seesaw. When two similarly weighted children get on, they can pass their weight back and forth. One is up, and the other is down. They switch. Sometimes they hover right about even in the middle, legs dangling above the ground. Each partner's weight supports the other's in the fun, and although sometimes they're down and sometimes they're up, their weight remains the same. Balance is critical to the success of the seesawing! If a child is really unlucky, and their partner jumps off suddenly, they crash down to the ground, with the wind knocked out of them. (Which is probably why you don't find old-school seesaws on many playgrounds these days!)

In a Hands-Down community, conversation and content ride the seesaw in a similar fashion. They maintain equal weight across the day and from conversation to conversation. However, sometimes the teacher is focused more on building the content, and conversation is more in the background. Sometimes the teacher is focused more on developing students' conversation skills, and the content is less of a focus. And sometimes there is equal attention on both. Regardless of where the focus lies, both goals are always present and of equal importance. Their weight doesn't change.

Figure 2.2 Striking a balance between content and conversation goals

How does this look? To the students, the Hands-Down Conversation structure looks the same. The difference is really in the mind and plans of the teacher (see Figure 2.2). Sometimes you will be listening for the students' ideas about the content and taking notes on content more heavily than on conversation. You'll be thinking about what whole-group and small-group math or literacy lessons you want to teach next to keep developing students' understanding of this content. You'll be thinking about which books, tasks, and problems you want to invite them to engage with next. At other times you will want to really focus on students' dialogue skills. When this is your focus, you will take more notes on the talk so that you can think about what elements of dialogue you will want to uncover next for your students and how you will offer students opportunities for meaningful practice. This brings us to our last teacher move.

Lift the Curtain on Dialogue

Children come to school with a robust verbal life and very capable talk skills that have been acquired by speaking with and listening to their families and communities. Our students' "virtual school bags" come equipped with an oral toolbox (Thompson 2002). These skills are highlighted and honored in a Hands-Down Conversation in a way that they are not in traditional classroom conversations characterized by frequent paraphrasing, reframing, and teacher evaluation. We also recognize that what have been traditionally called "academic" dialogue tools are a form of currency in our society that is used to make change, obtain influence, and access structures of power. So while we place great emphasis on making space in our classrooms to listen to the everyday talk that our students bring with them, we also know that providing opportunities for talk only during Hands-Down Conversations is not enough. We find that when we pull back the curtain on how this "academic" dialogue works, we can more fully provide the opportunity for every student to access these skills. By orienting students to these skills in short microlessons, we can increase students' participation and confidence in this type of dialogue, while simultaneously honoring and utilizing their "virtual school bags."

But don't worry! We are not suggesting you need to fit another focus lesson into your very packed school schedule. The beauty of teaching talk is that it *also* helps you teach the content. Remember that seesaw! We have found that an explicit dialogue microlesson can be done in about five minutes, before having a Hands-Down Conversation. Then the students are able to try out that new dialogue skill while *simultaneously* engaging in math or literacy content. You can fit these dialogue lessons in quickly before you have a conversation analyzing a graph together or making sense of a chapter in a novel you just read aloud. Keep in mind, although our talk lessons *are* specific and explicit, the ultimate goal is *not* formulaic talk. We try to never stop the natural flow of conversation or a child's natural speech patterns in order to enforce the use of a sentence stem or some other skill that we just taught in the lesson. In Section II of this book, you will find dialogue micro-lessons as well as examples within each micro-lesson of how you might give students opportunities to try out those dialogue skills in a Hands-Down Conversation about a genuinely interesting idea.

Let's Start Building

In this chapter, we've outlined four teacher moves that are critical to building a community where Hands-Down Conversations grow and flourish.

- Take a Curious Stance
- Decide When to Put Hands Down
- Balance Conversation and Content
- Lift the Curtain on Dialogue

You may find other ideas, tips, and thoughts that are important to you as you begin the exciting work of building your Hands-Down community. Whatever they are, we suggest you name them and jot them down. This way, you can check back in on your core considerations from time to time to keep yourself focused and grounded.

Chapter

3

Facilitating the Hands-Down Conversation

Terrific teachers have teeth marks on their tongues.

—Alfie Kohn, "A Dozen Essential Guidelines for Educators"

It's winter in Hannah's fourth-grade classroom. She has recently been reading a lot of fairy tales with her class, with a focus on teaching students to critically analyze the texts for the hidden and overt messages authors send. Right at the end of a conversation yesterday about how princesses are portrayed in fairy tales, one of Hannah's students brought up the movie *Frozen*. The students were quite animated in their desire to talk about this movie, so Hannah decided to come back to it again the subsequent day.

Hannah: So, Leah, you said something to us yesterday that really got everyone talking, but we ran out of time. Can I repeat your idea for us to keep talking about?

(Leah nods. Hannah looks down and reads from her notes.)

Hannah: Okay, you said, "But not all princesses actually *do* get married at the end. Like in *Frozen*, you know? Anna does, basically, but Elsa doesn't." Let's keep talking about this today. Who would like to start us off?

Juan: Okay, so here is what I wanted to say yesterday. *Frozen* still is about getting married and love. It's like all princesses are all about love. That's why it's a girl movie.

Leah: No. No, it's not! It's—

Christina: *Frozen* isn't like that. It's about sister love. Not getting married. I mean, Anna wants to, but, she doesn't actually get married anyway. To Hans or Kristoff.

Juan: She still is wanting to be married and stuff. I mean, my sister watches it all the time. And it's like the people who make movies for girls always make it about love.

Leah: It's supposed to be about how sister love is more important, though. *That's* true love, not the gross kind . . .

(Leah giggles and some others join her.)

Hannah: Can I say something for a minute? Juan was talking about what the people who made this movie want us to think. Remember, in this case, the author is Disney. So . . . what messages might Disney be trying to send us?

Beckket: So, I think Leah is right—Disney is saying that sister love is more important than getting married. Like Disney thinks families are important, I guess?

Sandra: But why did Disney have to have the love part with Anna and Kristoff anyway?

Juan: 'Cause it's a girl movie. And girls always watch that stuff.

In the vignette above, the teacher made careful decisions about when and how to insert herself in the conversation in order to elevate the dialogue without taking control. Knowing what to do with yourself as you facilitate a Hands-Down Conversation can be tricky and even a little awkward at first. This chapter is designed to help you define your role. Maureen Boyd and Lee Galda describe the teacher role in building "joint authority" in a conversation as having three parts: "They listen attentively; they allow time for other students to contribute; and when students contribute, these teachers build on what they offer and connect these offerings to the curricular focus" (2011, 13). Let's unpack these parts by considering what to do with your "physical self," your "listening self," and your "speaking self" as you facilitate a Hands-Down Conversation.

Your Physical Self

When having Hands-Down Conversations, we encourage our students to take the lead by removing ourselves from the circle. We position ourselves physically and mentally as listeners and note-takers rather than as directors of the conversation so that students stop "talking to the teacher" and start talking to one

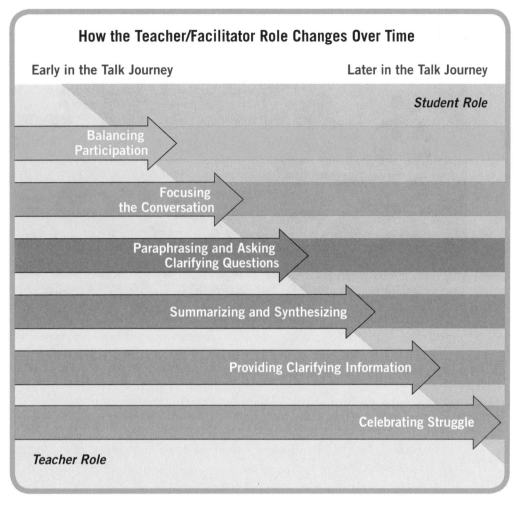

Figure 3.1 While both students and teachers are continuously approximating these moves throughout the talk journey, teachers encourage students to take on more of the work as time progresses.

another. This may feel awkward or even rude at first; however, the teacher's role traditionally carries so much power that it is often difficult for students to talk to each other without this physical shift. You may find as time goes on that it is not necessary to be as removed from the conversation physically. You'll know you can re-enter the circle if your students are looking at each other instead of at you!

Taking notes on your Hands-Down Conversations is also an essential part of your job because it helps you listen deeply to your students' words. We busy ourselves with our clipboard, pencil, and paper, looking downward at our notes instead of making eye contact with the class or the speaker. We find two note-taking methods particularly powerful and worthy of mentioning.

Figure 3.2 Christy sits outside of a Hands-Down Conversation, listening to students and taking a transcript.

Quick Transcripts

When we transcribe student dialogue, we attempt to write down our students' words very closely, with as little inference or analysis as possible. The result is what we call a "quick transcript." Taking a quick transcript allows us to capture a conversation that we can later analyze to see both who is talking and how much, as well as what kinds of ideas students are discussing. However, writing quickly enough to take a complete and exact transcript is a challenge! We deal with that in a couple of ways: Sometimes we try to take a transcript that captures as much of the conversation as possible, knowing that we will likely miss bits and pieces. Other times we do not try to keep up with every word said but rather listen for big ideas and jot those down in students' words. Depending on your personal skills and style, you can consider taking notes on the computer if you are faster or more comfortable typing than writing. Regardless of how we get the data, we use quick transcripts when we are interested in thinking about the *content* of the dialogue. They are also the tool we turn to when we are looking to see how students build on and connect to other speakers (e.g., when we are working on the dialogue skills in Chapters 6 and 7).

Teacher Tip

Our colleague Kathleen Maturan has experimented with using the voice memo app on her phone and the audio recording feature of PowerPoint on her computer, and has had great success with both of these tools. These tools allow teachers to review conversations at a later time.

Conversation Maps

Sometimes, especially as you are getting started with Hands-Down Conversations, you may be interested in who is participating in the conversation and how much. Conversation maps are our preferred tool for analyzing patterns of participation. To make one, quickly sketch a circle on a piece of paper and add students' names to indicate where they are sitting on the carpet. As the conversation begins, draw a line from student to student as they speak so that you can later reflect on the path of the conversation. You might jot down a few words or bits of conversation in the margins to help you think more about the content of the conversation, but the purpose of the conversation map is primarily to help you focus on patterns of participation, especially when you are working on some of the beginning-level dialogue skills in Chapter 4.

Teacher Tip

If your students have assigned spots in the circle, you can prepare copies of the Conversation Map Template, created by our colleague, first-grade teacher Allyson Gray (see Appendix B), with students' names already written in ahead of time. That way, you are ready at a moment's notice to draw a conversation map.

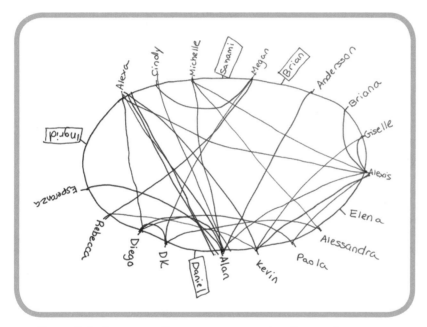

Figure 3.3 A conversation map can reveal patterns of participation in a conversation.

While it takes a bit of practice to become proficient at listening and note-taking at the same time, you will find any notes you are able to take during conversations to be invaluable tools. Kara Pranikoff emphasizes the importance of taking notes about talk, explaining that these transcripts inform our instruction in the same way that Running Records inform our reading instruction of beginning readers (2017). These notes will guide you as you think about what dialogue lessons and content experiences your students might need next in order to help them express their ideas and engage with others' ideas. They will also create a record for you to see growth over time, and they can even provide a powerful way for your students to reflect on their own growth.

At A Glance: Two Ways to Take Notes in the Hands-Down Conversation

Quick Transcript	Conversation Map
What? This is a record of what the children are actually saying.	**What?** This is a tool that helps you track who speaks to whom and how many times they speak.
Why? This helps you focus on the *content* of the conversation and the connective language students use with one another.	**Why?** This helps you track *participation* and other talk behaviors.
How?	**How?**
1. Use a clipboard and blank or lined paper. 2. As each student talks, write their initials or their first name and follow with as much of their verbatim comment as you can jot down.	1. Draw a circle and write the name of each student in their place around the circle. 2. Draw a star to indicate the first speaker. 3. Draw a line from that speaker to the next speaker. 4. Continue drawing lines to follow the conversation.

Your Listening Self

Figuring out how to listen is one of the challenging and interesting parts of getting started with Hands-Down Conversations. Instead of listening for particular content or answers, we have found it helpful at first to listen for two elements of conversation: disagreement and big ideas. When we do this, we train ourselves to focus on what is important and not become sidetracked by minor misunderstandings or unrelated comments.

Disagreement

Hands-Down Conversations thrive when we are talking about ideas that are open to interpretation. Therefore, it is critical to listen for differing ideas and opinions as we facilitate conversations. Sometimes these disagreements are easy to spot, but often they are lurking below the surface of students' comments. We do not expect students to always be able to pick out exactly what makes their thinking different from someone else's. That is where you come in. We need to listen carefully for the two (or more) different ideas emerging so we can highlight them to get students talking about something that is truly ambiguous (unless our students do it themselves!). For example, when Steve Miner's class was discussing the idea of beauty, several of the students were saying that "anything could be beautiful," when Charlie countered, "But, well, if something breaks and you try to fix it back and it doesn't look the same, then you start not liking it." Christy knew that the students in this group were just emerging in their ability to connect directly to other students' comments, but she wanted to make sure they probed more into this disagreement, since it really got at the heart of something important about beauty. So that's when Christy briefly entered the conversation, to make the following observation:

> *Can I interrupt for a second? 'Cause I hear something interesting. Some of you are saying, "Anything COULD be beautiful," but I also hear some of you saying, "If a beautiful thing breaks or gets old, it's not beautiful anymore." So there's something to talk about there.*

Christy's comment highlighted the emerging disagreement for the students to think about, and it allowed the students to go deeper into the question of beauty and individual perception. To read more about nurturing disagreement as a spark for Hands-Down Conversations in literacy and math, see Chapter 8.

Big Ideas

One of our greatest goals for dialogue is that students will be able to integrate all of their individual talk skills in order to build upon one another's ideas and come to a new and different understanding as a result of a conversation. In order to support students on their journey, we will have to listen carefully to see when a big idea is emerging. Often, one student starts to hit on something, and the conversation continues on around it, like a leaf in a swirling pool. You'll want to note that leaf so you can help students come back to it, either today or another time, if they don't do that themselves.

Think back to third-grade teacher Hannah's class conversation about *Frozen*. She noted that Juan was beginning to think critically about the author's message. His comment about "the people who make the movies" rose, as a new "big idea," above some of the debate about family love or romantic love. Hannah decided to highlight that big idea to talk about further, connecting it to her content goal for her students to become critical readers. As you refine your facilitation skills, you will start listening for other things, but at the beginning you can try focusing your listening for *disagreement* and *big ideas* to help you sort through the comments.

Your Speaking Self

So you've listened intently and you've heard a nugget of disagreement as your students are talking. Or maybe you've heard someone circling a big idea. What do you say now? How do you jump in without taking over the conversation? In a Hands-Down Conversation, teachers take on a different speaking role than what we may be used to, one that takes practice for both ourselves and our students. You have seen some snippets of our ultimate goal—conversations in which student voices are leading the way and teachers are facilitating *on the side* to help build to those bigger ideas or engage in productive disagreement. However, the amount of teacher facilitation varies with the students' age and experience with Hands-Down Conversations. You will need to do a little more talking during the first Hands-Down Conversations but will be able to decrease the amount you talk as students gain experience and maturity. The key is to insert your voice in ways that build capacity in students rather than making them dependent on your continual participation.

One way to develop this skill in yourself is to look ahead at the dialogue skills you will teach in the later chapters and model these skills before your children are ready to take them on themselves. Serravallo calls this the "proficient partner" move, in which the teacher inserts a comment or idea that helps elevate the level of conversation and then quickly passes back control (2010). Our goal in speaking is to play the role of someone who is slightly better able to listen, connect, and respond to the ideas that are being presented without taking the wheel and driving the direction of the conversation to match *our* ideas or opinions. When we've chosen to have a Hands-Down Conversation, we truly want the students to explore all available possibilities or perspectives and aren't trying to lead them to a single "best" idea or solution. That being said, we are still the teachers, and our role is to keep elevating the level of conversation so our students continue to build stronger dialogue skills and deeper understanding of the big ideas behind our curricular content. By keeping our language exploratory and our interruptions selective and brief, we can achieve our goals while still keeping the ball in the students' court.

We have listed some of the facilitation moves we find useful during Hands-Down Conversations in Table 3.2. As you move into the dialogue micro-lessons in Section II, you will notice that many, but not all, of these facilitation moves are the same ones we will teach our students to start taking over as we work our teacher voice out of the conversation. A few facilitation moves will remain the responsibility of the teacher only, at least in most elementary classrooms.

Teacher Tip

When we add a comment in a conversation, we always make sure it is as brief as possible. Sometimes we might even preface our comment with the question "Can I say something?" This communicates a critical message: "This is your conversation. I'm so interested in hearing your ideas, I only want to interrupt for a minute." And then we make sure our comment really is brief!

Table 3.2 Teacher Facilitation Moves

Teacher Move	Looks Like/ Sounds Like	When and Why to Use This Move	Micro-lesson in Which Students Learn to Take Over This Move
Talk So Everyone Can Hear Us	"Brandon had something important to say there; can you say that again a little louder, Brandon?" (Or a nonverbal signal to indicate volume)	This is something you can do in very early grades, or at the beginning of Hands-Down Conversations, but quickly turn over to the responsibility of the students. You will want to work on emboldening the speaker and/or having the students learn to ask each other to speak in a louder voice.	**Lesson 4.7** We Talk So Everyone Can Hear Us
Turn and Talk	"Let's take a moment to turn and talk about [restate an idea that has come up]."	This move can be used when everyone talks at once. But, if your students are working on learning to share the airspace, you won't want to jump in because they need the chance to try to work it out. Turn and Talks can also be used if no one is speaking and you have given sufficient wait time. You can suggest a Turn and Talk about an idea that was recently raised, to rekindle the fire.	**Lesson 4.8** Too Many Voices at the Same Time **Lesson 4.9** Chirping Crickets
Focus (or Stay on Topic)	"We can explore _____ another time, but today . . ." OR "Let's refocus on the idea we are talking about today, which is . . ."	You can use this move when the conversation is either straying to other topics or becoming focused on a "small idea" (such as a disagreement over a minor detail from the book you just read). Use this move with caution, however, as overuse can result in students' feeling that their ideas are not worthy of conversation.	**Lesson 5.1** Keeping the Conversation Focused

(continues)

Table 3.2 Teacher Facilitation Moves *(continued)*

Teacher Move	Looks Like/ Sounds Like	When and Why to Use This Move	Micro-lesson in Which Students Learn to Take Over This Move
Celebrate Struggle and Uncertainty	"Wow, you are really trying to express your understandings (or beliefs) about [the topic]. By thinking about each other's ideas, you will come to a deep understanding of [the topic]."	You might use this when you start to see students becoming uncomfortable with the fact that there is disagreement. This comment rewrites the narrative from "We are trying to figure out who is right and who is wrong" to "We are all working through this together." Depending on the level of discomfort, you could put a bookmark in the conversation until another day.	
Paraphrase or Ask Clarifying Questions	"So I think you said . . ." "Did you mean . . . ?"	Repeating students' comments or asking questions is a move you should use selectively. Do this *only* when you hear an idea that has great potential but wasn't stated clearly enough for other students to respond to. You will want to teach your students to take over this move as soon as they are ready.	**Lesson 6.1** Paraphrasing: Listening So Closely and Saying an Idea in Your Own Words **Lesson 6.2** Cloudy or Clear: Asking Clarifying Questions
Clarify	"There's some information I'd like to share that I think would be helpful to our conversation here . . ."	There will be times when students have a crucial misunderstanding, or they need some information to continue the conversation. You may decide at these times to insert yourself, without sounding like you are diminishing or correcting students' ideas. It is important that these interventions be brief.	

Table 3.2 Teacher Facilitation Moves *(continued)*

Teacher Move	Looks Like/ Sounds Like	When and Why to Use This Move	Micro-lesson in Which Students Learn to Take Over This Move
Summarize	"[Student] said _____. That seems important. Can we talk more about that?" OR "I'm hearing a little disagreement. There seem to be two ideas here: _____ and _____. Let's talk more about that."	This is your opportunity to state those two things you have been listening for: disagreement and big ideas. You should do this to focus the conversation and keep building toward a higher collective understanding. Summarizing will be the teacher's role for much of elementary school, but older students may be able to take on this skill at some point as well.	**Lesson 7.6** Summarizing

Power and Empowerment

We can be aware of how our physical, listening, and speaking selves all send messages to our students about their role in the conversation and in the learning. By recording your own contributions to your Hands-Down Conversations in your notes, you can later reflect on the impact your behaviors have on the conversations and the learning. Peter Johnston writes about the importance of setting up "symmetrical power relationships" in the classroom. He explains that in order to shift from a knowledge-performance model to one where students construct deep understandings together with each other and their teacher, it is important to disrupt the "typical asymmetrical expert-novice relationship" both among peers and between teacher and student (Johnston 2012, 53). This driving principle is at the heart of all of our teacher moves as we facilitate Hands-Down Conversations. It is a delicate balance to find ways to lift and extend our students' thinking while maintaining everyone's position as an equal contributor to the thinking work of our classroom. But it is possibly the *most* important work we do.

II

Orienting Students to Dialogue

The Micro-lessons

In Kassia's first weeks of teaching kindergarten, she had no idea what she was doing. Kassia had previously taught second and third grade, and then spent a couple of years as a math coach. During that time, she had become increasingly interested in kindergarteners' mathematical thinking, finally deciding to return to a classroom-teacher role to learn more about these fascinating five- and six-year-olds. To say she had *no* idea what to do might be an exaggeration, but in the intensity of returning to the classroom and facing the first few weeks of kindergarten, it did not feel that way.

One day at recess, Kassia lamented to her friend and experienced kindergarten teacher colleague, Mary Anne Buckley, "I don't know if I can do this kindergarten thing. They spend so much time wandering around the room and handing me tiny flecks of dust off the carpet. I can't get any teaching done!"

Mary Anne, in her infinite wisdom, did not provide any magical suggestions on the spot, but she did offer to come to Kassia's classroom and give her some feedback.

Mary Anne visited a few days later, during Kassia's writing workshop. Kassia had just finished reading aloud Suzy Lee's wordless picture book *Wave* (2008), the story of a little girl on the beach and a giant wave. Using the read-aloud as a mentor text, she taught a carefully crafted lesson on how writers can tell stories through their pictures. At the end of the lesson, Kassia sent her young writers off to their tables with stapled booklets, hoping to see something great start to happen.

After a few moments, Alonzo folded his paper booklet into a telescope and yelled to his tablemates, "Look at my eye!" Carla scribbled furiously on all of the pages for two minutes and then began to follow Kassia around the room, saying, "I'm done, teacher. I'm done, teacher." Molly grabbed all of the crayons from her table's basket in one fist and refused to share with anyone else at the table.

Meanwhile, Kassia scurried around trying to confer with students about their writing and jot meaningful notes about their ideas in her notebook. And while Kassia tried to ignore the crescendoing chaos surrounding her, she was silently dying of embarrassment that Mary Anne was witnessing this moment.

That afternoon after the kids went home, Kassia said to Mary Anne, "Okay, tell me what to do." Mary Anne laughed.

"September in kindergarten is messy," she said. "But this is what I did when I was visiting your class. I watched the students and thought about what they might need next. Some kids weren't sure what to do when they had written or drawn on all the pages of their booklet. You could teach them how to staple on more pages or how to put their booklet in their folder and get another blank one from the paper tray. And some kids didn't have enough crayons."

"Yeah, I saw that. Molly hoards them all."

"You can teach them about sharing the crayons. But you can also teach them about how to go to the supply area and get more baskets of crayons for their table."

"And what do I do about the kids who are wandering around? Did you see Alonzo's telescope?"

"Yeah, I was watching him. He went to the table after the lesson and looked around. He's not sure yet what to do in writing workshop. You might try teaching the kids to tell their stories to each other first on the carpet. That might help some of them have an idea of how to get started."

After she talked with Mary Anne, Kassia felt relief. Mary Anne had not offered her a magical solution, but what she did offer was something more powerful. Mary Anne taught Kassia that we can watch our students closely and ask, "What do they need next?" We can reframe the "problems" we see in our classrooms as guideposts that point us in the direction of what we might teach next. And perhaps most importantly, we can offer students tools that empower them to make their own decisions and bring their ideas to life.

What Is a Dialogue Micro-lesson?

In this section you will find micro-lessons that will support you as you observe your students' conversations and ask, "What do they need next?" An important part of the teacher's role in building strong classroom discourse is to pull back the curtain on dialogue and say, "Look, this is how it works!" But when you are trying to teach something really big, like classroom discourse, it can be helpful to pick out one next incremental step, just as Mary Anne helped Kassia do in her writing workshop. The dialogue micro-lessons in this section offer short and powerful ways that teachers can orient students to the tools of dialogue and suggestions on how to engage students in meaningful practice with these tools. It is important to note that the lessons in this section and throughout this book are guides, not scripts. To support you, we have written out words we might say in these lessons if you choose, but we encourage you to innovate and find the words to fit your teaching style and the students with whom you work.

When we teach micro-lessons to students, we do so in a predictable format. We begin by gathering the students in the meeting area, either in a Hands-Down Conversation circle or in a group next to their Turn and Talk partners. Then we present the micro-lesson, starting by describing why we have chosen this lesson today (based on what we noticed in their last conversation), and then teaching them the new talk or listening move. This part takes about three to five minutes. We then invite the students to try out this move in either a partnership, a group of four, or a Hands-Down Conversation with the whole class around the content we have chosen as the day's focus. During that conversation, we still pay attention to the content, but we are especially focused on watching for evidence that students are trying out the dialogue move we just introduced. We wrap up the lesson by reminding students of the new move, and perhaps highlighting a moment in which we noticed someone trying it out. Just like a regular Hands-Down Conversation, the micro-lessons can take place in any content area, in any part of your day. They are simply a quick addition to the beginning of a Hands-Down Conversation.

Which Dialogue Micro-lesson Do I Start With?

While the dialogue micro-lessons follow a general progression of sophistication, we believe that each of us should forge our own path, deciding which lessons to use and when, and crafting our own lessons that are responsive to our students' needs. You'll want to pay attention to the table entitled "If You Notice . . . You Might Try . . ." at the beginning of each chapter. These tables will help you determine which lessons in that chapter will be best suited for your Hands-Down Conversation community. It is important to note that we do not recommend delivering a micro-lesson before every Hands-Down Conversation. We want to use them only when we have observed a need, and when it feels as though the students might be ready to take that next step. Just as Mary Anne and Kassia considered what the next steps were in Kassia's writing workshop, we are careful not to bombard our students with too many new skills in too short a time frame. You'll also want to consider students' overall cognitive load and add micro-lessons at times when the content of the Hands-Down Conversation is more familiar. In the following "Sample Week" table, you can see how a teacher might use Hands-Down Conversations as a teaching tool across their day and week, and when they might decide to introduce new dialogue moves.

A Sample Week in a Hands-Down Classroom Community

	Monday	Tuesday	Wednesday	Thursday	Friday
Morning Meeting	HDC about a tricky classroom community issue or problem				Micro-lesson and HDC about a comfortable social or classroom topic*
Literacy Workshops			Micro-lesson and HDC on familiar content		HDC on new or challenging content
Math Workshop		HDC about new or challenging content		HDC followed by reflection on growth around yesterday's micro-lesson	

*Note: See Appendix C for a list of sample social topics for Hands-Down Conversations that can provide opportunities for practicing new dialogue skills.

Each lesson has a name and a number. Although the lessons throughout the book generally progress in difficulty, you will want to pick and choose what is best for your class, rather than going "in order."

This section describes some important information for you to determine if this lesson is the best "next step" for your students, and explains why this lesson is important.

6.6 Revising an Idea

There is never a bad time to focus on revising ideas through talk. Because the previous lessons in this chapter focus on becoming oriented to other people's thinking and becoming more intentional listeners, this is a particularly helpful time to introduce or return to a focus on revising one's own ideas. Lynn Simpson, a fourth-grade teacher featured in the Teaching Channel video "Improving Participation Through Talk Moves," summarizes what we hope all students will learn about revising their ideas: "Revising our thinking is permission to change our mind[s] once we are confronted with new information . . . When you're confronted with new information you should change your thinking. You should take what you learned, merge it with what you already know, and then come to a new understanding" (Teaching Channel 2019). We consider this lesson to be just one small step in a longer journey of creating a classroom where revision is encouraged and celebrated as a critical part of all learning and living.

This is where the teacher language begins. In order to "lift the curtain" on dialogue, we are very explicit in naming "what" we are teaching.

During the Dialogue Micro-lesson

What and Why? As we learn and talk with each other, our ideas are growing all the time. I have noticed you sometimes even *change* your thinking after you hear someone else talk or you get new information! That is so awesome, because that means your ideas are growing as you become a better listener and talker. When that happens to you, it is a great moment to tell us about, because it might help other people reflect on their thinking too.

We always want to provide a rationale to our students for "why" this dialogue move is important, and how it applies to them.

How? Here's one way you can talk about how your ideas are changing (*reference or draw parts of the anchor chart as you talk*):

1. As you listen to the conversation, check in with yourself. Notice when your brain says, "Oh, I'm changing my mind."
2. You can share that thinking with the group. You might say, "I used to think _____, but now I'm thinking _____," or "I want to change what I said before."

This section provides one possible set of manageable step-by-step directions for "how" to try this skill out. There are almost always other ways to implement this skill—this is one suggestion.

Revising Ideas

I used to think ___, but now I'm thinking ___.
OR
I want to change what I said...

Sample anchor chart for you to modify to meet your students' needs.

This is the moment when we give the students the opportunity to try out the move. It will be either in the form of a Turn and Talk, Conversation Club, or Hands-Down Conversation. In the lesson we suggest a format, indicated by the icon, and we show one example conversation topic. You will choose a format and conversation topic for your Guided Practice that makes sense for your students.

During the Hands-Down Conversation

Guided Practice: It Might Sound Like . . . As a class, we've been thinking a lot about what sorts of "rules" there are in our world about being a boy and being a girl. Yesterday we looked at a collection of toy advertisements and noticed what objects, colors, words, and people were in the ads. Let's put those back up on the screen today and talk more about them. What messages might these companies be telling us about being a boy or being a girl? Remember, as you listen to your friends talk, you might change your thinking. Please let us all know if you have one of those "I'm changing my mind!" moments!

Facilitation Moves As the Hands-Down Conversation unfolds, you will want to highlight and encourage any moments in which a child tries out this revision move. You want to make sure the message is loud and clear that changing your thinking isn't an admission of "being wrong," but a sign of reflective listening and thinking. You might say something like "This is so cool! Jannice is thinking about this in a new way because of what Tamara said!" or "Wow, Elias is listening *so* carefully that he is thinking about this a new way now." You can also prompt students to reflect on their thinking after a particularly provocative comment during the conversation by saying, "Hmmm, what Jorge just said is really making me think. Is anyone else thinking differently about things now? You can let us know if you are." As always, be selective about how many times you jump into the conversation. You can always save an encouraging comment for after the conversation is over.

This section has some suggested facilitation moves for you to keep in mind while your students are engaged in guided practice. It might include things you can listen for and wording to try out as you nudge and coach your students to take on the dialogue move.

After the Hands-Down Conversation

Reflect This conversation brought up some different ways of thinking. Turn and talk to your partner about what new ideas you are having now. How has this conversation changed your thinking?

Reinforce We are learning and growing from listening to each other. Isn't it cool to think about all the powerful thinkers in this class and in the world that we can listen to? Whenever you are talking with someone, you can notice those moments where you say to yourself, "I'm changing my mind," and talk about how your thinking is changing.

Teacher Tip

As you look for a subject for this Hands-Down Conversation, be sure to pick something that will lead to divergent thinking and multiple perspectives. This is usually true of Hands-Down Conversation topics, but it will be important to be especially mindful of this today.

This is an extra "Teacher Tip" to consider as you facilitate the Hands-Down Conversation or teach the lesson.

We rename the dialogue move in a generative way to encourage transfer and reinforce student approximations.

In some of the lessons we build in a moment for student reflection. You can choose to add a reflection to any lesson. This reflective moment encourages student self-awareness and agency in the discourse community.

...ng Ideas   **111**

The Micro-lesson Structure

As shown on pages 44–45, each dialogue lesson has three parts: "During the Dialogue Micro-lesson," "During the Conversation," and "After the Conversation." This format allows us to introduce a new talk or listening move, provide some talk time to practice it in a scaffolded way, and then reflect and rename the move at the end.

During the Dialogue Micro-Lesson, or "What, Why, How"

You will notice each lesson opens with a "What/Why/How" structure. This structure remains consistent throughout the book, which is an intentional choice. We want to provide our students with a clear explanation of *what* we are teaching them, a brief rationale as to *why* this tool is important, and then some step-by-step directions explaining *how* to try the tool out. This is a useful and familiar teaching structure to turn to for describing explicit skills. By using this structure, we help ourselves stay succinct and keep the lesson "micro" in size. It keeps us and the students focused on just one aspect of dialogue at that moment. That way, we can provide students with tools and tips and then quickly hand the conversation back over to them. The What/Why/How structure also provides explicit steps that allow a child to try a technique that is often quite complex, such as entering their voice into a conversation. You will note that we have laid out possible steps as a "how" for you to try with your students in our micro-lessons, but in most cases, there are *many* ways that people in the real world achieve these dialogue moves. You can also write your own "hows" that make sense to you and your own students.

During the Conversation

The most important work comes after the micro-lesson, when the students immediately "have a go" with these dialogue tools themselves, using and building on them to create new understandings through talk. This can happen in a Hands-Down Conversation, a small group, or a partnership. We call this "guided practice," since it is a conversational moment for the students that is scaffolded in some way (either by making the content lighter, providing supportive facilitation moves, or orchestrating partnership/small-group work to try out the skill). Our goal is for students to integrate these new talk and listening moves into their existing talk toolbox, and we look for evidence of this integration during the guided practice. In many of the lessons, we include "facilitation moves," which are suggestions for how you can encourage transfer of the new talk and listening moves during the guided practice.

Guided practice is also the point at which you might embed the talk and listening moves back into some content. In the "Guided Practice: It Might Sound Like . . ." section of each lesson, we provide an *example* of how you might give students an opportunity to try out the dialogue move immediately after you teach it. We use examples from classrooms in which we have worked, but we do not intend that you will use our sample topics for conversation with your students. Instead, you will select content that makes sense for your group of students. Remember, whatever you select, you'll want it to be something with room for ambiguity and plenty of opportunity for listening to multiple perspectives and ideas. Section III of this book will further support you as you plan for literacy and math Hands-Down Conversations, and Appendix C provides suggestions for sample social or class-community topics to talk about with your students.

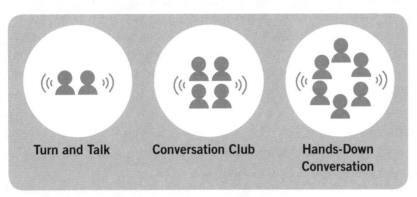

Figure II.1 Possible structures for student conversation

You'll notice that the guided practice part of the micro-lessons takes the form of Turn and Talks, Conversation Clubs, and Hands-Down Conversations (Figure II.1). We believe that all three of these formats for conversation have different benefits and allow children to talk and listen in different ways. As you plan a lesson, you will want to consider which guided practice format makes the most sense for your students in each conversation—it may be different from the one we have selected to highlight, and that is perfectly fine!

Figure II.2 Kindergarten students in Katie Keier's class take part in guided practice of a new talk skill in a Conversation Club.

After the Conversation

Sometimes, after trying out a new skill we pause for a reflective moment. This provides an opportunity for students to consider how their own talk is growing and changing. We have provided examples within some of the micro-lessons in the section entitled "Reflect."

Every lesson ends with a section called "Reinforce." This step takes place after the Hands-Down Conversation and provides an opportunity to remind students of the lesson focus of the day, and (hopefully) to name one or two moments you observed during the lesson when students were attempting to take on the new move. It can also be a chance for you to explain how students can go forward using this move in future conversations.

Anchor Charts

Anchor charts are a powerful tool that you can post in your room and refer back to during Hands-Down Conversations that take place days or weeks after the micro-lesson. In each micro-lesson, we provide an example of what an anchor chart for that lesson might look like; however, you will adapt them in ways that make sense for your students. We have found that anchor charts are most powerful when (a) the students are present during their creation, and (b) the charts are created with a minimal number of pictures and words. To create the charts with our students while still keeping our talk lessons truly "micro" in size, we usually half-complete the anchor chart before the lesson and draw or write in the "meat" of the chart with the students in front of us (Figures II.3 and II.4).

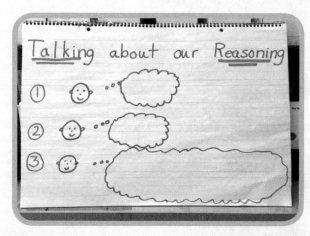

Figure II.3

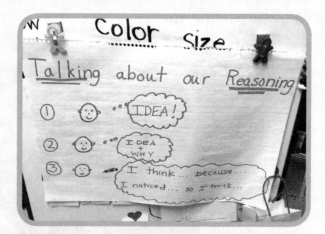

Figure II.4

For example, we may prepare the chart by writing the title of the dialogue move and the numbers 1, 2, and 3 on the paper. Then, while we teach the lesson to the students, we will sketch a little picture next to each number (or write a couple of words) to create a reminder of the skill. We try to put as few words on the chart as possible, thinking carefully about what students really need to remember. The chart should serve to jog their memory—it's not the entire lesson written out verbatim. We are also careful not to post too many anchor charts in the classroom at once. By listening to your students' Hands-Down Conversations, you will learn which anchor charts are the most useful to keep posted in your talk community.

Our editor and friend Tracy Zager stumbled upon a quote from the cookbook *The River Cottage Meat Book* that perfectly sums up how we feel about the micro-lessons in this book. "The recipes work, but don't feel bound by them. There are infinite prescriptions for borscht from Siberia to Ukraine. And it is well known that no two French chefs can agree on how to make the perfect pot-au-feu. Make mine once, twice if you really like it. Then next time make your own" (Fearnley-Whittingstall 2007, 274). Take the chef's advice here too! We hope these micro-lessons serve as a valuable resource, but even more, we hope you write your own lessons for your students, as you help them take on new ways of expressing their ideas through talk.

4

Jumping In

At a Glance: *You'll Know You're Ready for the Lessons in This Chapter When . . .*

- Students are able to come to the meeting area and form a circle or sit on the edges of the carpet. That's it! There are no prerequisite dialogue skills for starting Hands-Down Conversations.

- You will want to return to lessons in this chapter throughout the year as your class works together to refine your Hands-Down community.

As teachers of writing, math, and reading, we are very familiar with the idea that learning is a series of approximations. Hands-Down Conversations are also always works in progress. Just like the first time Kassia handed over the stapler to her students, handing over control of deciding who speaks when and how much will feel a little messy at first. You can bet that despite a careful lesson on stapler usage, there were many instances of jammed staples and crumpled papers as students took on the new responsibility. That's part of the process. It was worth the mess, because the stapler is an important tool that allows students to be more independent writers with the agency to make changes to their books. Similarly, learning the tools of talk empowers students' voices beyond the space of teacher-facilitated conversations.

You can expect that your first Hands-Down Conversations will be filled with bumps and stumbles. That is *exactly where you want to be*, because the first few conversations you have will give you information about where to begin in your work and help you decide what talk micro-lessons make sense for your students now. Let's see how two classrooms got started with Hands-Down Conversations. As you read, think about what the next steps might be for these two classes.

Beginnings

It is fall in Erin's fourth-grade class. Erin and Kassia have just launched Hands-Down Conversations and are collaborating to figure out what might be next for these students as conversationalists. The class is working together to make sense of a graph (Figure 4.1).

Kassia: So, let's talk about what we notice and wonder about this graph. Remember, we don't have to raise our hands. Who would like to start us off?

(There is silence. The students look at each other, at Kassia, and at Erin. There is some squirming and nervous giggling—the quiet can be uncomfortable! Finally, Marco raises his hand. Kassia gestures at Marco encouragingly, whispering "Remember, hands down," and looks down at the clipboard in her hand, hoping Marco will talk to the class, not to the teachers.)

Marco *(looking right at Erin)*: A lot of rhinos were getting killed.

(There's more silence. Marco nudges Harley, who sits next to him.)

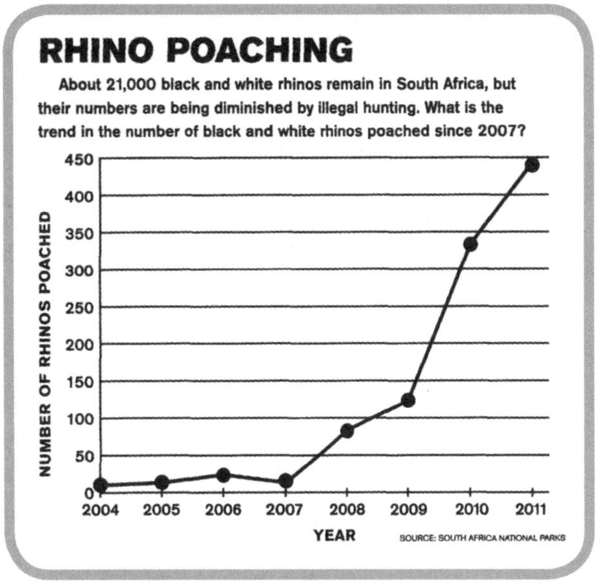

RHINO POACHING
About 21,000 black and white rhinos remain in South Africa, but their numbers are being diminished by illegal hunting. What is the trend in the number of black and white rhinos poached since 2007?
450
400
350
300
250
200
150
100
50
0
NUMBER OF RHINOS POACHED
2004
2005
2006
2007
2008
2009
2010
2011
YEAR
SOURCE: SOUTH AFRICA NATIONAL PARKS

Figure 4.1 Fourth graders made sense of this graph about rhino poaching.

Harley *(looking between Erin and Kassia)*: No rhinos were killed in 2004, and then in 2011 a lot were killed.

Jasper *(who sits next to Harley)*: Pass!

Kassia: Oh, remember, we aren't going in a circle. Anyone can speak . . . and no one has to speak.

(More silence follows.)

Now let's visit another classroom. Mary Beth Dillane has been trying Hands-Down Conversations with her second-grade students in various subjects for a few months now. Christy joins her class on a Wednesday morning to listen as they discuss the book Mary Beth has just read to them, *How to Heal a Broken Wing* (2017), by Bob Graham. The energy in the room becomes electric when Mary Beth picks up her clipboard and positions herself behind the circle, saying, "Let's have a Hands-Down Conversation about one big idea from this book: 'Responsibility.' Who would like to start us off?"

Eliza: I think you really shouldn't help birds or other animals 'cause they are wild.

Jason: No, no, you *should* help them if they need it. It's umm . . . hurt . . . and . . .

Eliza: I'm just saying, it could make the bird mother mad. I heard once at a nature center . . .

Adonis: *(interrupting)* Wait, you just talked, Eliza. Now it's someone else's turn. Jorge.

Eliza: I was just saying . . .

Adonis: Jorge, you talk.

Jorge: I, uh . . . I think you could help a bird maybe . . . if . . . ?

Eliza: *(interrupting)* I still didn't finish!

(Several other students join in, now all talking at the same time, trying to be heard.)

Does any of this sound familiar? Some of these conversations may even remind you of meetings you've attended as an adult! Everyone talks at once. Or no one talks at all. People are a bit confused about who is in charge, and to whom to direct their comments. Maybe one person emerges as a self-appointed leader, directing the conversation uncomfortably. These patterns can be challenging for a teacher to listen to without jumping in to "fix." They could even lead one to abandon Hands-Down Conversations altogether. There was plenty of reason at this juncture for Mary Beth or Erin to throw in the towel and say, "Well, I don't think these Hands-Down Conversations work for me this year. My students are just too chatty/quiet/bossy/new to English/young for this kind of talk." But they didn't. Instead of reverting back to taking control of the conversation, Erin and Mary Beth recognized that if they empowered their students with the tools of talk, they could work across the year to explore content and construct understanding in a deeper, more meaningful way (and maybe help these children navigate those painful adult conversations of the future!). Both of these teachers examined these early attempts with a problem-solving lens, just as Kassia and Mary Anne did with that chaotic kindergarten writing workshop, and asked themselves, "What's next for these students?" That's where the micro-lessons on dialogue come in.

Ready . . . Set . . . Jump

The lessons in this chapter will prepare you to "jump in" and orient students to the structure of Hands-Down Conversations so you can start trying them with your students right away. We have noticed there are recognizable patterns in the development of classroom discourse within this structure. For example, most students, regardless of their age or the content they are learning, need to spend time exploring these launching lessons to get going with Hands-Down Conversations. The purpose of the micro-lessons in this chapter is to establish the building blocks of the talk community, which will be constructed by both the teacher and the students. As you do the work in these lessons, students will get to know each other as conversationalists and begin to work together to create a safe place for everyone to express their ideas. You will also want to revisit this chapter as you work together to create a community. The later lessons in this chapter in particular are ones that classes come back to even when they are well into their work with Hands-Down Conversations. Some classes will probably spend more time exploring this chapter, whereas others may spend more time in the following chapters. Either way, we recommend starting with these lessons as you build the community in your class and set the stage for those deeper conversations and more complicated talk. It

ONE TIME . . .

One thing you can expect as you get started is some off-topic or just barely on-topic participation. This is especially true with younger students. We are all familiar with the "One time, my grandma . . . ." story that often peppers kindergarteners' and first graders' conversations. Let those errant stories go for now and resist the temptation to abruptly cut the child off. In *Comprehension Through Conversation: The Power of Purposeful Talk in the Reading Workshop*, Maria Nichols teaches us that before we work on building conversations that move mountains, we need to "have our learners focused and all members participating in the talk" (2006, 41). It takes time to orient students to the kind of academic conversation we hope for in the classroom.

The goal of the work in this chapter is to get everyone highly engaged, get lots of students confidently participating, and build a trusting classroom community that opens the door for students to be brave and take risks in sharing their thinking. If you find a conversation becoming totally derailed by off-topic exchanges, do a Turn and Talk to refocus. And if you want to work on focusing children on the topic at hand, you can do it there in the partnership. The ways we listen to all of our students' comments at this point, even off-topic comments, will send the message "You are important. We need your voice in our community!"

can be tempting to make a mental checklist of all the things your students aren't yet doing in their conversations at this point: "They aren't really listening to each other!" "That comment didn't connect at all!" Resist the urge to rush to teach everything at once. Focus instead on celebrating the skills students bring with them to the classroom and the community you are building with this first set of micro-lessons.

Splash!

So, you've got your clipboard and pencil ready to take notes.

Your students can gather in a circle.

You've got something to talk about—even if for now it's just issues with the class pencil sharpener.

You're ready.

Jump in.

If you notice . . .	You might try . . .
You're ready to get started!	**Lesson 4.1** What's a Hands-Down Conversation?
Some students are jumping into the conversation too quickly, and you know everyone needs processing time.	**Lesson 4.2** Wait Time
You're ready to introduce Turn and Talk partnerships.	**Lesson 4.3** Turn and Talk, Part 1: Getting Started
Students are ready to get to know their Turn and Talk partners better and learn more about intentional listening.	**Lesson 4.4** Turn and Talk, Part 2: Getting to Know My Talk Partner

If you notice . . .	You might try . . .
When students turn and talk, it's mostly a "share" time in which each person says one thing and then they are "done," without really listening to the other.	**Lesson 4.5** Turn and Talk, Part 3: I'm a Strong Listener
Students have had some practice with Turn and Talk partners and are ready to transfer these skills to small-group conversations.	**Lesson 4.6** Conversation Clubs
Students are mumbling or talking so quietly that other children can't hear them.	**Lesson 4.7** We Talk So Everyone Can Hear Us
The Hands-Down Conversation feels unbalanced in terms of participation.	**Lesson 4.8** Too Many Voices at the Same Time OR **Lesson 4.9** Chirping Crickets
You have a few students who dominate the whole conversation and/or a few students who rarely talk.	**Lesson 4.10** Self-Monitoring Voices
Your students have been working on various talk and listening moves (like those taught in Lessons 4.1–4.10), and you want to encourage individual growth and reflection.	**Lesson 4.11** Setting and Reflecting on Goals with Partners

What's A Hands-Down Conversation?

As soon as students are able to gather on the carpet in a meeting area, they are ready to have a Hands-Down Conversation. You may think you should wait until class rules and norms are established, but it is even easier if students learn that this is a regular part of the classroom from day one. That being said, however, you can start Hands-Down Conversations at any point in the year.

During the Dialogue Micro-lesson

What and Why? Students, one of the ways we can talk to each other in our classroom is by having a Hands-Down Conversation. A Hands-Down Conversation is when we talk together about an idea, but we don't raise our hands. We want to have these types of conversations in our room because they give us all a chance to hear each other's amazing ideas. A Hands-Down Conversation is the same thing you have during a family meal or when you're sitting with a group of friends. It's what grown-ups do at work meetings and with friends too. Today I'll teach you how we have this kind of conversation.

How?

1. Sit in a circle where everyone can be seen and you can see everyone.
2. Listen for a quiet space to slide your voice in so there is just one voice at a time.
3. Don't raise your hand.
4. Share your idea.

During the Hands-Down Conversation

Guided Practice: It Might Sound Like . . . Today we will start by having a conversation about this idea: "It would be better if it was winter all the time than if it was summer all the time." (*Any classroom community issue or social topic like this is a good way to start. Everyone has access to these ideas. We recommend forming the launch as a statement instead of a question because we've found students are less likely to give one-word responses. Begin with a few moments of Turn and Talk before the Hands-Down Conversation to allow students to get some ideas out.*) Let's give it a go. Remember, you don't have to wait for me to call on you. Who would like to start us off?

Facilitation Moves During these first Hands-Down Conversations, your main role is that of listener and noticer. This focus sends the clear message to students that these conversations belong to them. Look down at your clipboard, and wait, wait, wait to jump in, even if the talk seems to be a bit chaotic (or quiet). You may be surprised to see what actions students take to try to organize the conversation! Take lots of notes—this data will help you figure out what to teach next. Remember Alfie Kohn's teeth marks? There are many moments during Hands-Down Conversations when biting our tongue is the most important facilitation move we can make. When the conversation has gone on long enough, or when there is a natural break in the conversation, go ahead and interrupt with a quick summary of some of the ideas you heard and reinforce students' efforts in this new way of talking.

After the Hands-Down Conversation

Reinforce Wow, today I noticed that we heard from six different students! And even more students shared their ideas in the Turn and Talk. You each got your idea into the conversation. So, remember that whenever we have a Hands-Down Conversation, we will listen for the silence and then share our ideas one at a time, without raising our hands.

> ### Teacher Tip
>
> Some crosstalk is part of most authentic conversations. Getting your voice in and out of a conversation is an imperfect science, and some people are more comfortable with crosstalk than others. In many cases, brief crosstalk does not interrupt the flow or comprehension of the conversation and does not need to be managed by the teacher. If you do note crosstalk getting in the way of conversation, you will want to design a micro-lesson to support students in how to manage it.

4.2 Wait Time

Many of us tend to be a little uncomfortable with silences during conversation. In the classroom, teachers often fill in silence by restating their question, offering support or "hints," or calling on students to try to participate. However, most of us, even those who think we don't need it, benefit from wait time to organize our ideas before speaking. This lesson might, at first glance, seem a little obvious, but that is the beauty of many of these micro-lessons—we are uncovering and making transparent the little behaviors and moves that make dialogue successful. And we have found that sometimes this lesson is as much a reminder for us as teachers as it is for the students.

During the Dialogue Micro-lesson

What and Why? We need wait time before we start to talk so that we have a chance to get our thoughts ready. At the beginning of our Hands-Down Conversations, it helps us to take a moment for wait time, before we begin talking. Today I'm going to teach you what we do during that time.

How?

1. Sit with your hands down and voice off.
2. Think: What do I really want to say about this?
3. Rehearse it or practice it in your mind.

During the Hands-Down Conversation

Guided Practice: It Might Sound Like . . .  Earlier today, in science, we read an article together about the large "trash island" that is floating in the Pacific Ocean. I've put the article back up on the SMART Board to refresh your memory. Remember it was called the "Great Pacific Garbage Patch"? I've been thinking a lot about that ever since we read it and I bet you have too. Let's talk a little about that now. We'll start with quiet wait time to collect your current thoughts and ideas about this problem. Remember, hands down and no talking while we organize our thoughts. This is your wait time. (*Try to wait a full thirty seconds if you can. Resist the temptation to fill the time with additional talk or reminders. Try silently counting or watching the clock.*) Okay, who would like to begin our conversation?

Facilitation Moves While giving wait time before beginning a conversation is always a good idea, you should also listen for additional moments when more individual thinking time may be needed to refocus the conversation. For example, you might hear several students starting to make comments that are "false starts," such as "I uh . . . uh . . . I don't know" or "I um . . . I forget." A little of this is natural, but if you hear several of these in a row, you can interrupt, saying, "It sounds like you all are really thinking hard about this and need some time to gather your ideas before we talk. Remember, so-and-so just said _____. (*Repeat the last comment or summarize the conversation so far.*) Let's have some wait time to think about how you'd like to respond to that. (*Wait twenty seconds and start again.*)"

After the Hands-Down Conversation

Reinforce Remember, any time you are about to talk to someone, or even while you are having a conversation, you can take a moment of wait time to get your ideas ready. You might say, "Let me think for a minute." In our Hands-Down Conversations, we'll give everyone time to think before we talk by not speaking and not raising our hands.

> ### Teacher Tip
>
> As students begin to take on more leadership in the conversation, you can teach them that anyone can ask for more thinking time by saying something like, "Can we have a minute to think about that?" or "I think we should stop and write about this in our journals for a minute."

Turn and Talk, Part 1

Teaching students how to turn and talk is so important that we have written three lessons on the topic. (And you'll likely invest even more time across the year helping students learn to dialogue in partnerships!) In a Turn and Talk moment, students can gain confidence and sort out their ideas in a safe space. They can prepare for sharing something with the whole group, or process what they have just heard. This lesson is about the logistics of Turn and Talk. It is not yet about really listening deeply, but just physically moving our bodies to prepare for conversation. Depending on your class and the age of your students, you may want to reteach this lesson several times over the course of a few days until this behavior is natural and fast—it could even be made into a little game to get the physical movement quick. Some students will come with previous Turn and Talk experience, and you will be able to move on after you have established the talk partners.

During the Dialogue Micro-lesson

What and Why? Today we are going to learn how to turn and talk with our talk partner. You will get the chance to talk with this person many times. Today we are going to get good at quickly moving our bodies into position to have a conversation. We turn our bodies to talk to a partner because it helps us be better listeners and talkers and lets our partner know that we want to hear their ideas.

How?

1. Turn your whole body so that you face your partner.

2. Ask: "Do you want to go first?" Decide who has the "Big Ear" role and who has the talking role.

3. Switch roles.

4. Listen for when I ____. (*Describe your preferred signal for getting students' attention, such as raising a hand, ringing a chime, or saying, "One, two, three. Turn and look at me."*) That signal means it's time to turn back around to face the whole group again.

Getting Started

During the Turn and Talk

Guided Practice: It Might Sound Like . . . Here is a chart of your Turn and Talk partners. We will keep these partnerships for a while, and then change them. Move to sit with your partner now. *(You will probably want to ask students to sit next to their talk partners from now on when you are going to have a Hands-Down Conversation.)* Earlier today we checked out books from the library for the first time. When I say, "Turn and talk," you will turn your whole body to your talking partner and talk to them about the books you chose from the library today and what kinds of books you love to read. Ready . . . Turn and talk!

Facilitation Moves As partners talk, circulate, complimenting and adjusting physical behaviors—not worrying too much yet about the content of the talk. You might try interrupting the talk a couple times to let the students practice your "signal" for returning to the group, and then have them turn and talk again, so the movement becomes fluid. Once students are familiar with Turn and Talks and are having longer conversations, you may start to let them know when their Turn and Talk time is coming to an end by saying something like, "We'll finish up our thoughts for now in one minute," and then give them your established signal, so that ending the Turn and Talk feels less abrupt.

After the Turn and Talk

Reinforce So remember, when you are talking to another person, even in the cafeteria, you can sometimes make your bodies face each other. This is one way we get ready for listening and talking.

Teacher Tip

We highly recommend establishing "talk partners" for each subject and keeping them the same for a month or so. This way, students can really get to know their partners and still have many talk partners across the year. We form these pairs more or less randomly—we don't advocate any kind of "ability grouping" for talk partnerships. Turn and Talk trios can be supportive of some students as well.

Turn and Talk, Part 2

As a classroom builds the dialogue community, it is crucial to recognize that each individual has different talk patterns and preferred indicators of listening. Cultural norms, family values, and individual hardwiring bring a beautiful diversity to human communication that we want to honor in our classrooms. For example, strong eye contact can be perceived as hostile or even rude by some, whereas others feel it is rude when a person does not make eye contact. Individuals also vary in their comfort with proximity to a speaker. The Hands-Down Conversation classroom honors these variations. Beginning to appreciate and understand these differences can start with the Turn and Talk partner. This lesson helps students begin to get to know their talk partner's preferences and style.

During the Dialogue Micro-lesson

What and Why? Everyone likes to be listened to. Doesn't it feel good when someone really shows you that they care about what you are saying? The interesting thing is, each of us shows that we are listening in different ways. Today we are going to learn how our Turn and Talk partner likes to be listened to so we can be a good talk partner for them.

How?

1. Take a moment to think about what behaviors you would like someone to do when you talk to them. What do you want their body to look like? Their face? What do you want them to say? Nothing? Lots of things? How do your family members show that they are listening to each other? Let's write some of these ideas down here on our anchor chart.

2. Now, tell your partner what kind of listening you like. Remember to look at the anchor chart for ideas to get you going. And tell your partner something you do NOT like a listener to do! (*With younger students you might assign Partner A and Partner B and tell them which partner will talk first.*)

3. Switch and listen to what your partner likes.

Teacher Tip

Model the "How" of this lesson with one student or a partner-teacher in front of the students before asking them to try it out.

Getting to Know My Talk Partner

During the Turn and Talk

Guided Practice: It Might Sound Like . . . Now that you have learned a little about your partner, we are going to try listening just the way our partner likes. Today we are not going to have a whole Hands-Down Conversation. We are just going to practice having a conversation with our Turn and Talk partners. While you talk, see if you can make your body and voice show your partner that you are listening in a way that makes them feel heard. Now turn and talk about this: "Snakes are dangerous, or snakes are not dangerous. Why?"

Facilitation Moves As partners are talking, circulate, asking students to pause their conversation while you check in with them. "So, James, do you feel like your partner is listening to you? Yes? That's great. Can you give her some feedback about exactly what she's doing well?" Keep in mind that we are not necessarily trying to get everyone to conform to *our* ideal of what a listener should look like. We can transfer this power to the students. A student may be very comfortable with his talk partner interrupting him midsentence and jumping in. That is fine, as long as both partners are okay with that!

After the Turn and Talk

Reflect Take a moment to tell your partner one thing they did today that made you feel like they were listening.

Reinforce Today you got to know your Turn and Talk partner a little better and try out being a good listener for them. We will have a lot of opportunities to keep working on this with your partner. But *whenever* you are having a conversation with someone, you can watch their body and face for clues about what behaviors they like in a listener.

This lesson sets the stage for deeper listening and paraphrasing to clarify understanding, which we will build upon in Chapter 6. Listening to understand is a difficult skill that develops over time. It's okay right now if the students don't fully understand their partners' ideas and are just making attempts to hear them. In kindergarten and first grade, full development of this skill may take a good portion of the year for some students (in terms of social maturity). Therefore, you will want to keep circling back to reteach and reinforce this lesson periodically. Although many older students have some listening skills in place, we have found that it is still worthwhile to teach them this lesson before moving on to deeper listening moves.

During the Dialogue Micro-lesson

What and Why? Students, you have been working on being excellent Turn and Talk partners and showing your partner that you are listening. Today I want to teach you that when you turn and talk, you have another important job. You will listen to your partners' idea SO well that after they talk, you will understand both their idea AND your idea! We do this because when we listen to other people's ideas it helps our ideas grow too!

How?

1. When you are the "Big Ear" partner, keep your body facing the talker and show that you are listening just the way your partner likes it.

2. When they are talking, try to understand their idea so well that you could tell everyone about it when we come back to the circle.

3. Switch.

4. Switch again if you have time! Keep talking and listening the *whole* time until the teacher calls you back to the circle.

5. Try sharing your idea *or* your partner's idea in our Hands-Down Conversation.

Turn + Talk:
I'm a Strong Listener
1. talk → Listen
2. Think → their idea
3. Try sharing your partner's idea!

I'm a Strong Listener

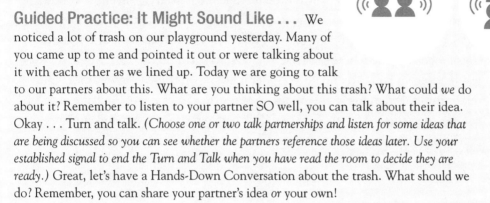

During the Turn and Talk and Hands-Down Conversation

Guided Practice: It Might Sound Like . . . We noticed a lot of trash on our playground yesterday. Many of you came up to me and pointed it out or were talking about it with each other as we lined up. Today we are going to talk to our partners about this. What are you thinking about this trash? What could *we* do about it? Remember to listen to your partner SO well, you can talk about their idea. Okay . . . Turn and talk. (*Choose one or two talk partnerships and listen for some ideas that are being discussed so you can see whether the partners reference those ideas later. Use your established signal to end the Turn and Talk when you have read the room to decide they are ready.*) Great, let's have a Hands-Down Conversation about the trash. What should we do? Remember, you can share your partner's idea *or* your own!

Facilitation Moves During the Hands-Down Conversation today, you will be especially focused on whether the Turn and Talk conversations are informing what students say to the whole group. You might hear a student referencing something they discussed with their partner earlier (even if they don't explicitly say, "My partner said . . ."). Note this so you can reinforce it after the discussion. You might enter the conversation during a slow moment and say, "Remember, you can share your partner's ideas too, not just your own." Another helpful move is to have a second Turn and Talk, mid-conversation, to process what has already been said and provide another opportunity for students to hear more ideas from their partner.

Teacher Tip

As you listen to students turn and talk, consider whether to circulate and listen a bit to several partnerships or just stick with one pair and really listen to the whole conversation. While we offer recommendations for your listening throughout the micro-lessons, both options are good teacher listening moves.

After the Hands-Down Conversation

Reinforce Wow, I noticed that Jasmine shared her partner Sam's idea with us today. She must have been listening so well. Sam, I bet that felt good to have your partner listen to you, right? Remember, any time you are talking with another person, your job is to listen so well that you can understand their idea *and* your idea.

Conversation Clubs

As students deepen their skills as listeners and talkers through their Turn and Talk partnerships, it is helpful for them to extend this practice to small groups, which we call Conversation Clubs, adapted from Serravallo's work with Read-Aloud Clubs (2010). Conversation Clubs offer students opportunities to further develop, in small groups, these talk and listening moves, which they can transfer both to the whole-group setting and to small-group work where there is less teacher support. You might consider building on these Conversation Club relationships by having these groups meet for small-group work outside of the whole-group time. As with Turn and Talk partners, we recommend students remain with the same Conversation Club for a month or so in order to develop and refine working relationships with the people in the group.

During the Dialogue Micro-lesson

What and Why? We've been doing a lot of thinking with our Turn and Talk partners. Today you and your Turn and Talk partner will meet with another Turn and Talk partnership. This group of four people will be your Conversation Club. We'll meet with our Conversation Clubs any time we want to talk about ideas in a small group. These clubs will allow us to talk about more people's ideas than we do in a Turn and Talk, but still be in a small group.

How?

1. Look at our Conversation Club list to see who you and your Turn and Talk partner will meet with.

2. Find your Conversation Club and make a little circle together so everyone can see and hear each other.

3. Share the conversation. Listen and talk. Ask each other questions. Try to keep the conversation going.

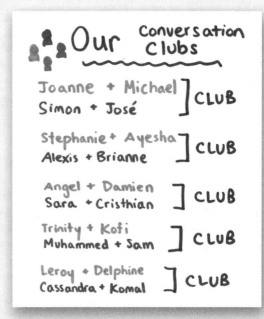

Our Conversation Clubs

Joanne + Michael
Simon + José] CLUB

Stephanie + Ayesha
Alexis + Brianne] CLUB

Angel + Damien
Sara + Cristhian] CLUB

Trinity + Kofi
Muhammed + Sam] CLUB

Leroy + Delphine
Cassandra + Komal] CLUB

Figure 4.2 A Conversation Club chart helps students quickly find their group.

During the Conversation Club

Guided Practice: It Might Sound Like . . . Since today is our first day working with our Conversation Clubs, we're going to try out this "Would you rather?" question: Take a look at the pictures of the two choices. Would you rather be able to grab a handful of mini candy bars from this bag? Or would you rather have one king-size candy bar? There's no right answer—you're practicing really listening to the members of your club. And if someone doesn't explain *why* they chose the handful of mini chocolate bars or the single giant chocolate bar, you can ask them! Try to keep the conversation going for a while.

Facilitation Moves Since this lesson is more about establishing behaviors, you will want to circulate around, listening briefly to several coaching groups and giving them a little feedback before moving on. If you see a group has concluded its conversation, you might stop by to ask a question, such as "How do you know your club members are listening to each other?" "What will you do if someone isn't talking much in your Conversation Club?" or "How can you keep your conversation going?" Remember, you're not looking for a right answer from students here, but rather working to support the Conversation Clubs as they develop ways of talking together as a group.

After the Conversation Club

Reflect The kids in the class next door are starting their Conversation Clubs later today. Now that you've met and talked with your club, what listening and talking tips do you have for those students as they get started with their Conversation Clubs?

Reinforce Getting to share ideas with your Conversation Club will be both interesting and challenging. Sharing a conversation with more than one other person can be tricky sometimes, but it's also fun to hear and build on different people's ideas. We'll keep meeting with our Conversation Clubs and getting to know one another as people and thinkers.

> ## Teacher Tip
>
> Over the next few days, have students meet in their Conversation Clubs in a few different content areas. Having multiple opportunities to talk about different ideas helps students get to know each other within the context of these new groups.

We Talk So Everyone Can Hear Us

We've all facilitated classroom conversations in which some students speak so softly that they cannot be heard—by their teachers or their classmates! Sometimes we, as teachers, jump in and say, "Speak up, please," or restate students' words for them. Other times we may be hesitant to ask these students to talk louder because we are just so happy that they are talking at all—however quietly. In these situations, most students are unable to hear the ideas of the quiet speakers, and the class is dependent on the teacher to intervene. Empowering students to help each other monitor voice level sends the message that all voices are important and that we all have a responsibility to make sure we hear each other's ideas. When we teach this lesson, we tell students: "All voices are important and should be heard. We can use our strong speaking voices, and we can help our classmates make their voices heard."

During the Dialogue Micro-lesson

What and Why? When we have a conversation, it is important to talk in a strong voice that everyone can hear. Sometimes people speak so quietly that we cannot hear them. We can send them a respectful signal to speak with a stronger voice. This is important because all of us—the people with louder voices and the people with quieter voices—have important ideas. We need to make sure we can hear everyone's important ideas.

How? Talk so everyone can hear your voice. Help make sure we can hear each other's voices.

1. Start to say your idea.
2. Watch for our class signal that anyone in the class is having a hard time hearing you.
3. Our class signal will be touching your ear. (*Model how to do this in a respectful way that conveys the message but does not interrupt the speaker.*)
4. If you see the signal, change your speaking voice to try again with more volume.

Figure 4.3 Christy models a signal the community members might use to remind each other to speak louder.

During the Hands-Down Conversation

Guided Practice: It Might Sound Like . . . Today we're going to do a "Same or Different" routine. Just like we have done before, you can argue for ways they are the same and ways they are different. Let's turn and talk with our partners about what we're thinking. (*Listen in to a couple of partnerships. You might ask a student if they would be willing to start the Hands-Down Conversation.*) Let's come back together. Remember that because everyone's ideas are important, we will all use strong voices so we can hear each other. And if you can't hear someone—that happens sometimes—you'll show them our class signal in a respectful way. Kendra, would you be willing to start us off with your idea?

Facilitation Moves One particularly useful move as children are taking on new talk and listening moves is to play the role of the "ghost partner" during a Hands-Down Conversation (Serravallo 2010). For this skill, that might mean that you crouch behind a student and whisper, "Can you hear him? No? Remember, you can ask him to speak louder by touching your ear." As always, use this kind of prompting judiciously, as over-prompting can result in students' relying on you to do this work for them rather than taking it on for themselves.

> ### Teacher Tip
>
> Establishing a nonverbal class signal to communicate that you cannot hear someone can provide a helpful and respectful way for students to remind each other to speak louder. However, it's also okay for students to simply say, "Could you speak a little louder, please?"

After the Hands-Down Conversation

Reflect Let's turn and talk with our partner for a moment to reflect. Could you hear everyone's voice? Was the signal helpful and respectful in this conversation? What can we keep working on? I'll come around and listen in on your conversations so that I can hear what you want to keep working on in our next conversation.

Reinforce When we let someone know that we can't hear them, we're telling them, "Your ideas are important! We want to hear them!" We will all keep working on using strong speaking voices in our class and everywhere.

4.8   Too Many Voices at the Same Time

As you launch Hands-Down Conversations, one of the first challenges you and your students will work together to problem-solve is how to share the conversation so that one person (more or less!) speaks at a time. It can be tempting to replace hand-raising with another external way of monitoring turn-taking, such as having a talking stick that one must hold in order to speak or giving students a certain number of "talking chips" that they have to contribute to a pile each time they speak. We strongly discourage these practices! If we want students' dialogue skills to transcend the classroom space, we need to teach them how to balance listening and speaking in authentic ways. This balance of listening and speaking takes practice, for sure, but we are continuously amazed at how students of all ages take this on and are successful with it. We launch this lesson in a Conversation Club because it can be easier to develop this skill in a small group and follow that up with practice in a Hands-Down Conversation.

During the Dialogue Micro-lesson

What and Why? Sometimes in Hands-Down Conversations, lots of us have ideas—and many of us want to share them at the same time! It can be hard to figure out how to get your voice into the conversation. Today I'm going to teach you some ways that you can listen for the space in a conversation and slide your voice in. Being part of a conversation means talking *and* listening. It is important to figure out ways we can all do *both* of these things.

How? Here's one way you can slide your voice into a conversation:

1. Listen for space in the conversation. This sounds like someone finishing their idea or a little bit of quiet.

2. Lean in and say, "I think . . ." to slide your voice in and get your idea started.

3. If you hear someone else start to speak or see them lean forward to speak at the same time, you might say, "You can go first."

Slide your voice into a Conversation
1. Listen for space shhh
2. Lean in — I think...
3. I think... oops! — You can go!

During the Conversation Club

Guided Practice: It Might Sound Like . . . Today we're going to practice by meeting with our Conversation Clubs. Remember that a Conversation Club is two Turn and Talk groups, so four people. If you need help remembering who you and your Turn and Talk partner will meet with, you can check out the chart here. When I say, "Turn and talk," you will make a little circle with these four people and practice sharing the conversation—listening for the space and sliding your voice into the conversation when you're ready. Today we're going to practice by talking about this "Which One Doesn't Belong?" image of spirals (Figure 4.4). What do you notice? Which spirals might go together? And which one do you think doesn't belong? Why? Okay, turn and talk.

Figure 4.4 Which one doesn't belong? (Danielson 2016)

Facilitation Moves As groups of four talk in their Conversation Clubs, choose a single club to listen to. If you notice only a couple of people are doing most of the talking, you might teach kids how to invite someone else into the conversation. You might say, "When you realize you've done a lot of talking, you can decide to shift to a listener role and invite someone into the conversation. You can say something like, 'What do you think about this, Cate?'"

You can notice and name the talk moves you want to encourage by saying something like this: "When Jason and Aaron started talking at the same time, Jason kept the conversation going when he said, 'Go ahead, Aaron,' and let Aaron speak first." Be sure to spend some of the time listening and taking notes on how students are talking in their Conversation Clubs. Listening is your best tool for thinking about what is next for your learners.

After the Conversation Club

Reflect Today we've thought a lot about how to share the conversation. As I was listening to Conversation Clubs today, I heard Jason and Aaron start to talk at the same time. Jason said, "Go ahead, Aaron." That helped everyone get their voices into the Conversation Club. Turn back to your club and talk about what went well in your conversation. What was a little tricky?

Reinforce Anytime you are talking with a group of people, you can watch for clues that other people are trying to speak at the same time. When you see one of those signs, think about offering, "You can go first." You can find ways to share the conversation whether you're with your Turn and Talk partner, with your Conversation Club, in a Hands-Down Conversation, or even chatting with friends after school.

> *Teacher Tip*
>
> The purpose of the sample anchor charts is to offer ideas for supporting students with visuals and words as they take on new dialogue moves. Just as we encourage you to adapt the talk micro-lessons in this chapter, we hope you will also adapt these anchor charts to meet the needs of your students.

4.9 Chirping Crickets

When launching Hands-Down Conversations, the challenge for some classes is too many voices talking at one time. Some classes, on the other hand, have just the opposite challenge! Students in these classes are unsure of how to begin a conversation without the teacher's frequent prompting, so no one says much at all. When no one is speaking, we might be tempted to institute something like round-robin sharing, in which each student takes a turn speaking as we go around the circle. Instead, we can use more authentic facilitation strategies to generate conversation, such as giving students time to turn and talk or allowing them to prepare for the discussion by writing or drawing about their ideas ahead of time.

During the Dialogue Micro-lesson

What and Why? Sometimes when we have a Hands-Down Conversation, we're not sure about how to get the conversation started or how to keep it going. You might be thinking, "Should I start talking or should I wait for someone else to talk?" You might be feeling nervous about sharing a new idea. You might not have an idea to share yet.

How? When we're having a hard time starting a conversation or keeping a conversation going, there are a few strategies we can use to get us warmed up: (1) turn and talk with our partners, (2) draw and write on our own before we talk, or (3) both!

> ### Teacher Tip
> While this lesson is especially appropriate when you are first launching Hands-Down Conversations, it can be useful at other times as well. For example, students may become silent when engaging with new or difficult content. This could be a productive time to teach or return to this lesson.

During the Hands-Down Conversation

Guided Practice: It Might Sound Like . . . Yesterday we worked on figuring out different ways four people could share a brownie equally. We came up with lots of ways we agreed on, but we couldn't agree on this one (Figure 4.5). It seemed like we needed some more time before we were ready to talk about whether this brownie was cut into equal fourths or not. Here's what we're going to do: In your math journals, you're going to draw and write for a few minutes about your thinking on this question. You might write, "This brownie is cut into equal fourths" or "This brownie is *not* cut into equal fourths." Then write and draw a little about *why*. How do you know? When we come to the circle, we'll share our thinking and our notebooks with our Turn and Talk partners before we share our ideas in a Hands-Down Conversation.

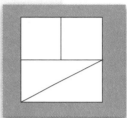

Figure 4.5
Students debate whether this brownie is cut into fourths.

Facilitation Moves Talking about journals with a partner is a skill that will develop over time with practice. You can build in scaffolds at the beginning or coach partnerships in the moment if they need support. Here is a structure for sharing journals you might use with students in need:

1. Person A opens her journal and shares an idea. She should put her journal where both people can see it.

2. Person B listens and responds to what Person A has shared.

3. Switch roles.

4. Compare your ideas. How were they the same and different?

This structure may seem a bit rigid—there are many different ways to productively discuss journal work—but teaching one way to get started can help students learn to use the journal as a useful tool in their conversations.

During an actual Hands-Down Conversation, if things get very quiet, you can increase participation by verbally or nonverbally encouraging students to share what they have written or talked about with their partner. Sometimes just pointing at a particular student's journal with an encouraging smile and whispering "Share!" is enough of a confidence boost to get a student talking. Then you can quickly get out of the way again.

After the Hands-Down Conversation

Reinforce Whenever we are not sure about how to get a conversation started or how to keep it going, we can pause the conversation to turn and talk or to write and draw. Anyone in our class can suggest that we stop and do this if they notice there are not a lot of people talking.

4.10 Self-Monitoring Voices

When you notice some students are talking too much and others' voices aren't being heard, you might use this lesson. Keep in mind that not all students will share in every whole-group conversation you have, and that is okay. However, we do want to teach students to self-monitor their own levels of participation so we can allow for a more equitable balance of voices and opinions without the teacher always orchestrating this. We might think we want to teach only the "quiet" students how to speak out, and only the "loud" students to pipe down, but in reality, each of us can be "quiet" or "loud," depending on the situation, so this is a valuable lesson to teach everyone at the same time.

During the Dialogue Micro-lesson

What and Why? In some conversations you might talk a lot and in other conversations you might talk just a little, or not at all. Sometimes you might be like this. *(Refer to the "talker" side of the anchor chart.)* You're talking and talking and doing less listening. And sometimes you might be like this. *(Refer to the "quiet" side of the anchor chart.)* You're not sure how to get yourself into the conversation. Today I'm going to teach you how you can think about which kind of talker you are being in this conversation, and how to make a plan to take action. Monitoring our voices will help us make sure we hear lots of different ideas in our class, including our own!

How? Ask yourself, "Which kind of talker am I in *this* conversation?" *(Note: We are careful not to label or identify students as "quiet" or "talkative." Instead, we help students reflect on the ways they participate in different kinds of conversations.)*

If you are feeling talkative, try this	If you are feeling quiet, try this
1. Wait. 2. Think: Is this the most important thing I must share with everyone today? If yes, say it! 3. If no, you can wait, or try inviting someone else into the conversation. Say, "Maria, what do you think?"	1. Think: What do I really want to try to say today? 2. Listen for a space. 3. Lean in with your body. 4. Say "I think . . ." or "My idea is . . ."

During the Hands-Down Conversation

Guided Practice: It Might Sound Like . . . Take a moment to reflect on the conversation we had yesterday after our read-aloud. Think about which kind of talker you were in that conversation. Turn and talk to your partner about the ways you participated yesterday. Then, make a plan for what you will try during our Hands-Down Conversation today. Make a little goal for yourself and tell your partner your plan. It might sound like this: "I'm going to listen to three people first before I talk." Or it might sound like this: "I'm going to talk one time today." After our Hands-Down Conversation, you'll tell your partner how you did today.

Facilitation Moves As partners talk about their goals for this conversation, listen in and take notes. You may notice that some students see themselves very differently than you or their peers see them. (We'll never forget when one of our most talkative students declared, "I'm shy. I need to talk more.") In other cases, students may be quite aware of themselves and not be ready to make changes. (One student asked us, "What if you know you're quiet and you don't want to change?") Try to avoid "correcting" students' goals or forcing particular goals. Let the partners help keep each other accountable.

> ### Teacher Tip
>
> When trying to get a more even balance of participation without controlling the conversation yourself, you can specifically invite someone to start the conversation who might be otherwise hesitant to join in. You can use this same move when you're concluding the conversation by asking, "Is there anyone who hasn't gotten to speak who would like to have 'the last word' for today?"

After the Hands-Down Conversation

Reflect Turn and talk with your partner about how your goal went today. Were you successful? What worked for you? What was tricky?

Reinforce Remember, when you are in a conversation, even at lunch, you can ask yourself, "Which kind of talker am I being right now?" and then take action to make sure that everyone in the conversation has a chance to be heard.

4.11 Setting and Reflecting on Goals with Partners

We want students to know that throughout their learning about conversations, they can reflect and set goals for themselves and check in on their progress. This lesson demonstrates one way to do this work in which all the students set individualized goals and check in with their partners about their progress. You can also consider setting a group goal as a class or inviting students to write privately about their goals in a notebook.

During the Dialogue Micro-lesson

What and Why? As talkers, we've been thinking a lot about ____ and ____. *(Refer to the previous talk micro-lessons you have taught that you want to be at the top of students' minds as they set goals—either from this chapter or another!)* When you are learning to do something new or to get better at something, you can set a goal for yourself. Setting a goal reminds you of what you are working on and how you are going to get better at it. Today I'd like to help you set a goal for your role in our conversation.

How? Here's one way you can set a goal:

1. Think back to some things we have been working on. *(Refer to the anchor chart(s) from one or two lessons—here we refer to Lesson 4.7, We Talk So Everyone Can Hear Us, and Lesson 4.5, Turn and Talk, Part 3: I'm a Strong Listener, but you can reference any lessons you want students to think more about.)* Some of you may be working on speaking loudly and clearly when you talk. Some of you might be working on being a strong listener for your Turn and Talk partner.

2. Think for a few moments about what *you* are working on most right now. Is it speaking clearly? Being a strong listener? Something else?

3. Tell your partner your goal and listen to your partner's goal.

4. You can try using this sentence: "I'm working on . . . so today I'm going to . . ." Make sure to tell your partner *what* your goal is and *how* you're going to work on it.

During the Turn and Talk and Hands-Down Conversation

Guided Practice: It Might Sound Like . . .

Today we are going to talk about how hard things have been at music, since Ms. Pauly is out for maternity leave. I know that has been rough. Maybe we can talk through this together and think of some ideas to make it go better between our class and the guest teacher. Let's start by talking with your Turn and Talk partner about what we could do. Remember your goal! Go ahead and talk. *(After giving partners a couple of minutes to talk, transition to a whole-group Hands-Down Conversation.)* Now we are going to share our ideas with the whole group about music class. Keep your conversation goal in your mind while we talk about music class—are you working on having a strong voice, being a strong listener today, or something else? Who would like to start us off?

Facilitation Moves As you listen to students set goals with their partners, you may want to walk around and jot down some of these goals. Reflecting on your students' goals can help you think about ways that you, as the teacher, might continue to support students in reaching their goals. For example, if a student shares that their goal is to get their voice into the whole-group conversation at least once, you might support that by listening to them during the Turn and Talk and suggesting, "Now that is an idea I think we could all benefit from hearing when we come back together as a whole group! Would you be willing to start our Hands-Down Conversation by sharing your idea?"

After the Hands-Down Conversation

Reflect So today you were thinking about a personal goal for the conversation. Take a moment to reflect on how that went. Now, share with your partner how it's going with your goal. Is there anyone who would like to tell the whole group what they were working on and what they're discovering?

Reinforce Remember, any time you are learning something new—in conversation, or in life, you can set a goal and keep it in mind to help you make progress. It is important to know that most people don't achieve their goals in one conversation. You can keep thinking about and reflecting on your goal as you talk—both here in school and outside of the classroom.

> ### Teacher Tip
>
> We sometimes ask students to write or draw their goals on a sticky note and keep this sticky note in front of them during the conversation. This note can help remind students what they are working on, and it gives you a quick bit of visual information that you can use for prompting students during the conversation.

Chapter

5

Talking About Our Ideas

At a Glance: *You'll Know You're Ready for the Lessons in This Chapter When . . .*

- Students have some experience both listening and talking with Turn and Talk partners and Conversation Clubs.

- Students may be starting to monitor their own level of participation in conversations, balancing the roles of listener and speaker.

- Students, for the most part, speak at an audible volume in whole- and small-group conversations.

- Students are taking on some of the basic turn-taking moves of Hands-Down Conversations from early in Chapter 4 but the moves may not be "mastered." You do not need to "finish" Chapter 4 before proceeding to this chapter. However, Chapter 5 will be more productive if you have done some work to collaboratively establish the norms of classroom conversation.

It's a warm afternoon in early October when Jill and her class of first graders return to the classroom from recess and make their way to the rug, skipping and loudly singing songs from their music class earlier in the day. "Let's take a look at this," Jill says, as her students gather and settle in on the rug. Jill projects a photograph of a pile of multicolored toy ocean animals. "This is the Counting Collection that our friends Gabriel and Andre counted yesterday." The chatter and squirming subside a bit.

"Hey, I've never seen that one before!" shouts out Jessie. The first graders are familiar with Counting Collections, an instructional activity in which students organize, count, and record how many objects are in their collection, but this

Figure 5.1 An unorganized Counting Collection of ocean animals

collection of fish is new to them. (For more on Counting Collections, see *Choral Counting & Counting Collections: Transforming the PreK–5 Math Classroom* (2018), edited by Megan L. Franke, Elham Kazemi, and Angela Chan Turrou.)

"Oh yes!" continues Jill. "This is a brand-new collection I've just added to the Counting Collection box. And this is a photo of what the collection looked like *before* Gabriel and Andre counted it."

Jill looks over to where Gabriel and Andre are sitting on the rug and winks. Gabriel and Andre are two wiggly kids, in the joyous (and sometimes frustrating!) way that so many first graders are. Yesterday, they spent a long time sorting and playing with the toy fish but finally buckled down to count their collection after brainstorming with Jill about how they might organize the fish to help them keep track of their count.

"Gabriel and Andre aren't going to tell us how many fish there are . . . *yet.* And they aren't going to tell us how they counted . . . *yet.* We want to hear some of your ideas first. How *might* you organize and count this collection? And *why* would you count it this way? Turn and talk to your partners about that."

After the Turn and Talk, Jill comments, "This is really interesting. You have a lot of *different* ideas all about this *one* collection of toy fish. Let's listen to some of our ideas about how we might count this collection and *why* we might count it that way. Who can start us off in a Hands-Down Conversation?"

During the Turn and Talk, Jill listened to Cameron, who is usually hesitant to share his ideas in the whole group, and she encouraged him to join the Hands-Down Conversation. "Go ahead, Cameron," Jill says when she sees he's willing to share.

Cameron: I noticed there are a whole bunch of fish there. There's a lot of them! You could make a long, long line of fish across a table and count them.

Elsie: I would use that bag they came in. I'd dump them all out and then count them while I put them back in.

Flor: You can also make groups.

Antonio: Yeah, you can count by tens, fives, or twos. Or threes. Threes are hard, though.

Caitlin: You could make groups of different colors and count the colors.

Olivia: Wait, are we going to count these fish today or not?

Alan: You could go get a hundred chart and put the fish on there!

Peter: Oh yeah, I did that yesterday with my button collection!

Jill: You have lots of ideas about how you might count this collection. Today some more partner groups will get to count this collection, and when we come back together to reflect, we'll hear from those people *and* look at the picture of what Gabriel and Andre's collection looked like *after* they counted the fish! We'll think more about *why* they might have organized and counted the way they did.

What do you notice about this conversation? Take a few moments to skim back over the transcript and reflect on what stands out to you before reading on. Here are some things that we noticed:

- Most of the students were enthusiastically engaged. Students cared about each other's ideas. And, of course, it didn't hurt to throw in a new collection and a bit of suspense. (Everyone wanted to see what that photograph of Gabriel and Andre's counted collection looked like . . . but they had to wait until later to see it!)

- In the Turn and Talk partnerships and the whole-group Hands-Down Conversation, almost all of the students who spoke shared relevant ideas that made sense and drew upon their math experiences.

- There is evidence of listening! Some students' comments connected to and built upon other students' ideas. Other students nodded in agreement when they heard an idea that matched what they were thinking.

- Although Jill asked students to explain *why* they might organize and count the fish collection in the way they chose, most students did not talk much about their reasoning. *Why* would they make a line with the fish while counting, group by tens, or use a hundred chart?

We don't doubt that the students have solid reasons for these decisions. We believe all students are reasoners from the moment they walk into our classrooms (and long before!). However, most students can benefit from collaborative work on *how* to talk about their reasoning. The micro-lessons in this chapter offer some ways to help students more clearly articulate their own thinking. Most elementary school students are working to communicate their ideas to each other in a way that is understandable and convincing. We want to help them work toward clarity of expression by taking some time to focus on them as speakers.

As we focus on helping students develop as speakers, we cannot forget the importance of growing as listeners as well. This reciprocal relationship and responsibility between speaker and listener are things we want students to understand, and to keep in mind ourselves. Bridie Raban explains that "interactive conversations involve both speakers and listeners who take care to ensure that they understand what is being talked about. They use verbal and nonverbal behaviors to supply information on the process of their co-construction of meanings, and both take a responsibility for the meanings that are shared" (2001, 33). All the work we have done in Chapter 4 on listening in partnerships and Conversation Clubs will continue to be referenced and refined at this stage.

As we take on the goal of teaching students to talk about their ideas clearly, there are two important considerations we like to keep in mind.

1. Speaking clearly is more than just putting words together in a grammatically correct construction. When we speak, we are constructing ideas based on our perspective, which comes from our previous experiences and learning. Adults who are clear communicators are aware of this, and work to help their listeners understand their point of view, providing necessary context along the way and checking in for understanding. Young students, as Raban observes, often "inappropriately assume that everyone knows what they know, and although this may be true in a close family context, away from that familiar group children need to learn to be far more explicit" (2001, 29). Learning to consider your audience and their understandings is something that comes with maturity but can also be supported and taught along the way.

2. We want to value and recognize the ways students naturally speak and express themselves, while helping them learn how to communicate with a diverse group of listeners. This doesn't mean that students must only talk "school," as this inevitably privileges some students and shuts down others. Instead, as Emdin puts it, "when teachers engage in dialogues with students that privilege unique voices, the students feel validated for who they are rather than who the teacher expects or desires them to be" (2016, 67). For example, in a classroom with many students who are bilingual in English and Spanish, some students might express their ideas in a combination of both languages. We would encourage students to speak in the way that is

comfortable to them. In addition, we would want the students who aren't bilingual to monitor their own understanding and, when necessary, respectfully say, "I'm not really sure what you mean there, can you say more about that idea?" Learning to listen to and value other people's ideas when they are expressed differently than the way you would say them is an especially important consideration for white teachers and students who, as a group, work and live in systems that privilege their needs over others'.

One last thing to note in the first-grade class's Counting Collection conversation is the teacher's (Jill's) role as a listener. When Antonio suggested counting the ocean animals by tens, fives, or twos, Jill could have said, "Oh, that would be a quick way to keep track and count!" When Alan and Peter suggested using the hundreds chart, Jill could have commented, "A hundred chart can help you keep track of the count and remember what the written number looks like." But she didn't. Instead she listened. She thought about the students' ideas and what kind of talk and listening moves they were using. And she thought about how she might structure discussion in future math classes (and in other content areas) to support students' learning about sharing their ideas and their reasoning. Developing these talking and listening skills takes time, of course, as most worthwhile things in teaching and learning do. The good news is that the more opportunities students have to talk about their reasoning and engage with the reasoning of others, the more robust and nuanced their reasoning becomes.

Figure 5.2 Kassia listens carefully as two students share their reasoning.

If you notice . . .	You might try . . .
Students are sharing ideas and opinions that may be unrelated or tangentially related to the topic of conversation.	**Lesson 5.1** Keeping the Conversation Focused
Students are sharing opinions and ideas, and might be trying to explain their reasoning, but it isn't very clear yet.	**Lesson 5.2** Supporting with Reasoning, Part 1: The Why Behind Our Ideas
Students are supporting their ideas with reasoning and are beginning to consider what kinds of evidence best supports their ideas.	**Lesson 5.3** Supporting with Reasoning, Part 2: Digging Deeper into the Why
Students are sharing ideas without monitoring how their partner(s) are understanding their ideas.	**Lesson 5.4** Am I Being Clear?

Keeping the Conversation Focused

Sometimes a conversation will become derailed by a comment that other students feel the need to argue with or address, creating a distracting sub-conversation. For example, a group of students might be discussing the character motivations in a book, and one student might comment, "When Sam ate breakfast alone, he was ignoring the other characters because he was sad." Another child might respond, "It wasn't breakfast, it was lunch." And then the conversation turns into a debate about whether it was breakfast or lunch. We want to teach all students to monitor whether their thoughts are directly related to the topic at hand. As with all of our micro-lessons, we are looking for approximations. Sometimes off-topic comments are just part of life for children and adults alike! The key is to create enough awareness of staying with a topic that these comments don't take over, and we keep the conversation going.

During the Dialogue Micro-lesson

What and Why? When we have a Hands-Down Conversation, we want to make sure that we say things that are connected to what we are talking about right now. We do this because when we all work together to think about one thing, we can learn something new or figure out something interesting. But staying focused on the topic can be hard! Sometimes, our conversations might make you think about something else from another time or place that is a *little bit* connected to our conversation but not very much.

How? So, here's one way you can stay focused on the topic (*reference or draw parts of the anchor chart as you talk*):

1. Stop and think for a moment before speaking.
2. Ask yourself: "Is this exactly what we are talking about today?"
3. If yes, lean in and say, "I think . . ."
4. If no, put that idea into your pocket. Save it for another time.

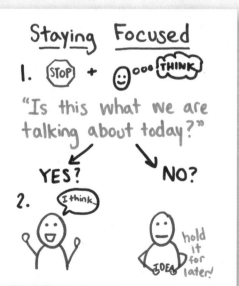

During the Hands-Down Conversation

Guided Practice: It Might Sound Like . . . Today we are going
to think a little more about the poem we read, called "The Vacuum Cleaner's
Revenge" (Janeczko 2001). I'll put it back up so we can see it. Let's think about the
perspective of the vacuum cleaner. What is it feeling and thinking? In a moment
we are going to have a Hands-Down Conversation, and we'll keep our talk focused on
the perspective of the vacuum cleaner. Here are some things you might talk about today:
How does the vacuum cleaner feel? What is it thinking? Why is it acting that way? (*On a
chart, the teacher jots a list—feel, think, act—with some picture support for these categories.*) If
you feel yourself ready to say something, you might check this list and ask yourself, "Does
my idea fit with this conversation?"

Facilitation Moves As the conversation gets going, focus on jotting down the
content of student comments and checking to see how they fit with the bigger topic. If
you find that students are sharing off-topic comments, you can try redirecting them in a
way that honors their thinking. A helpful prompt that presumes positive intention on
the part of the speaker is this: "How do you see that related to _____ [current conversational topic]?" (Cazden 2001, 89). This question allows the student an opportunity to
clarify why he made the comment, perhaps surprising everyone with
an interesting connection. If you hear the conversation veering off
topic, you can use prompts like these to gently redirect it without
shutting students down: "Let's check back in with our topic today"
(*and refer to your list*), or "Let's refocus on the idea we are talking
about today, which is _____."

Teacher Tip

When teaching this talk move, you
might want to purposely start the
conversation with a slightly narrower
(but still open-ended) topic, as in
the above example, rather than
something broad, like "What do you
think about the vacuum cleaner?"
Slightly narrowing the focus may help
students decide whether comments fit
with the topic.

After the Hands-Down Conversation

Reflect Today we focused on making sure our conversation stayed
right on topic. We were talking all about the vacuum cleaner's
perspective—how it feels and thinks and why it acts the way it does.
Take a moment to turn and talk to your partner about an idea you
wanted to say or something you *did* say that really fit well with this
conversation topic.

Reinforce Any time you are in a conversation, you can think
about what everyone is talking about. Then, before you speak, ask yourself, "Does my
idea fit with this conversation or should I save it for later?"

Supporting with Reasoning, Part 1

One of the most important elements of dialogue is engaging with the reasoning of others. In order to do this well, we need to continually work on making our own reasoning clear and understandable. In elementary school, we want to teach students to start naming the influences that shape their thinking. Students' beginning attempts at justifying their ideas might not yet be robust. ("I think triangles all have three sides because I saw a triangle yesterday.") However, at this stage, we can encourage these attempts at justification and press students to develop their ideas. In this lesson and the following one, we have provided a sample guided practice for both math and literacy. Although there are many similarities between how we reason in literacy and how we reason in math, it is important to think about the unique characteristics of reasoning within each content area as well. As you read, consider what is similar and different about the ways we reason in literacy and math. How might we harness the similarities to strengthen reasoning across content areas?

During the Dialogue Micro-lesson

What and Why? When we are explaining our ideas, we can tell people *why* we think the way we do. Giving reasons is helpful to listeners, because then they understand our ideas better.

How? Here's one way you can explain your reasoning to your listeners (*reference or draw parts of the anchor chart as you talk*):

1. When you have an idea, ask yourself, "What made me think this way?"

2. Think: Did I notice something, or do I know something that made me think this way?

3. Then share. You might say, "I think ____ because ____," or "I noticed/know ____ so that makes me think ____."

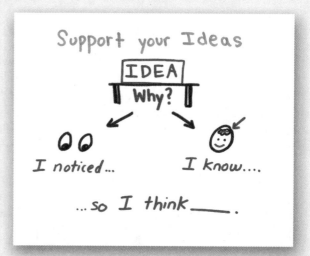

The *Why* Behind Our Ideas

During the Turn and Talk

Literacy Guided Practice: It Might Sound Like . . . We've been reading the book *The Secret School* (Avi 2003) together. You've noticed that there are a lot of "funny" objects in the book, and different ways of talking, which we call "dialects." I noticed several of you brought those things up when talking with your Conversation Clubs. That's because this book takes place in a different setting than the time and place that we live in, right? Let's think more today about the setting of this book: Elk Valley, Colorado, 1925. Although we didn't live there and then, we can put together the clues the author gives us to imagine what it would have been like. Let's take a moment to jot down some ideas about the setting in our readers' notebooks before talking with our partners, so we can think about the reasons behind our ideas. You might start by writing something like this about the setting: "I think that it was ____, because ____." Or "I think that it felt ____, because ____." After you write, we will have a Hands-Down Conversation.

Literacy Facilitation Moves While the students are writing, you can circulate, prompting students to talk through the *why* behind their ideas. Then, as the facilitator during the Hands-Down Conversation, you will take careful note of students' attempts to support their reasoning, so you can highlight and reinforce those either during or after the conversation. If you notice evidence of reasoning, and you want to reinforce that mid-conversation, you can interject, saying, "Can I just interrupt for a minute? I want you to notice what Marco did there. He explained his ideas about how he thinks it is really cold there by telling us about a TV show he saw about skiing in Colorado. That made it so easy for us to imagine and understand his thinking." On the other hand, if students aren't supporting their thinking, you can choose a few moments to enter the conversation and prompt an individual after they have shared a particularly interesting idea, saying, "Wow, let's think about that idea some more. Can you tell us *why* you think that?"

> ## Teacher Tip
>
> It is possible that the previous experiences or ideas students refer to may be misremembered or rooted in partial understandings. That is okay! The idea is that students are learning to support their thinking, and partial understandings can be highlighted as helpful in-process thinking.

Math Guided Practice: It Might Sound Like . . . Take a look at this jar of gumballs. I'm *wondering* if there are enough gumballs in here for us all to have one, but I don't really know. Before we count them, let's estimate how many gumballs we think there *might* be. What seems like an estimate that's not too low or too high? Take a moment and think. When you're ready, open your math journal and write down your estimate *and* your reasoning—why you think what you think. Your idea might sound like this: "I think there are ___ gumballs because . . ." Or it might sound like this: "I noticed _____, so I think there are ___ gumballs." When we've all had time to think and write, we'll share our estimates and our reasoning with our partners.

Math Facilitation Moves Just as in literacy conversations, you can support students' efforts to explain their reasoning by noticing and naming the reasoning they're using. "Ah, so, Carla, you came up with your estimate of twenty by thinking about how many layers of gumballs are in the jar." If a student doesn't share their reasoning, or if the reasoning is vague, you can nudge the student by saying, "What makes you think that?" Showing genuine curiosity in students' ideas encourages them to keep working to explain their ideas, even in moments of difficulty.

After the Turn and Talk

Reinforce We have worked hard today to back up our thinking with evidence and reasoning. It is important to remember that any time you are having a conversation with someone, you can think about how you are supporting your ideas. That will make your ideas easier to understand.

Supporting with Reasoning, Part 2

Our goal in this lesson is for students to be aware of different types of evidence and consider which type of reasoning best explains the *why* behind their idea. Some reasoning is best done by using evidence from within the "text" you are working. Our use of the word *text* is broad—the book, passage, image, symbol, or problem that you have in front of you as you begin the conversation. When we support our idea using information from within the text, we are pointing to evidence "right there" that everyone can access to make our point. A different but equally important way we support our ideas in conversation is by referring to previous experiences, background knowledge, or other texts. Students can learn to consider when personal experience or previous learning would most effectively support an idea, when it is more impactful to point to evidence that is "right there" in the text, and when our thinking represents a combination of within- and outside-the-text reasoning.

During the Dialogue Micro-lesson

What and Why? I have noticed that when you are talking with each other, you are supporting your ideas with reasoning. You're telling us *why* you think what you think. Sometimes our *why* is something we notice right there in the book or problem we're talking about. And sometimes our *why* is something we know from our own lives, such as something we've learned before, or another book we've read or problem we've worked on. When we explain our reasoning—when we talk about the *why* behind our ideas—we can choose the kind of evidence that makes the most sense.

How? Here's one way you can choose the best kind of evidence for your idea *(reference or draw parts of the anchor chart as you talk)*:

1. Think about your idea. Ask yourself: "Why do I think that's true?"
2. You might support your idea with
   * something you notice "right there" in the text or problem;
   * something we've learned before;
   * something from your own life; or
   * a combination of these kinds of reasoning.

3. Decide which evidence will support your ideas. It is especially helpful if you can bring something to the conversation that we aren't already thinking about. You might want to choose information from "inside" the text if the proof is right there to see, but no one seems to have noticed it. You might want to choose information from "outside" the text if you have a new experience or some previous learning to refer to that we have not talked about yet.

During the Hands-Down Conversation

Math Guided Practice: It Might Sound Like . . . Do you remember when we estimated how many gumballs were in the jar yesterday? After we estimated, we counted the gumballs, and there ended up being twenty-six gumballs in there! Well, today we're going to estimate how many gumballs are in this *big* jar! Remember, when you estimate you're going to think about *why* your estimate makes sense. Your reasoning might have to do with something you notice about the big gumball jar right here. Or your reasoning might have to do with something you already know or have thought about before. And sometimes it might be a combination. Take a moment to write down your estimate and reasoning. Then we'll have a Hands-Down Conversation about what gumball estimates might make sense and why.

Math Facilitation Moves Noticing and naming students' ideas can be a helpful teacher move, especially as children are taking on a new skill or idea. In this lesson, you may want to notice and name the different kinds of reasoning students are using, relating their reasoning back to the categories of reasoning they learned about in the micro-lesson. It might sound something like this: "Shana said she thought about layers. She thinks there are about fifteen layers of ten gumballs. She used her noticings about the big jar *right here* to help her make a reasonable estimate. Gabriel said he thinks there are one hundred gumballs in the big jar because it looks four times bigger than the little one. He was using something he *already knew*—that there were twenty-six gumballs in the little jar—to help him solve this new problem. *And* he was using something he noticed right here—that the big jar looks about four times as big as the small jar."

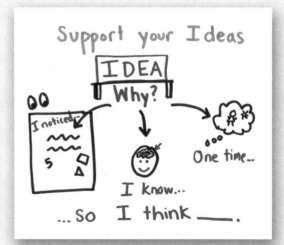

Digging Deeper into the *Why*, cont.

Literacy Guided Practice: It Might Sound Like . . . We have been thinking about the setting in *The Secret School*, by Avi, and helping each other think about what it might be like to live in this different time and place. We are going to dig a little deeper into the setting today and see how we can both gather clues from the author right there in the text *and* use our own experiences and knowledge to understand the setting in this historical fiction. Let's start by doing a little writing in your reader's notebooks. You can try organizing your journal with a T-chart. On the left side, write down something you are thinking about life in Elk Valley, Colorado, 1925. On the right side, explain what made you think that way. *(You can refer to the anchor chart about different types of reasoning as you say this.)* Was it something you read or saw in the text? Or was it an experience or previous learning you had? Let's think together more about what it was like living at that time. *(You can show one example and circulate it. Then, after a few moments of writing, launch the Hands-Down Conversation on this topic.)*

Literacy Facilitation Moves As students are writing and speaking, just as in math, you can help name the kind of reasoning they are doing. You can point out, for example, "Jana thinks that most of the people in this town didn't have a lot of money, because the characters all have bare feet. She is helping us understand the setting by finding clues *right there* in the story." Or "Alexis told us he thinks that at this time white children and black children couldn't go to school together, because he learned last year that schools in our country used to be segregated by law. Alexis shared some previous learning with us that helps all of us understand the setting of this story a little bit better."

After the Hands-Down Conversation

Reinforce Whenever you're thinking about your reasoning—why you think something—you can choose a kind of reasoning that makes sense for the situation. You might choose (1) something you notice "right there" in the text or problem, (2) something you've learned before, (3) something from your own life, or (4) a combination of those kinds of reasoning.

5.4 Am I Being Clear?

As we talk, it is important to consider how our audience (the listeners) is receiving the information. Monitoring oneself for clarity of expression is a complex skill. It requires both metacognition *and* an ability to consider the perspective of the listener. This skill will take practice and experience. Nevertheless, there are definitely aspects of this skill that elementary-age students can begin to take on, including watching their listeners for signs of interest and understanding, checking in for understanding, and learning that it is okay to revise and restate their idea.

During the Dialogue Micro-lesson

What and Why? When we are speaking, we need to think about whether we are being as clear as possible. We need to know if the listener understands us. This is important because if they don't understand us, they can't talk to us about our idea.

How? Here is one way you can make sure your listeners understand what you are saying:

1. As you are talking, look at the listeners. Do they look confused? Their faces might look like this (*refer to drawing on the anchor chart*). Or they might even say to you, "I don't understand your idea."

2. If you can't tell whether they understand, you can ask, "Does that make sense?" and watch to see if the listeners nod or shake their heads.

3. If you think they don't understand you, you can try to be clearer. You could

    a. restate your point: "What I'm trying to say is . . ." or

    b. clarify with an example: "For example . . ."

Am I Being Clear?

1. IDEA

2. Does that make sense?

3. What I mean is...

For example ...

During the Conversation Club

Guided Practice: It Might Sound Like . . . We've just started thinking
about measurement. Today we're going to start by taking a look at these two boxes.
Shin-hee says that Box A is bigger. Myra says that Box B is bigger. Which box do
you think is bigger? How could you figure out if you're right? Think for a moment
on your own. There might be more than one way to think about this question. When
I shake the egg shaker, you'll talk with your Conversation Club. You'll listen and talk
about your ideas about the boxes. As you're talking, you can look at your group to see
if they're understanding your idea. If you think they're unsure of your idea, you can ask,
"Does that make sense?" or say, "What I'm trying to say is . . ." Remember, when you're
listening, your job is to work hard to understand your group members' ideas and kindly
let them know when you need more information.

Facilitation Moves We focus on just meeting within the club this time, so
students aren't trying to read the faces and assess the understanding of the entire class
yet. A good initial step is working toward clearly communicating with a small group.
During this Conversation Club meeting, we recommend listening to and coaching just
one club's conversation. As students start talking, you might prompt a club member
by saying quietly to them, "Look at Julia's face. She looks a little
unsure. See if you can say it again a different way." Or you might
just quickly prompt: "Try giving an example!" You also can remind
the club members to ask each other clarifying questions when things
aren't clear, giving them the chance to work toward more understanding within this foursome. As with any facilitation, you will
want to be judicious in your decision to interrupt, choosing just a
couple of times to prompt the students so your voice does not take
over the conversation.

> ### Teacher Tip
>
> Check out Lesson 4.6 to learn more
> about starting and using Conversa-
> tion Clubs in your classroom!

After the Conversation Club

Reflect Let's take a moment to talk with your club about how you worked to understand each other today. What was hard to understand? What helped make things clearer?

Reinforce Any time you are speaking, it is important to check in with your listener
to make sure they understand you. Watch their body and their face, or you can ask them
if they understand! You can even try checking in when you are talking with your friends.

Chapter

6

Listening
and Linking Ideas

At a Glance: *You'll Know You're Ready for the Lessons in This Chapter When . . .*

- Students are mostly able to express their own ideas.

- Students are taking turns sharing ideas that are topically related, but not explicitly stating the connection to each other's ideas.

- With a facilitation move from the teacher, students might be starting to see how their idea connects or contrasts with another student's idea.

In late March Christy meets with Tanya, a first-grade teacher, to plan their literacy coaching time together. They decide to focus on word study after Tanya notes that many of her students have been struggling to apply their learning on the "silent *e*" spelling pattern to their writing. Together, Christy and Tanya hatch a plan to try exploring this spelling pattern through an inquiry approach, knowing that this approach often increases engagement and curiosity and surpasses a more typical "sit and get" approach of learning word-study patterns.

This approach to word study also provides multiple opportunities for Hands-Down Conversations. Tanya's students have participated in Hands-Down Conversations several times a week since the beginning of the year during both their reading and math workshops. Tanya has focused her micro-lessons on speaking at an audible volume, balancing participation, and staying focused on the topic at hand. The students have done some work together on explaining the *why* behind their opinions. This will be the first time that they try exploring a word study concept with the Hands-Down Conversation structure.

The teachers begin the inquiry by setting up a provocation for the class to notice and wonder about how the silent *e* works at the end of words. Christy and Tanya ask the students to "hunt" in their books for words that end in silent *e*, write the words on sticky notes, and create a class bank of "silent *e* words" on a poster. The students inspect these words to see how the spelling pattern works—how the silent *e* "changes" the vowel sound from short to long. They also spend time identifying and discussing words that *don't* work the way they expect (the words *love* and *have*, for example). When Christy and Tanya meet to plan the next lesson, Tanya reports that during social studies the previous day, when students were trying to write the word *landscape*, most of them did not apply the silent *e* or any other appropriate spelling pattern that would help make the long *a* sound in the second half of the word. Tanya and Christy decide to seize on this point as a teaching opportunity and bring the word into a Hands-Down Conversation. They ask the entire class to "give it a go," spelling the word *landscape* on individual whiteboards and then talking with their partners about what they are thinking.

Let's listen in as the Hands-Down Conversation begins:

Christy: So, you've tried writing this tricky word, *landscape,* and you've talked with your partners about some of the things you are thinking about how this word works. Now let's have a Hands-Down Conversation as a whole class about this word. You could talk about a tricky part, something that you are sure about, or something you noticed you and your partner doing differently. *(Christy jots* tricky, sure, *and* different *with a little symbol next to each on the whiteboard as reference.)* *(See Figure 6.1.)*

Christy: Who would like to get us started?

Neysa: I knew how to spell *land*, and I knew how to spell *cape*, and I thought I should put on an s and it made it *scape*.

Eddel: I wrote *land*, and *scape* sounds like when you escape from a scary forest or like from a mysterious island.

Veronica: I know how to spell *escape*, so I just took away the *e*. And I knew *land*.

Jose: I know the word *and* is inside *land*.

Portia: I only knew how to spell *land*. So I just sounded out *scape*. I just said the sounds.

Figure 6.1 A visual reminder of some options for conversation

(Several children make a nonverbal sign for "I have a connection.")

Christy: *(gesturing toward Eddel)* You can add on to Portia's idea, since you had a connection!

Eddel: I think *scape* has at the end *e*. If I say "scape," I didn't hear the *e*. Like "land . . . scape," you just hear that *p*. The *p* says its name, but you don't hear the *e*, I think?

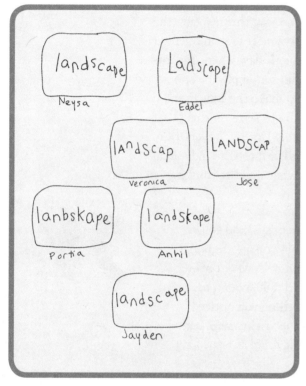

Figure 6.2 Several students' attempts to spell the word *landscape*

Christy: Oh, so you're saying that you put an *e* on the end even though you can't hear it? And Portia, you said you "sounded it out," but I see on your board that you still put that *e* on the end too! Eddel, you must be wondering why she put that *e* on just like you! Hmmm, that is really interesting. Did anyone else do that and want to say something about it?

Anhil: It's probably 'cause it's a silent *e*.

Neysa: 'Cause it's a "bossy *e*." I put it 'cause some words have a "bossy *e*." It's not in every word. It's like the *e* is saying "Say your name" to the *p*.

(Christy makes note of the misconception Neysa has here but listens to see if any other students say something about it.)

Anhil: If the *e* wasn't there, it would say "land-scăp." So the *e* makes the *a* say its name.

Jayden: If it wasn't there, it would say "land-scăp," 'cause the *e* makes it . . . well it makes the *a* say what the *a* should sound like.

Christy: I think you are talking about something really important here. A lot of you put a silent *e* at the end of the word. You're trying to figure out why this word needs a silent *e* or "bossy *e*," and what that *e* does to the other letters in the word. Tomorrow, we are going to explore a few more words with the *e* at the end and see if we can work together to write a rule to explain this silent *e*.

As we consider this vignette, we can see the students have already learned a lot about Hands-Down Conversations. Let's examine, for a moment, all that they are doing as young conversationalists without any teacher prompting or redirection.

All the speakers are

- taking turns,

- speaking clearly so that everyone can hear,

- making space for a variety of different voices to be heard, and

- staying on topic.

Some students are

- supporting their reasoning "within the text," by breaking the word *landscape* into smaller parts and considering how each of those parts might be spelled; and

- supporting their reasoning "outside the text," by referring to prior knowledge about the meaning of the word parts, other similar words, or spelling "rules" they have learned or heard about.

So, what is next? Once students have established some initial talk and listening moves in Hands-Down Conversations and are expressing their thinking, we want to examine whether they are actually (1) listening to one another and (2) connecting to one another's comments. If you look back through the previous vignette, you will notice that none of the students referred explicitly to their classmates' comments, even though we get a sense *at times* that they are listening to each other based on the connectivity of their comments. The beginning of this Hands-Down Conversation sounds a little like "round-robin sharing," in which each child makes their comment without building toward a bigger idea. Near the end, Neysa says that "the *e* is saying 'Say your name' to the *p*." Anhil and Jayden clearly disagree with that idea, understanding that the *e* is influencing the sound of the *a* in that word instead, but they aren't yet ready to ask Neysa a clarifying question or note how their thinking differs from hers. Tanya's students have encountered and engaged with each other's ideas from their very first Hands-Down Conversation, but they aren't yet noticing and naming the similarities or differences between their ideas or doing the crucial work of testing their ideas against other people's ideas without teacher prompting.

There is evidence, however, that *with* Christy's facilitation, the students are able to listen and link their ideas. At the point at which Christy suggests that Eddel add on to Portia's comment, the conversation begins to move on to the big idea of the silent/bossy *e*, which carries the rest of the conversation. Christy restates the connection between Portia's and Eddel's comments because Eddel did not explicitly state it. But once Christy states the connection, it opens the door a little wider to explore exactly what this "bossy *e*" is all about. Highlighting the friction between these ideas allows other students to enter the emerging debate and weigh in with their own thoughts on the matter. Now the students start talking about this "rule" that Tanya taught them earlier in the year and begin trying to make it their own. Cazden summarizes Vygotsky's and Bakhtin's thinking on this topic by saying, "When we transform the authoritative discourse of others into our own words, it may start to lose its authority and become more open. We can test it, consider it in dialog . . . with other ideas, and 'reaccentuate' it in our own ways" (2001, 76).

With Christy's support, the students tested the "silent/bossy *e*" rule in the context of the word *landscape*, and started to push against each other's ideas about how the rule works and what it means. Through the Hands-Down Conversation, the students could move forward to help each other with a collective new understanding about when and how to apply that spelling pattern (or "rule"). The fact that the students are not yet explicitly connecting to and pushing against each other's ideas on their own, but are able to start doing so with just a little nudge from the facilitator, indicates that this move is on the horizon for them. These students are now ready to learn some ways to connect to one another's ideas.

Why This Talk Move?

So, why is explicitly connecting to other people's ideas an important learning step?

Before this point, students are often thinking about and sharing their *own* ideas. In order to grapple with important ideas and move everyone's thinking forward, students must learn to really listen, understand, and respond to each other's thinking. And we, as teachers, must provide many opportunities for students to practice and fine-tune these talk and listening moves.

Figure 6.3 Students listen and connect to each other's ideas.

Learning to connect to other people's ideas takes time and purposeful practice. Students may initially rely heavily on sentence frames, for example, and this may make their language sound a little unnatural or contrived. Furthermore, students' connections to each other's ideas may be very surface level at first. Accept these approximations. Highlight them. When you do, you encourage students to continue playing with and innovating on these conversation moves. Just as the very young child learns to talk by spending extended time experimenting with and trying out new words, your students will make these new ways of talking in the classroom their own. You can support your students much in the same way a parent supports a child learning to talk—by meeting them right where they are and celebrating each approximation toward fluency with dialogue. The lessons in this chapter will guide you and your students in taking these important steps toward connective conversation.

In Chapter 7, students will continue this work as they learn to listen, understand, and respond in ways that allow them to collectively build on and push against each other's ideas.

If you notice . . .	You might try . . .
Students are using talk moves and demonstrating listening behaviors, and are ready to refine their listening moves. One clue that students are ready for this work is when they repeat the ideas of others in a conversation.	**Lesson 6.1** Paraphrasing: Listening *So Closely* and Saying an Idea in Your Own Words OR **Lesson 6.2** Cloudy or Clear: Asking Clarifying Questions
Students are most interested in their own ideas and haven't yet discovered the power and excitement that come with listening to understand what others think. Perhaps only a few students in the room are considered "listen-worthy" by their peers.	**Lesson 6.3** Looking Inside Our Brains: Curiosity About Other Ideas
Students are expressing their own isolated (and perhaps somewhat unrelated) ideas in conversations and are ready to learn more about connecting their ideas.	**Lesson 6.4** Same or Different? OR **Lesson 6.5** Adding On, Part 1: Linking Ideas OR **Lesson 6.6** Revising an Idea

Paraphrasing

One of the first steps in connecting more deeply to other people's ideas in a conversation is learning how to put your own ideas "on pause" in order to really listen and work to understand someone else's idea. Teaching students to paraphrase each other serves several purposes: (1) Paraphrasing sends the message to the speaker, "Your ideas are important and worthy of my attention and curiosity." (2) Paraphrasing intentionally slows the conversation down in order to focus on understanding an idea before building on it. (3) Paraphrasing offers the speaker an opportunity to clarify or refine their ideas. In this lesson, the key isn't that the listeners use the sentence stems or even get the speaker's ideas exactly right. The key is that they attempt to keep their own ideas on hold and think about what the speaker is saying first. This takes time and practice. You will likely want to come back to this lesson at various points throughout the year, as your students mature and grow as conversationalists and thinkers.

During the Dialogue Micro-lesson

What and Why? You all listen to each other's ideas all the time in our classroom and outside of our classroom. But today I am going to teach you how to listen *so closely* to someone's idea that you are able to say their idea in your own words. This is important because we all want to make sure we really understand each other's ideas so that we can build on them later.

How? Here's how you can listen closely and really understand someone else's idea (*reference or draw parts of the anchor chart as you talk*):

1. Get your big listening ear ready. Push your own ideas to the corner of your brain for a moment. Listen *so closely* to the speaker's idea.

2. Say the speaker's idea in your own words. You can start with this: "I think you're saying . . ."

3. Check with the speaker: "Is that right?"

4. Listen to anything the speaker adds.

During the Turn and Talk

Guided Practice: It Might Sound Like . . .   Take a look at this set of pictures. We're going to do a "Which One Doesn't Belong?" routine today. Just as you have done before, you'll think about your own idea about which picture doesn't belong and why, but in a moment you're going to push that idea to the corner of your brain and focus on listening *so closely* to your partner's idea and saying their idea in your own words. (*Provide wait time for individual think time.*) Okay, let's turn and talk!

Facilitation Moves   During Turn and Talks, as teachers, we sometimes have a tendency to stand "above" the conversations, scanning the group and looking only at the visual behaviors of partner talk. However, that behavior should be mostly automatic and solid for your class at this point. (If it isn't, revisiting Lessons 4.3, 4.4, and 4.5 may be helpful.) Since we are teaching students to respond with comments that are connective in this lesson, we recommend listening to one partnership and paying close attention to the listener's responses. You can whisper-coach the listener to help them try out paraphrasing if they need support, saying, "Try explaining her idea back to her now," or "You can ask her 'Do you mean . . . ?'"

After the Turn and Talk

Reflect   Let's reflect for a moment on how we are doing as listeners. What is hard about listening to your classmates' ideas? Were you thinking about what your classmates said today? Or did you find yourself thinking more about your own ideas? It's okay! We all do it! Take a moment to jot your reflection on a sticky note for me, and we will talk more about this during our next Hands-Down Conversation.

Reinforce   In any conversation, when you want to make sure you understand someone's idea, you can repeat it in your own words and check with them before adding on your own idea.

> ### Teacher Tip
> Remember that when learning new talk and listening moves, it can help to lower the level of cognitive demand in the content-area focus for the moment. Revisiting a familiar but particularly interesting book, graph, image, or idea is one way to do this. Or you can ask Conversation Clubs to talk about a lighter question (see Appendix C) to help groups learn to work productively.

6.2 Cloudy or Clear

We all talk in rough draft form, often expressing partially formed ideas or changing direction midsentence. This lesson orients students to the idea that it is okay if you do not fully understand someone's ideas and gives them the tools to ask clarifying questions and work to understand the speaker's message. Asking questions is another important part of being an active listener. It is also important to communicate the idea to your students that when someone questions you, it is because they are interested in your idea, not because you are wrong.

During the Dialogue Micro-lesson

What and Why? Part of your job in a conversation is to listen and work to understand other people's ideas. Sometimes even when you're listening closely, you won't be sure what the person is trying to say. That's okay! We are all working out our thinking as we talk. You can ask questions to help yourself understand your classmates' ideas. We know that everyone's ideas are important, and asking questions will help you understand them. When someone asks you to say more about your idea, it is because they are curious and want to make sure they understand it.

How? Here's one way you can ask clarifying questions (*reference or draw parts of the anchor chart as you talk*):

1. When someone is talking, ask yourself, "Do I *really* understand what they're saying? Am I clear or cloudy on their ideas?"

2. If you're cloudy on someone's ideas, ask them a question. The question might sound like this: "Can you say more about . . . ?" "Do you mean . . . ?" or "Why do you think that?"

3. Listen closely to what the person says. Check again to see if you're cloudy or clear on their ideas.

Asking Clarifying Questions

During the Hands-Down Conversation

Guided Practice: It Might Sound Like . . . Today we're going to be looking back at the graph about animal sleep. We've seen this graph before, and there was so much to notice and wonder about, we're going to take another look. As you listen to your classmates in our Hands-Down Conversation, notice when you feel clear and when you feel cloudy about other people's thinking. You might try out one of our questions if you need more information to understand.

Facilitation Moves During the conversation, you'll want to reinforce any attempts the students make at asking each other questions. For example, you could say, "Wow, you were working so hard to understand each other's ideas as you talked. Isabel really wanted to understand Asher's thinking about where this graph came from. When she asked, 'Are you wondering who figured out how many hours the animals sleep?' that helped us understand Asher's thinking." If none of your students are trying out clarifying questions, you can encourage the behavior by whispering to a student seated near you, "Did you understand Josiah? See if you can ask him a question to help us all."

After the Hands-Down Conversation

Reinforce Whenever you're not clear about what someone is saying, you can ask a question to help yourself understand what they're thinking.

> ### Teacher Tip
> We want students to learn how to use questions as a listening tool—not as a weapon to interrogate and break down a classmate's argument, courtroom style. This is an important balance to strike, and may be a necessary distinction to make, depending on the personalities and age of your students.

We want our students to listen to each other not out of compliance, but out of genuine curiosity about their classmates' ideas. Our colleague Ellen Rogers thinks a lot about cultivating a stance of curiosity among her students and inspired us to write this lesson. This stance of curiosity about other people's ideas is something we must model for our students all day long, to show them that we believe the ideas of all students (not just a few) hold worth. From there, our students can grow their curiosity and interest in each other's ideas as well. But while the community-building aspect of this skill takes place implicitly all day long, we can also explicitly teach and highlight this skill. It is important to note that this lesson asks students to apply some of the strategies from Lessons 6.1 and 6.2.

During the Dialogue Micro-lesson

What and Why? When you listen to someone, you get to find out some of what that person is thinking in their brain. Isn't that interesting? We can't *really* look inside there, but listening to what someone says is one way to get a glimpse into their head! And every brain in our class is a little different. When you find out what someone else is thinking in their head, it helps you grow the ideas in *your* head too. Today we will think about how we can try to "look inside" each other's brains and be *so* curious about what our classmates are saying.

How? Here's one way you can learn about someone else's thinking (*reference or draw parts of the anchor chart as you talk*):

1. Get ready to be the listener. Say to yourself, "I'm curious. I wonder what my partner thinks about this!"

2. Listen closely to your partner so you can really find out what's going on in their head!

3. Take a moment to think about what they just said. Ask yourself: "What did I find out? Do I need to ask a question or paraphrase to 'check in' on my understanding?"

4. Say something about their idea.

Curiosity About Other Ideas

During the Turn and Talk

Guided Practice: It Might Sound Like . . . (*Our colleagues Sanya Chopra and Yolanda Corado Cendejas developed this great topic for a Hands-Down Conversation.*) We have been inquiring about the genre of fantasy together. Take a look at the books we have read together so far (*teacher gestures toward the chalkboard tray, where three recently read fantasy picture books are lined up*). With your Turn and Talk partner, you are going to discuss the definition of fantasy books. What makes a book a fantasy book? Partner Bs, you will start the conversation today. Partner As, get ready to be curious. Say to yourself, "What does my partner think? I am about to peek right into their head!"

Facilitation Moves This is another time when we recommend you try to coach just one Turn and Talk partnership rather than bouncing around the room or watching the pairs talk "from above." This will give you valuable feedback about how they are taking the lesson in, and provide you with opportunities to remind students to try this talk move. After listening to the speaker, you might engage the listener in a short side-conversation about the idea presented, perhaps with prompts like these: "Wow, did you hear what she said?" "That was a really interesting idea, wasn't it?" "What do you understand about her idea?" "What do you want to say to her about that?"

After the Turn and Talk

Reinforce Whenever you are listening to someone talk—in our classroom or at home—you can think about how, when a person talks, you get to see inside their head. How cool! When you are curious about other people, who knows what you might discover!

> ### Teacher Tip
> When choosing which partnerships to listen to during Turn and Talks, you might consider focusing on students who tend to be quieter during Hands-Down Conversations. The Turn and Talk format may be more comfortable for these students, and potentially provide a better opportunity to check in on the development of their dialogue skills as well as the content of their ideas.

Learning to disagree with others' ideas respectfully is a cornerstone of dialogue. However, we all have seen evidence of adults who are still learning how to do this, because it is a talk move that takes conscious effort. Once students are really starting to understand their peers' ideas, they are ready to get into this part of the talk journey. This lesson introduces students to a first step: noticing and naming the similarities and differences between stated ideas and/or perspectives. We want to teach students how to talk about someone's idea rather than disagreeing or agreeing with the individual, because disagreement can sound a little rough around the edges at first, and we want to ease into having debates without shutting down our more hesitant speakers.

During the Dialogue Micro-lesson

What and Why? You've probably noticed that this classroom is full of great thinkers. We all have different ideas and perspectives. Our job is to try to understand our own ideas *and* others' ideas too. One way you can think about others' ideas is by looking for ways that another person's idea is similar to or different from your own ideas. When we name the differences in our thinking, it helps us each look more carefully at *why* we are thinking a certain way. And that can help us change and grow our ideas into something even bigger!

How? Here's one way you can notice and name the differences between your own ideas and other peoples' ideas (*reference the anchor chart as you talk*):

1. When you hear an idea, ask yourself, "Does this idea sound the same as or different from what I was thinking?"

2. Then you can tell the group what you've noticed. You might start by saying, "I agree/disagree with that idea because . . ." or "I am thinking about this a little differently . . ."

> **Same or Different?**
>
> □□ I agree with
> ___'s idea because...
>
> □△ I disagree with
> ___'s idea because...
> OR
> I'm thinking about
> this a little differently...

During the Turn and Talk

Guided Practice: It Might Sound Like . . . Let's try this out first with
an idea I heard someone say the other day in the cafeteria. "We should have
pizza *every* day as a lunch choice." Turn and talk to your partner about that idea.
Remember, listen for the differences and similarities in your ideas, and talk about
them! (*Circulate, listening to several pairs and prompting students:* "Does their thinking
sound similar to or different from your idea?")

Now, let's try talking about another idea. Yesterday, we read the book *Marvelous Cornelius: Hurricane Katrina and the Spirit of New Orleans* (2015), by Phil Bildner. During our
Hands-Down Conversation yesterday, one of you said, "The hurricane seems good 'cause it
made people help each other." But some of you really disagreed with that idea. Turn and talk
a little more about this. (*Write the following statement on the board:* "In this book, Hurricane
Katrina ended up being a good thing.") You might try using these sentence starters (*refer to
anchor chart*) to talk about the differences and similarities in your ideas with your partner.

Facilitation Moves The more we, as teachers, orient students to each other's
ideas throughout the day, the more they will take this move on in their own thinking
and talk. Consider how you can model, in authentic ways, thinking about how ideas are
connected. As partners solve a story problem, you might say, "What
you're trying here reminds me of Darius's idea that he shared in our
Number Talk yesterday." When conferring with a reader, you might
point out, "So you really think differently than this author. It seems as
if she thinks _____, but you're thinking _____." Reflecting aloud on
how students' thinking influences your own thinking is also powerful.
"Last night I went out for pizza, and I was thinking about what you
all said in our conversation about whether saying no to plastic straws
makes a real impact in our world. In some ways, I understand your
argument that _____, but I'm also thinking _____." Our goal in this
work is to nurture a community in which we are constantly working
to understand both our own thinking and the thinking of others.

> ### Teacher Tip
>
> In Lesson 7.1, we teach students how
> to agree with parts of each other's
> ideas and disagree with other parts,
> rather than having to make a binary
> choice. This lesson sets the stage for
> that future development.

After the Turn and Talk

Reflect What idea did you hear from your partner that you hadn't considered before?

Reinforce Remember, whenever you are listening to someone speak, you can listen
for how their idea sounds the same as or different from your own thinking.

Adding On, Part 1

Learning to add on to someone's thinking in a conversation is complex work that involves simultaneously holding on to two sets of ideas—your own and those of someone else—and comparing and connecting those ideas. It is not surprising that when students first learn the phrase "I'd like to add on," what follows is often only tangentially related to the original idea or just states the same idea again in their own words. That's completely normal! This lesson helps students begin to notice that something said in a conversation is related to their own idea and to try to articulate this connection by adding on.

During the Dialogue Micro-lesson

What and Why? As you listen to a conversation, you'll start to notice that other people's ideas are linked to yours. It's like linking paper clips together one by one to make a chain. Sometimes an idea you've thought of in your mind will connect to an idea that someone else says aloud. That means it might be a good time for you to share your thinking. Talking about how our own thinking connects to other people's thinking helps us grow an idea.

How?

1. Listen closely to someone's idea.
2. Think: Does my idea connect to this idea? Do I have something more to say?
3. You might say, "I'd like to add on to Amin's idea," or "Yes, and I also think . . ."

Linking Ideas

We can link our ideas to say more and grow big ideas together.

Yes, I also think...

I'd like to add on...

IDEA

Linking Ideas

During the Conversation Club and Hands-Down Conversation

Guided Practice: It Might Sound Like . . .   Yesterday we were working on some true or false equations. When we looked at the equation $5 + 4 = 4 + 5$, Kati said, "That's true because you can change around the numbers but it still equals the same thing." I'm wondering if we can talk about Kati's idea more. Is it always true? Sometimes true? Never true? As we're talking with our Conversation Clubs and then in the Hands-Down Conversation, you can try to find a space where you might add on to someone's thinking.

Facilitation Moves   As students are learning exactly what it means to build productively on someone's ideas, they sometimes benefit from a teacher noticing and naming this work. You can do this briefly while listening to a Conversation Club or the Hands-Down Conversation. Be as specific as you can in your feedback: "I noticed that Amari said, 'Switching doesn't work for subtraction.' Right after that Nora said, 'Like five minus one is not the same as one minus five.' Nora gave an example of Amari's idea. That's one way you can add onto someone else's idea."

After the Turn and Talk and Hands-Down Conversation

Reinforce   Sometimes you'll hear an idea that you want to say more about. You can add on to someone's idea like a paperclip in a chain.

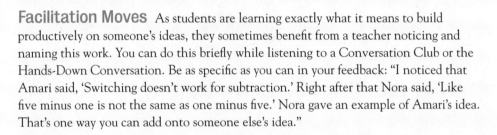

> ### Teacher Tip
>
> While this lesson focuses on helping students link related ideas, in Lesson 7.3 we expand on this topic by helping students add on in ways that deepen and grow understanding around an idea.

6.6 Revising an Idea

There is never a bad time to focus on revising ideas through talk. Because the previous lessons in this chapter focus on becoming oriented to other people's thinking and becoming more intentional listeners, this is a particularly helpful time to introduce or return to a focus on revising one's own ideas. Lynn Simpson, a fourth-grade teacher featured in the Teaching Channel video "Improving Participation Through Talk Moves," summarizes what we hope all students will learn about revising their ideas: "Revising our thinking is permission to change our mind[s] once we are confronted with new information . . . When you're confronted with new information you should change your thinking. You should take what you learned, merge it with what you already know, and then come to a new understanding" (Teaching Channel 2019). We consider this lesson to be just one small step in a longer journey of creating a classroom where revision is encouraged and celebrated as a critical part of all learning and living.

During the Dialogue Micro-lesson

What and Why? As we learn and talk with each other, our ideas are growing all the time. I have noticed you sometimes even *change* your thinking after you hear someone else talk or you get new information! That is so awesome, because that means your ideas are growing as you become a better listener and talker. When that happens to you, it is a great moment to tell us about, because it might help other people reflect on their thinking too.

How? Here's one way you can talk about how your ideas are changing (*reference or draw parts of the anchor chart as you talk*):

1. As you listen to the conversation, check in with yourself. Notice when your brain says, "Oh, I'm changing my mind."

2. You can share that thinking with the group. You might say, "I used to think _____, but now I'm thinking _____," or "I want to change what I said before."

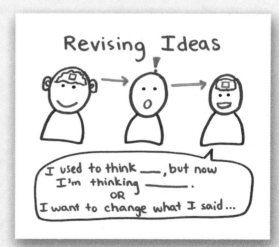

Revising Ideas

I used to think ___, but now I'm thinking ___.
OR
I want to change what I said...

During the Hands-Down Conversation

Guided Practice: It Might Sound Like . . . As a class, we've been thinking a lot about what sorts of "rules" there are in our world about being a boy and being a girl. Yesterday we looked at a collection of toy advertisements and noticed what objects, colors, words, and people were in the ads. Let's put those back up on the screen today and talk more about them. What messages might these companies be telling us about being a boy or being a girl? Remember, as you listen to your friends talk, you might change your thinking. Please let us all know if you have one of those "I'm changing my mind!" moments!

Facilitation Moves As the Hands-Down Conversation unfolds, you will want to highlight and encourage any moments in which a child tries out this revision move. You want to make sure the message is loud and clear that changing your thinking isn't an admission of "being wrong," but a sign of reflective listening and thinking. You might say something like "This is so cool! Jannice is thinking about this in a new way because of what Tamara said!" or "Wow, Elias is listening *so* carefully that he is thinking about this a new way now." You can also prompt students to reflect on their thinking after a particularly provocative comment during the conversation by saying, "Hmmm, what Jorge just said is really making me think. Is anyone else thinking differently about things now? You can let us know if you are." As always, be selective about how many times you jump into the conversation. You can always save an encouraging comment for after the conversation is over.

After the Hands-Down Conversation

Reflect This conversation brought up some different ways of thinking. Turn and talk to your partner about what new ideas you are having now. How has this conversation changed your thinking?

Reinforce We are learning and growing from listening to each other. Isn't it cool to think about all the powerful thinkers in this class and in the world that we can listen to? Whenever you are talking with someone, you can notice those moments where you say to yourself, "I'm changing my mind," and talk about how your thinking is changing.

> ### Teacher Tip
>
> As you look for a subject for this Hands-Down Conversation, be sure to pick something that will lead to divergent thinking and multiple perspectives. This is usually true of Hands-Down Conversation topics, but it will be important to be especially mindful of this today.

Chapter

7

Growing Ideas Together

At a Glance: *You'll Know You're Ready for the Lessons in This Chapter When . . .*

- Students are able to express their own ideas with evidence and clarity that are developmentally appropriate.

- Students are sharing ideas that are topically related and showing evidence of listening to each other, perhaps by linking ideas to previous comments.

Christy joins Margaret Summers's third-grade class one chilly winter afternoon. Margaret has just finished reading the book *Galapagos George* (2014), by Jean Craighead George, which relates the true account of the evolution of the Galapagos turtles in a narrative form. Margaret asks her students to form a circle for a Hands-Down Conversation. They move with ease into a circle next to their talk partners. Margaret reminds them of a bigger concept they have started talking about in science, and across subjects, for the past couple weeks: adaptation. She gives students a few moments of wait time to ponder what they are thinking about adaptation now, in light of Jean Craighead George's book. Then Margaret places a card with the word *adaptation* written on it in the middle of the circle as a visual reminder for her students and grabs her clipboard to take notes. Let's listen in to a part of the conversation:

Margaret: Who would like to start us off? Sonia, go ahead.

Sonia: I think the author was talking about the adaptation of the one kind of turtle, George, but she didn't really clarify what happened to the other turtles. So, I'm wondering about that.

Blake: Yeah, I agree with Sonia. I think she could have clarified that. Like, what happened to the other turtles? We only knew about George.

Minuh: I think that the turtles had to adapt 'cause they had a new environment. When they went to the new islands, they had to change.

Sam: I'd like to add on to that. The turtles had to change when they lived on the new islands because the islands were different. They had different kinds of plants and trees there for the turtles to eat.

Figure 7.1 Third graders gather in a Hands-Down Conversation to discuss their ideas about adaptation.

Jenny: So they became the "long necks," to reach and get the tree leaves.

Lamont: Well, I think all creatures adapt in new environments. We have to. Like if a human was put in an environment with just water, they eventually would have to adapt to living in water.

(*Several students start talking at once, but they make space for Luke, who hasn't had a turn to talk yet.*)

Luke: Yes, I agree with Lamont. You have to adapt. Or you die.

Darnell: No, that's not true. Like if you move to a new country, you could choose to just not eat the food there and just eat the kind of food you are used to. You wouldn't die.

Jenny: You have to learn the new language, though, don't you, Darnell?

(*Several voices try to enter the conversation again.*)

Danish: No, you don't! You could just talk to your family and your friends from your country there.

Luke: Okay, so maybe you don't *always* die. But most of the time I think you do.

Minuh: I got two baby sisters and I had to adapt to that. Being a big brother.

Jorge: I have a little brother too. And I had to adapt.

Jalina: I think you do have to change. You have to adapt. But you might not *die*.

Margaret's students demonstrate some impressive dialogue skills as they engage in this discussion. They have clearly put in a lot of effort as a community to become stronger listeners and talkers during this school year with Margaret, and in their previous grades.

- Students are negotiating who speaks and when. For the most part, they're balancing the roles of listener and speaker.

- Students are expressing themselves clearly and are focused on a single topic.

- Several students are supporting their ideas with reasoning from within the text (the book, in this case) or from outside the text (life experiences, providing examples, etc.).

- Their comments link to at least one other idea in the conversation.

- Students are showing evidence that they are listening to each other without any prompting or redirection from the teacher-facilitator. Sometimes they are repeating something a previous speaker said, agreeing or disagreeing with them, and, on one occasion (Jenny), even posing a clarifying question to challenge the previous speaker's theory. One student (Luke) revised his thinking as he listened.

These students are using discourse to develop and test theories, push against one another, and struggle with ideas together. They understand the power of clear communication and are working to present their ideas in a way that is convincing to their classmates. It would be tempting to say they're doing just fine as conversationalists and move our focus to literacy and math content. And yet, when we look closely at the conversation, we can see some exciting developments on the horizon for this community of students.

In *Comprehension Through Conversation: The Power of Purposeful Talk in the Reading Workshop*, Maria Nichols tells us about the goal of classroom dialogue: "Through this constructive process, participants achieve a whole that is greater than the sum of its parts—ideas that are bigger and better than any individual may have conceived on their own" (2006, 7). We see definite evidence that Margaret's students are starting to utilize one another's ideas to understand the very big concept of "adaptation." To take their conversation skills a step further, we can now teach them to more carefully analyze the ideas of their classmates and look for shades of gray in their arguments that they might either agree with or respectfully refute. We can support students as they use more robust reasoning and make their arguments clearer. We can also teach these students to track the trajectory of a conversation and the development of ideas, and to synthesize their classmates' comments, thus moving the group discussion and understanding forward. Margaret's students circle around some very interesting and debatable big ideas regarding adaptation, in both humans and animals, but no one steps up to highlight these ideas or acknowledge their significance yet. They could further a conversation like this by naming one of the theories someone has touched on and leading their peers to dig in to just this idea for a while. A student could say something like this: "So we're saying humans can decide whether they adapt but animals have no choice?" Or a student could highlight a debatable concept, saying, "So do we think we have to adapt to survive or not?" When students take on some of this summarizing language, they take on greater decision making and ownership of the conversation. They negotiate, as a group, which questions to pursue and which ideas to dig into. There will always be a role for the teacher, too, in this work, but we should challenge ourselves to share this role with students whenever possible.

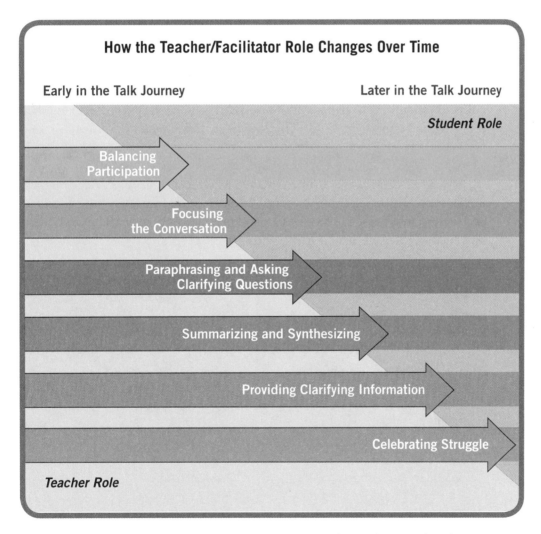

Figure 7.2 While both students and teachers are continuously approximating these moves throughout the talk journey, teachers encourage students to take on more of the work as time progresses.

In this final chapter of micro-lessons, we move from teaching students about their individual roles as talkers and listeners within a conversation to really focusing on how we collaborate as a class community to grow ideas together. One way to think of this, for both ourselves and our students, is to use the analogy of taking a trip or a journey with our conversation. In every Hands-Down Conversation, we want to arrive somewhere new as a class, not just stay in the same spot. This "somewhere new" isn't always a neat resolution or agreement; sometimes it means that we've come up with new questions or become uncertain of an idea about which we were previously so sure. But regardless of where our journey takes us, we make the trip together. Therefore, compromises are sometimes necessary—we have to help each other navigate the way and leave some side roads and detours unexplored for the moment. We also help each other by identifying stops and pointing out landmarks along the way. By doing so, we can keep track of our conversational journey and make sure we are moving forward.

Some of the lessons in this chapter require conversational and developmental maturity. It often takes some time to learn how to focus on the good of the collective group. As students work toward this goal, they can keep refining their listening and expressive skills. The lessons in this chapter are lofty, but they are important lessons to experiment with in elementary school. And, we would argue, these are essential lessons when we consider how leaders are developed in our world. A leader is not the individual who repeatedly voices her own ideas louder than anyone else in the room. A leader is the individual who listens to and understands those ideas voiced around her, merges them with her own ideas, and expresses herself in a clear, inspiring way.

If you notice . . .	You might try . . .
Students are agreeing and disagreeing with each other but often see it as a binary, all-or-nothing choice.	**Lesson 7.1** Analyzing an Idea
When students disagree with an idea, they state their own idea without giving evidence or a justification for their disagreement.	**Lesson 7.2** Refuting a Claim

If you notice . . .	You might try . . .
Students are beginning to connect their ideas to other ideas in the conversation. They might be saying, "I'd like to add on . . . ," but the relationship between their comment and the previous one is unclear, or it's a restatement.	**Lesson 7.3** Adding On, Part 2: Growing Ideas
The conversation "doesn't go anywhere" or keeps circling back to the same few ideas over and over.	**Lesson 7.4** Staying Together: Taking a Conversation Journey
Students may be clunky or abrupt in the way they bring up a new point, leaving other listeners confused about where the conversation is going.	**Lesson 7.5** Taking the Conversation to a New Place
Students are ready to take on even more ownership of the direction of the conversation.	**Lesson 7.6** Summarizing
You, as a teacher, are noticing many interesting things about your class's dialogue. You're ready to write your own dialogue micro-lessons.	**Lesson 7.7** The "Last Lesson": Writing Your Own Talk Micro-lessons

7.1 Analyzing an Idea

You either agree or disagree. You're either right or wrong. We've all been in conversations in school and in the greater world in which people hold so tightly to their own ideas that they dismiss all thinking that does not completely align with their own. Learning to see the shades of gray between opposing ideas is critical as both an academic skill and a life skill. In this lesson, we encourage students to see both similarities and differences between ideas simultaneously. We teach students that agreeing or disagreeing often isn't a binary choice; you can agree with parts of an idea and disagree with other parts. This lesson builds on the work of Lesson 6.4, Same or Different?

During the Dialogue Micro-lesson

What and Why? Sometimes we think that we have to completely agree or completely disagree with someone's idea, but actually many times we may agree with *part* of someone's idea and disagree with another *part* of it. Talking about the parts we agree with and the parts we disagree with helps us think more deeply and build stronger ideas as a class.

How? Here's one way you can consider how someone's thinking is both similar and different to your own (*reference or draw parts of the anchor chart as you talk*):

1. Listen to someone's idea. (Here's a tip: you're *really* going to have to use your close listening here.)

2. Think: What *parts* do I agree with? What *parts* do I disagree with?

3. You might say, "I agree with what you said about _____, but I think differently about _____," or "I see what you mean about _____, but what about _____?"

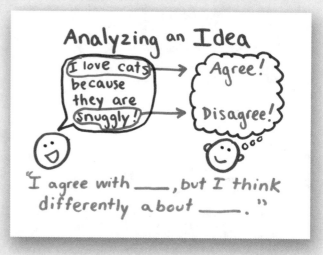

During the Turn and Talk and Conversation Clubs

Guided Practice: It Might Sound Like . . . We're going to try this out together. Imagine you hear someone say, "Video games are bad for kids." Turn and talk with your partner about this idea. How might you talk about which parts of this idea you agree with and which parts you disagree with?

Now let's try this out with another idea that some of you have been playing around with in the last couple of days: "Fractions are small." Turn and talk to your Conversation Club this time. Just as you did in our video game conversation, think about which *parts* of this idea you agree with and which *parts* you disagree with.

Facilitation Moves As you listen to one or two Conversation Clubs talk, you might hear students *saying* that they agree or disagree with each other, even when that isn't entirely true. For example, José says, "Fractions are small. You can share a sandwich with four people and that makes a small fraction," and Kay responds, "I agree fractions are small. You can share a lot of sandwiches with four people and those are a lot of fourths." In this case, Kay *says* she agrees, but she really is adding new information to José's comment and demonstrating some different thinking that, if it were highlighted, could move both of their ideas forward. As the facilitator, you can name this difference for them, saying, "You both are thinking fractions are small, but Kay is thinking about it a little differently. She said _____ (*repeat her words*). Let's talk more about that."

> ### Teacher Tip
>
> You will want to make sure that you choose a topic for this conversation that leads toward opinions that are not black and white in nature. One way to do this is by launching the conversation with a "controversial statement," such as in the video game and fractions examples in this lesson.

After the Conversation Clubs

Reflect I've noticed that sometimes when someone disagrees with your idea, or even part of your idea, it can feel uncomfortable. Why do you think this is? What can we say to ourselves when we're feeling this discomfort? Write your thinking down on a sticky note. You can keep your reflection in your notebook just for you, or you can share it with me by passing it to me on our way to PE class in a moment.

Reinforce There are times when we completely agree or disagree with an idea. But more often, we hear parts we agree with and parts we disagree with. Talking about these parts helps us grow and even change our ideas.

7.2 Refuting a Claim

As students learn the subtleties of agreeing and disagreeing (Lessons 6.4 and 7.1), some common patterns of talk often emerge. Here's one we've noticed:

Student 1 states a claim (e.g., "If a number has a two in it, it's even," or "The main character is a bully").

Student 2 disagrees (e.g., "Not all numbers with twos in them are even," or "The main character is not really a bully").

End of discussion.

These students are listening to and engaging with each other's ideas. They're off to a great start! They're ready to learn how to use evidence to refute a claim. In this lesson, we orient students to the notion that when you disagree with an idea, you have to say why you disagree.

During the Dialogue Micro-lesson

What and Why? We have thought a lot about how agreeing and disagreeing with each other's ideas helps all of us grow in our thinking. Today we're going to think more about how, when we disagree with an idea, we can say *why* we disagree and give reasons why we think the idea is not true or is just partly true.

How? Here's one way you can help your listeners understand why you disagree with an idea or part of an idea (*reference or draw parts of the anchor chart as you talk*):

1. Sometimes you will hear an idea that you disagree with. You may think, "I don't think that's true," or "I don't think that's always true."

2. Ask yourself, "What is my evidence that this is not true or not always true?"

3. Share your idea. It might sound like this: "I don't agree with that because . . ." Or it might sound like this: "I don't think that is always true because . . ."

During the Hands-Down Conversation

Guided Practice: It Might Sound Like . . . Let's try this out. For practice, I've chosen an idea that we've thought a lot about recently: "The number twenty-three is even because there is a two in it." Yesterday, almost all of you decided at the end of math that you didn't agree with that statement. Now we're going to practice how you can say *why* this isn't true.

Facilitation Moves When practicing this talk move, we find it helpful to start out by giving students a statement to disagree with. This clearly presented claim is a scaffold. Eventually, students will need to transfer this skill into all their conversations, learning to support their thinking with reasoning and refute murkier claims they encounter in conversations, without scaffolding. Nonetheless, we find it helpful to practice and give feedback around this talk move in guided practice, and then reinforce it throughout many other conversations thereafter.

After the Hands-Down Conversation

Reinforce When Kiana said that twenty-three couldn't be even because you can't split it into two even groups, she was supporting her idea with evidence in a way that helps us understand why she disagreed with the idea that twenty-three is even.

> ## Teacher Tip
>
> Look for opportunities to reinforce talk moves, such as refuting a claim, in other conversations after they have been introduced in a micro-lesson. You can briefly interject by noting what a child has done: "When Rochelle said _____, she was telling us *what* could not be true, and she was telling us *why* it couldn't be true." And then briefly name why that move is important: "That evidence helped move our thinking forward."

Adding On, Part 2

This lesson builds upon the ideas in Lesson 6.5, Adding On, Part 1: Linking Ideas. After students are linking their ideas and noticing a little about which thoughts are related, they can begin to focus on building upon an idea that is on the table. We try this in a Turn and Talk first, asking students to connect their comment by adding on to an idea the other person just said. The big shift here is to really respond to what your partner said, not the thought that was already in your head. This can be hard for adults too, so it will take ongoing practice! Since growing an idea through talk is challenging, the first time you explicitly teach this lesson, we suggest practicing it with a social topic before moving to content-area conversations that require a heavier cognitive load.

During the Dialogue Micro-lesson

What and Why? You have all been working on listening to each other's ideas and noticing how you can link or "add on" to something someone else has said. Today we are going to learn how to say something *new* about another person's idea. This will really help us move somewhere new with our conversations and grow bigger ideas.

How? Here is one way you can build upon your classmates' ideas (*reference or draw parts of the anchor chart as you talk*):

1. Listen closely to someone's idea.

2. Think: What ideas do I have about that? or What can I say about what they said?

3. Tell how that person's idea helped you grow something new. You could try saying, "What *you* said made me think _____," or "When you said _____, it made me think _____."

Growing Ideas

During the Turn and Talk

Guided Practice: It Might Sound Like . . . Let's try first talking about this idea with your partner: Is there a superhero who you like the best? Why? Partner B will share first. Partner A is going to listen so carefully and talk about Partner B's ideas. (*Listen in to the partner talk.*) Okay, wrap up your conversations and come back together.

Now let's talk about a math idea for a bit. Take a look again at these two pictures of pizzas. Yesterday I asked you to write about this question: "How much of each pizza is left?" Some of you said one-fourth of each kind of pizza is left, and others of you said one-fourth of the cheese pizza is left and two-eighths of the pepperoni pizza is left. This time Partner A will share first, and Partner B will work really hard to add on to what Partner A said. Remember, you could try saying, "What *you* said makes me think ____."

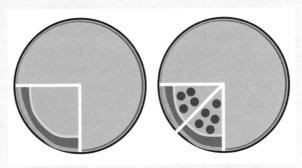

Figure 7.3 How much of each pizza is left?

Facilitation Moves Select a couple of talk partnerships to listen to. Position yourself behind the listener (Partner B). If you hear Partner B adding on, you can highlight this move, saying, "You just took what your partner said and added something new to it! You're growing ideas!" If Partner B doesn't add on to Partner A's comment (perhaps they move on to their own idea or just repeat back their partner's idea), try encouraging them by whispering, "What does *what she just said* make you think?" Sometimes, the "listener" will not really have been listening the first time around, and they will find it necessary to ask their partner to repeat what they said. That is good practice and learning!

After the Turn and Talk

Reinforce Today, when I was listening to you talk, I heard how you are trying to grow each other's ideas. (*Share an example you heard.*) Any time you are in a conversation, you can listen for ways that you can add on to another person's idea and grow something new!

> ### Teacher Tip
> If it is a struggle for students to hear and comprehend their partner's ideas, it might be worth returning to some of the "Listening and Linking" lessons in Chapter 6.

Staying Together

In this lesson we introduce the idea of a conversation as a journey. We use this analogy here to help students see that (1) we are functioning not just as individuals in this conversation but as a unit, and (2) in order to achieve our common goal, we will have to stay together and head in the same direction. This lesson teaches students to start tracking the conversation journey and learning to monitor whether their contribution will help the conversation keep moving forward. We come back to this "journey" analogy in other lessons in this chapter.

During the Dialogue Micro-lesson

What and Why? Our conversations are a lot like a journey. We all start the trip together and begin talking about something. When we all stay together on the journey, we can arrive at a new place, and develop a whole new understanding, perspective, or question. This means we all have to make a mental map of the conversation and track where we are. We have to decide whether our comments will help the journey move forward or will take us in different directions.

How? Here's one way you can help us stay together on the conversation journey:

1. Listen to what your classmates are saying. Think to yourself: What are they talking about right now? Can I say something about this?

2. When you think of something to say, hold onto it and wait for an opening or quiet moment.

3. As you wait, keep listening. If the conversation moves on to a bigger or slightly different idea, stay with us on the journey! Put your idea down for now and start thinking about what you can add to this new part of the conversation.

Taking a Conversation Journey

During the Hands-Down Conversation

Guided Practice: It Might Sound Like . . . Recently we read
Princess and the Peas, by Rachel Himes, which is a new take on the traditional
tale "The Princess and the Pea." In the Author's Note in the back of the book,
Rachel Himes tells us the reason she wanted to make her tale about cooking
black-eyed peas instead of about feeling a pea under a mattress. She says, "I decided
to rewrite the story to be about the things that I think are truly important—love and
family" (Himes 2017). Let's think about this decision and the other choices Rachel
Himes made as an author to keep some parts of the tale the same and change others.
What are your thoughts on these changes and choices? Did they result in a different
message, as she hoped? Let's have a Hands-Down Conversation about this. As we do,
we will really listen to each other and see how we are moving along together in the
conversation. Remember to try to share something that goes with what we are talking
about so we all stay together.

Facilitation Moves As the conversation unfolds, one possibility to support your
students with this skill is to draw a map to use as a silent visual cue to the students,
helping them track the big idea that is currently on the floor for discussion. Instead of
writing a transcript today, put a piece of chart paper on the easel. Sit
just outside the circle as always, but where you are visible. When you
hear the conversation circling around a big idea or concept, jot that
down on one part of the chart. As the big idea shifts, write the new
topic somewhere else on the paper and draw a line between them (see
the anchor chart for an example of how the map might look).

After the Hands-Down Conversation

Reflect What you tried today is a challenging skill. It can be hard
to think about what you want to say and keep listening at the same
time. Turn and talk with your partner about how it feels to listen and
think at the same time.

Reinforce Any time you are having a conversation with our class,
or a group, you can think of it as a journey and make sure we stay
together. If the conversation has moved on, think of something you can say about this
new bigger idea, instead of taking us in a different direction.

> ### Teacher Tip
>
> Another part of staying together on
> the conversation journey is learning
> how to go back to a previous comment
> or idea. We can teach kids this skill
> too, using segues such as "I'd like to
> go back to what _____ said," or "Can
> we talk more about . . . ?" This kind
> of language helps cue the rest of the
> class that a shift in topic is occurring.

In this lesson, we teach students how to use "signposts" when we are talking, to alert people when the conversational journey is moving to a new place. We want students to have the flexibility to bring up new subtopics, or slightly shift the conversation if it makes sense to do so. However, it helps the listeners follow the conversation if the speaker signals this shift.

During the Dialogue Micro-lesson

What and Why? Sometimes as you're listening to a conversation, you might want to add a new idea, or bring up something slightly different for everyone to talk about. When you do this, you will want to take everyone with you on the journey! So you'll want to give us a sign that you're moving to a new idea in the conversation.

How? Here's one way you can let people know that you are taking the conversation to a new place (*reference or draw parts of the anchor chart as you talk*):

1. You might notice that either
   a. we are all saying the same thing over and over, or
   b. there is a lull, because no one is sure what else to say about that idea.

2. You can take us to a new place in the conversation journey by bringing up a new idea for us to talk about.

3. Give us a signal that you're taking the conversation somewhere new by saying something like this: "Another idea I'm thinking about is . . ." or "What do you all think about . . . ?"

During the Hands-Down Conversation

Guided Practice: It Might Sound Like . . . Yesterday we took a first look at this piece of art by Faith Ringgold called *Tar Beach 2*. You did a lot of careful observation, and we have listed on this T-chart all the things we saw (objects, people, etc.) and all of our conjectures or ideas about the things we noticed. We spent a lot of time talking about how the kids Cassie and Bebe are depicted here, lying on their backs looking up, and again here, flying above the city. Similarly, the dad is shown both seated at the table and standing on this skyscraper here. Today, let's talk about *Tar Beach 2* some more and see what ideas we can grow together. What is this piece of art making you think about "perspectives" or "point of view," both in this painting for the characters Faith Ringgold created and in *our* lives? Remember, as we go on our conversation journey, you might decide at some point to take us to a new place along the way. If you do, please let us know.

Figure 7.4 *Tar Beach 2* by Faith Ringgold

Facilitation Moves As students have this conversation, you might decide to track the journey by sketching a little map in front of them, as in Lesson 7.4. You can point out those moments when someone moves the class to a new place, jotting it on your map, and offering some of the "signpost" language retroactively: "Miguel, you are taking us somewhere new. You can let everyone know by saying, 'I have a new idea to talk about.'" It isn't essential that the student actually mimic your language in this case; you are just helping the students identify those moments when the conversation is shifting and moving into a new subtopic. These cues both help the speakers learn to recognize when they have slightly changed topics and help the listeners follow along. As with any of the micro-lessons, you will want to keep practicing this skill so you can release more of the responsibility of tracking these shifts to the students and have them rely less on your words (and your map!).

> ### Teacher Tip
> You'll want to choose a broad topic for students to practice this skill, so there is room for them to take the conversation in a variety of directions.

After the Hands-Down Conversation

Reinforce Whenever you are having a conversation, you can notice those moments when you or someone else has brought up a new topic or idea, and think about letting everyone know, so we can all stay together.

Up until now, this role has been part of the teacher's job as facilitator. It is a challenging talk move, but a valuable one for students to try out and be aware of. Think about a conversation you have had when you were trying to work out a problem or better understand an issue. It was probably helpful when someone in the conversation occasionally recapped or summarized what had been said. This summarizing moves the conversation forward. At this stage in our teaching, we can try handing over some of this responsibility to our students. The move of summarizing builds on the moves of repeating and paraphrasing (Lesson 6.1), so you might try this lesson if some of your students are using those talk moves well.

During the Dialogue Micro-lesson

What and Why? As a class, we are all working together to grow ideas and take interesting journeys with our conversations. One thing you can do to help us move forward is to summarize, or review, where our conversation has been so far and guide us to where it could go next. This is like what a tour guide might do on a bus trip. They tell us about the journey so we can all keep track of where we are going and keep together on the bus.

Teacher Tip

You may want to teach this lesson on two separate days, since it has two different "Hows", or you could explain both at the same time, depending on your class.

How? Here's one way you can summarize a conversation to help move us forward and build bigger ideas (*reference or draw parts of the anchor chart as you talk*):

1. Listen for when you hear a big idea to talk about. It might be something someone says quietly that sounds like we could talk a lot about or it might be something that everyone seems to be talking about just a little bit and we should probably discuss more.

2. Tell us all what you heard. You could say, "I think we should talk more about _____," or "It seems like we all are talking about _____."

Another way to summarize is this:

1. Listen for something people seem to disagree about or have different ideas about.

2. Tell us the two sides of the argument that you hear, so we can try to talk more about them. You might say, "Some people think _____, but other people think _____," or "So do we think _____ or _____?"

During the Hands-Down Conversation

Guided Practice: It Might Sound Like . . . Since we have been reading realistic fiction, we have been thinking about external and internal influences on characters. We know that when a character changes, both the ways a character is on the inside *and* the things that happen to the character on the outside are important to consider as causes for that change. Let's think about that more with a book we've read lots of times this year. *Mango, Abuela, and Me* (Medina 2015) is one of our favorites! Today, let's have a conversation about this question: What was more powerful in making Mia change her relationship with Abuela? External or internal factors?

Facilitation Moves To support students as they take on the responsibility of summarizing, you can point out when a big or debatable idea emerges but let the students name the big idea. Your facilitation move might sound like this: "I hear a disagreement emerging. Can anyone help us summarize our conversation so we can talk more about the two sides of this debate?" or "Hmm, this sounds like a big idea to talk about. Who can name a big idea emerging that we could grow together?" Students will not be proficient in this skill initially and may not name the big idea exactly as you would. That's okay—we don't want to get into a "guess what the teacher wants us to talk about" situation by correcting them or trying to look for another child who might summarize it better. As always, we will want to applaud approximations and retain student ownership of the conversation. There is always tomorrow to keep talking.

After the Hands-Down Conversation

Reinforce Whenever you are having a conversation, you can help grow ideas by summarizing the conversation. You can listen for big ideas and disagreement and tell people what you hear so they can try to talk more about those things.

7.7 The "Last Lesson"

Choosing a talk micro-lesson should always be in response to the students in front of you. While we hope many of the micro-lessons in this book will be useful to you in your classrooms, we also expect that you will want to write your own micro-lessons. Talk micro-lessons are always about honoring and building on the many ways students express their own thinking and engage with one another's ideas. Talk micro-lessons are never about "fixing" student talk. This "last lesson" offers you, the teacher, a behind-the-scenes look at how we plan talk micro-lessons to help students build on their talk and listening moves.

Creating a Dialogue Micro-lesson

What and Why? Students come into our classrooms everyday with brilliant ideas. They also come with their own ways of talking about those ideas and engaging with the ideas of others. As teachers, we can help students continue to develop as productive communicators who work together to build ideas and theories about the world around them.

How? So, here's one way you can create your own dialogue micro-lessons:

1. Using data collected from a transcript, conversation map, or more informal noticings, reflect on these questions: Who is talking? What talk and listening moves are students already using?

2. Decide: What's next? What talk and listening moves are students just beginning to approximate? What new learning about talk might be most helpful to them right now?

3. Write: Think about *why* and *how* you use this talk move when you yourself talk to friends or colleagues. Use the what/why/how structure to write down a way to explain the move to your students.

4. Choose a content area in which to "launch" this micro-lesson. Remember, if you expect the talk or listening move you're working on to be challenging, it's a good idea to start with a familiar content-area idea or a social topic.

5. Give students a chance to "have a go" at the new move. Consider which format will be most supportive to try the move out: Turn and Talk partners, Conversation Clubs, or a Hands-Down Conversation.

Writing Your Own Talk Micro-lesson

Facilitation Moves When you plan a talk micro-lesson, it is helpful to anticipate the kind of in-the-moment support students might need. What prompts will you use to remind, reinforce, and coach students to take on the skill? Jot these prompts down in your lesson plan and have them ready. Remember that prompts should be as lean as possible and used judiciously, since we want students to have an opportunity to try talk and listening moves with their peers.

After the Hands-Down Conversation

Reflect and Reinforce Many times, we think of a "lesson" as a singular unit, something you do once. However, with most talk and listening moves, we use the initial talk micro-lesson to orient students to the move, and then offer many follow-up opportunities to try out this move across content areas and across days, providing feedback and reinforcement as children take on the move as their own.

Teacher Tip

The more you listen to students talk, the more talk and listening moves you will notice coming from them. Consider highlighting students' talk and listening moves through micro-lessons codesigned by students. For example, you might hear a student disagree with their partner's idea while discussing a book. With the student's permission, you can craft a micro-lesson around this way of pushing one another's thinking by offering counterexamples.

III

Exploring the Crossover

Conversations in Literacy and Math Classrooms

After a summer thunderstorm, Christy and her two young daughters pulled on their rain boots to go outside and play around in the puddles that had accumulated on their driveway. On this afternoon, questions and exclamations of discovery bounced back and forth between the girls like a tennis match.

"What happens when you mix mulch into this one?"

"Try using this shovel—it lifts the mulch."

"But the stick can stir it better."

"Why is this one so much deeper than the others?"

"Look! The puddle disappears when I jump in it!"

"If you put a piece of chalk in the puddle, can it still write?"

"How did I get mud into my underwear?!"

Of course, the girls' puddle explorations required no adult instructions or interventions from Christy. Children intuitively know that every puddle can be tested in an endless variety of ways.

Years ago, Kassia watched a group of her third graders engage in a similar exploration as they built a "troll trap" during recess. As a few kids used sticks to dig a hole at the edge of the playground, Jo, a wiry eight-year-old girl, yelled out, "We've got to fill this hole with water! The troll will be here any minute!" Children raced to a nearby puddle to fill their water bottles before returning to dump the water into the troll-trap hole. After several kids emptied the contents of their water bottles into the hole, they began to notice that the water was not filling the hole as they had expected, but instead was seeping quickly into the ground.

"What's wrong with this hole?" Jo asked, dismayed.

"We need to block the water from going into the ground!" shouted Alex.

The rest of the kids responded immediately to the call to action (after all, a troll was on the way!):

"I'll get some grass!"

"Wait! We should put mulch in the hole first."

"No, I have a plastic baggie in my lunchbox we can put at the bottom of the hole."

"I'll bring more water!"

The kids looked up at Kassia, curious to see if she was watching or would stop them. She quickly averted her eyes. Technically, it was probably against some school rule to pull up grass and create a large soupy hole on the edge of the playground. But the troll scenario was too fascinating to intervene in, and recess would be over in a few minutes anyway.

We can understand a lot about how children learn by watching them play, whether they are the children in our own families or the children we teach. Children ask questions through their play. They follow their own curiosity, developing and testing theories along the way. In play, children don't feel the need to hurry up and find "the answer." They are comfortable lingering with ambiguity and unresolved questions. As they play, they debate ideas, revise theories, or simply live with conflicting theories.

So when we come into the classroom, it is important to remind ourselves that we are never "starting from scratch" with children. Children are brilliant, and our goal, as teachers, should always be to build on children's competence. While school is a place where traditionally there has been little room for the sorts of "puddle poking" that Christy's daughters and Kassia's third graders engaged in, we can choose to open the classroom door and let in the ways of thinking that children are already doing outside of school. The work of a Hands-Down Conversation community is to constantly seek a space in which both teachers and students can linger with ideas and construct meaning together.

Planning for Hands-Down Conversations in Math and Literacy

As literacy and math coaches, we spend a lot of time talking together about the ways children negotiate and create shared meaning. Working in the same schools as classroom teachers and then as coaches has given us many opportunities to compare notes over the years about how children think and talk.

"Do you know Armando and Caetie in Mr. Miner's class?" Christy would begin. "Listen to what they said when we were reading *Big Red Lollipop*" (Khan 2010).

"Oh yeah, I know them. Armando said something to the class about fractions last week that completely surprised me," Kassia would reply. And off we would go into a conversation about the ways children construct ideas and the ways we facilitate talk and learning.

It is through many of these conversations over the years that we have explored the crossover between literacy and math. While there are certainly many differences between literacy and math learning, it is the common ground that interests us the most. Our students develop as mathematicians and readers simultaneously, and the boundaries between these subjects (and others) are often more rigid in the minds of teachers than in the minds of children. Rather than keeping each subject in its own box, we can build classroom communities in which ideas and ways of thinking cross content-area borders. The conversations we have in literacy and math can strengthen and reinforce one another and lead to ways of thinking that go beyond any one subject area.

By sitting alongside children and teachers in both math and literacy classrooms, we

WHERE DO THE DIALOGUE MICRO-LESSONS FIT IN?

Within the planning process of each Hands-Down Conversation, we pause to think about how we want to weave in further opportunities to develop dialogue. We consider which dialogue micro-lessons we have taught the class recently, and what they are approximating in their most current conversations. We decide whether we would like to teach a new talk or listening move or reinforce ones we have already thought about together as a class. We keep in mind that we may not want to immerse students in brand-new content *and* new talk moves all in the same lesson. The "Week-at-a-Glance" sections in Chapters 8, 9, and 10 are examples of how content and talk develop alongside each other. As you read the chapters in Section III and start planning for Hands-Down Conversations, consider how you can work to strike a balance between teaching dialogue and content in your classroom.

have found three types of conversation to be particularly powerful across the content areas. These conversation types build on children's intuitive ways of thinking and get at the heart of what it means to be a reader, a mathematician, and a community member. The three chapters in this section explore these three types of conversations.

In Chapter 8, "Nurturing Disagreement," students construct arguments and engage with each other's ideas.

In Chapter 9, "Developing Theories Together," students build on patterns they notice to make conjectures and develop theories.

In Chapter 10, "Engaging with the World," students critically analyze the messages that texts send and decide together how to respond.

Throughout the next three chapters, we invite you to join us as we plan and facilitate Hands-Down Conversations across the elementary grades in both math and literacy. The examples you will read about in this section are intended to get you started. Once you begin looking, opportunities to have these kinds of conversations will present themselves everywhere.

8

Nurturing Disagreement

There has never been a more important time to teach young people to suspend judgment, weigh evidence, consider multiple perspectives, and speak up with wisdom and grace on behalf of themselves and others.

—Mary Ehrenworth, "Why Argue?"

In the 1950s, Alice Stewart, a physician and scientist, became the first person to make the connection between X-rays during pregnancy and childhood cancer. Stewart's discovery came at a time when X-rays were a new and exciting technology, and the controversial findings of a woman doctor and scientist, as you might imagine, were met with significant resistance from the medical community. "No one wanted to know," said Margaret Heffernan in "Dare to Disagree," her TED Talk about Alice Stewart (2012). In order to convince the medical community of the risks of getting X-rays during pregnancy, Stewart had to do more than simply present her data; she had to become an expert in crafting her argument. A statistician named George Kneale, with whom she worked, became her partner in preparing for this argument. George Kneale "saw his job as creating conflict around her theories," and together they learned the power of collaboration in which "thinking partners aren't echo chambers." In her TED Talk, Heffernan reflects on this idea: "I wonder how many of us have or dare to have such collaborators?" (2012).

Argumentation Across Literacy and Math

Many of us, in our work and in our personal lives, have felt discomfort around disagreement, and our hesitance to engage in disagreement has perhaps even led to missed opportunities to grow our own thinking and the thinking of those around us. Angela Barlow and Michael McCrory write that "disagreements provide students with the impetus to think deeply about mathematics in an effort to make sense of a situation. The discourse that surrounds the disagreement allows students to organize their thoughts, formulate arguments, consider other students' positions, and communicate their positions to their classmates" (2011, 531). By nurturing disagreement in *all* subject areas, we encourage students to engage in argumentation, the process by which we use reasoning to consider ideas and theories about what is true.

In the field of literacy education, Stephen Kucer reminds us that a reader's purpose, perspective, background knowledge, and the context in which they are reading all play a role in determining the meaning they walk away with. "The author does not solely determine the importance of ideas" (2005, 162). We believe that this is just as true in math as it is in literacy. There is no special list of prerequisite skills required to construct meaning from a text (in the broadest sense of the word). Students do not need to wait for the teacher to tell them what to think or if they are "right." The right to create meaning in literacy and math belongs to everyone, and we can live that value by engaging in rigorous debate, by saying to all students, *this text is yours to figure out.*

> ## WHAT WE NEVER DEBATE
> While we believe nurturing disagreement about both academic and social issues is a productive way of considering perspectives and constructing ideas, there are some topics we *never* ask students to debate. In recent years some teachers around the country have given students assignments to take on a "Nazi's perspective" or to "consider the argument" for slavery. It is never okay to debate or encourage "perspective taking" in a way that denies the humanity of an individual or group of people.

We believe that students who experience debate in a way that values *listening* equally with *talking* develop several powerful qualities:

1. Agency. We construct meaning both individually and collaboratively.

2. Intellectual risk-taking. We reflect on and dissect our own thinking and others' thinking.

3. Open-mindedness. We work to understand multiple perspectives.

At the heart of conversations that nurture disagreement is the idea that considering different perspectives and bringing a skeptical lens to an idea is a productive way of building understanding. As students become more familiar with argumentation as a way of thinking across literacy and math, they become more generous in the ways that they listen to each other, consider each other's ideas, and revise their own ideas.

Planning to Disagree

So, how do we plan for Hands-Down Conversations that nurture disagreement? The planning process for both literacy and math conversations follows a similar trajectory:

1. **Choose and understand an important content goal or big idea you want students to explore.** Consider what work might be good "next steps" for your students based on their current understandings. Then consider the authentic processes readers and mathematicians engage in as they do work around these ideas.

2. **Select a "text" that allows you to engage in the content work.** The "text" may be a book, a poem, an image, a quote from a student, a graph, or a problem.

3. **Anticipate students' thinking and what understandings they will bring to the text.** As you anticipate student thinking, it is possible that you will go back and revise your text or even choose a different text altogether if you realize that your text does not encourage the kind of thinking you are hoping to highlight.

4. **Plan time for immersion in the text.** Before asking students to engage in debate around the text, you will want to give them some time to digest, play with, notice, or develop a connection with the text. This could be brief, such as providing some wait time to consider the text before a conversation begins. Or it could be more extensive, such as reading a book to students a few times or inviting students to work on a math problem in pairs before coming to the conversation.

5. **Plan a launch and facilitate conversation.** Decide how to build debate and uncertainty around the text.

Table 8.1 Some Ways We Can Launch "Disagreement" Hands-Down Conversations

Type of Launch	What Is It?	Examples
Offer a Debatable Idea Always/ Sometimes/ Never	Offer a debatable idea and ask students to decide if it is always, sometimes, or never true.	• Wolves are bad. • Fractions are small.

Table 8.1 *(continued)*

Type of Launch	What Is It?	Examples
Offer a Debatable Idea Choose a Side	Ask students to choose a side of a debate. Use descriptors that are subjective or hard to quantify, such as *better*, *bigger*, *good*, or *right*.	• Let's talk about this: Jack is good or the giant is good. What do you think? • Odd numbers are better or even numbers are better.
Pose a Debatable Question	Ask a question about an idea that is open to multiple answers and interpretations.	• Would you rather ____ or ____? • Which one doesn't belong?

Note: *See Chapter 2 for more on crafting launches for Hands-Down Conversations.*

In this chapter, we invite you into both reading and math conversations that nurtured productive disagreement in Kelsey Friend's first-grade class. Kelsey's classroom is a community bursting with conversation. She works hard to foster student ownership and agency through both the lessons she plans and her interactions with her students. Kelsey works to notice power inequities in her class and find ways for everyone to belong to the community and have their voice heard. To do this work, Kelsey continually models being a curious listener and is frequently found crouching down in her classroom, listening intently to her students' thoughts and ideas. Her words reflect her genuine desire to deeply understand the ideas children bring to the table. She often says to students, "Tell me more about your idea; I really want to understand it," and "So tell me if I've got this right. You're saying . . ."

As you take a look at our planning process for both of the conversations, consider how this process might work in *your* classroom. You can use the following "Week at a Glance" to see how this work played out in math and literacy across a week in Kelsey's classroom. The examples and ideas we present here will be just the tip of the iceberg. We know you will find many more ways and opportunities to nurture disagreement among your students and within your content areas.

Figure 8.1 Kelsey listens intently to understand her first graders' big ideas.

Week at a Glance: Nurturing Disagreement in Kelsey's Classroom

Monday	Tuesday	Wednesday	Thursday	Friday
Micro-lesson on Supporting with Reasoning (Lesson 5.2) and Conversation about social topic (Appendix C)	Reading: Read aloud *Chameleon, Chameleon* for the first time, for enjoyment.	Math: Quick review of Supporting with Reasoning (Lesson 5.2) and Hands-Down Conversation about question: "Box A is bigger or Box B is bigger?"	Reading: Interactive read-aloud of *Chameleon, Chameleon*	Reading: Quick review of Supporting Ideas with Reasoning (Lesson 5.2) and Hands-Down Conversation about *Chameleon, Chameleon*

Nurturing Disagreement in Math

1. Choose and understand an important content goal or big idea.

While we often begin our math planning by unpacking grade-level standards, it is also important to connect these standards to the bigger ideas of mathematics that span across the grade levels within and beyond elementary school. Getting in the practice of asking ourselves, "What are the big ideas here?" and "Why does this matter?" can help us make sure that we put our teaching focus in the right place and don't get lost in the weeds. For example, one of the second-grade state math standards in Virginia asks students to compare whole numbers using the greater-than, less-than, and equal-to symbols. In her first year of teaching second grade, Kassia spent a lot of time helping students remember which symbol was which and giving them tips like "Look at the tens digit first." (Never mind *why*!) Later she began to ask herself, "But what's this standard *really* about?" She learned that the big idea behind the standard asking students to compare two-digit numbers is constructing an understanding of how our place value system works as well as thinking about how numbers relate to each other. (Is one number a lot bigger than the other? Would they be pretty close together on a hundreds chart?) The more we ask ourselves these kinds of questions about the big ideas of mathematics, the more we put our energy into what really matters and the stronger the foundation we build for children's mathematical learning.

> Since Kelsey's first-grade class was about to begin a unit on measurement, we wanted to remind ourselves of the big ideas around measurement for young learners as we planned. We began by thinking about the idea that "many different attributes can be measured, even when measuring a single object" ("Big Ideas," Erikson Institute Early Math Collaborative website). This idea, while it may seem simple to adults, is fundamental to many subsequent measurement understandings including ideas around measurement units, tools, and precision.
>
> We also knew that young students already have ideas and experiences around measurement that they would bring to the conversation. (What is big? What is small? Who is the tallest?) We wanted to make space to listen to these ideas in our Hands-Down Conversation and consider how we could build upon them throughout the unit.

2. Select a "text" that allows you to engage in the content work.

Most math textbooks and curricular resources are written with very little room for ambiguity or differing perspectives. Christopher Danielson, the author of *Which One Doesn't Belong?* (2016b) and *How Many?* (2018) and a math educator who

LEARNING MORE ABOUT THE BIG IDEAS OF MATHEMATICS

Deeply understanding the big ideas of mathematics is a career-long journey for every math teacher. Each professional article or book we read and each mathematical interaction we have with a child adds a new layer to our understanding. Here are two particularly helpful resources that we return to again and again as references for understanding the big ideas of elementary math.

- *Understanding the Math We Teach and How to Teach It, K–8,* by Marian Small

Each chapter of this book focuses on a different area of mathematics and opens with an "in a nutshell" textbox containing several bulleted big ideas that are explored in detail within the chapter. Small also offers a variety of open questions throughout these content chapters, many of which are perfect for Hands-Down Conversations.

- Erikson Institute Early Math Collaborative website (earlymath.erikson.edu/why -early-math-everyday-math /big-ideas-learning-early -mathematics/)

Focusing specifically on early childhood mathematics, this website outlines the important math concepts young children should explore. Clicking on a big idea leads you to short articles, videos, and classroom resources on that topic.

delights in asking ambiguous questions and listening to children, writes that, "ambiguity is an important source of mathematical activity that is too often overlooked in favor of certainty in math classrooms" (2016b). It is no wonder that so many students see math as a subject in which you're either right or wrong, good or bad!

We can create space for ambiguity in math "texts" in several ways:

A. We choose a problem from our curriculum and give it a "makeover" in order to create ambiguity and room for debate.

B. We use an instructional routine that, by design, invites multiple perspectives. Throughout this book you've read about "Which One Doesn't Belong?" "Would You Rather?" "Same or Different?" and other routines you can lean on when planning for Hands-Down Conversations.

C. We use our students' words or the words of "some people." Many times, a debatable idea or theory will emerge from student discussions or student work. Other times, the teacher can plan for debate by using the phrase "Some people say/think . . ." and inviting debate around this idea.

While we often think of the "texts" of our math teaching as a problem from a math curriculum, it is helpful to remember that a text can also be a photograph that invites student thinking, a graph from a newspaper, a quote from a student, or simply a debatable idea you have come up with.

As Kassia began to think about a text that would help Kelsey's first graders explore the big ideas of measurement that she and Kelsey had chosen, she remembered a task she had seen in several curriculum resources. In this task the teacher shows students a bucket (or other container) and asks, "How can we measure this bucket?"

Students might say, "We could see how much water it holds," or "We can measure how tall the bucket is with cubes," or "We could see how much string it takes to go all the way around the opening of the bucket." While this bucket conversation might elicit *some* of the ideas Kassia hoped to focus on in their Hands-Down Conversation, something about it felt lacking. With the bucket question she was left wondering:

- Why does this matter?

- Why should I bother listening to what other people have to say about this question?

The bucket question, despite its shortcomings, inspired a new text for Kelsey's classroom. Rather than ask, "How could we measure this bucket?" they could ask students to look at two different boxes and debate which box was bigger.

After coming up with this idea, Kassia spent some time in her neighborhood recycling area, rifling through possible box choices. She wanted to choose two boxes that looked very different from each other and two boxes that could each be the "bigger" box in different ways. The boxes became the text and, unlike the bucket question, the choice of boxes and the term *bigger* invited ambiguity, nuance, and disagreement.

3. Anticipate students' thinking and what understandings they will bring to the text.

In their article "Orchestrating Discussions," Smith, Hughes, Engle, and Stein discuss five teacher practices that are critical to facilitating productive whole-class math conversations. The first practice, anticipating, "requires considering how students might mathematically interpret a problem, the array of strategies (both correct and incorrect) they might use to solve it, and how those strategies and interpretations might relate to the mathematical ideas the teacher would like his or her students to learn" (2009, 551). The process of anticipating student thinking allows us, as teachers, to access understandings students may bring to a text and respond in more thoughtful and robust ways.

As Kassia stood in the neighborhood recycling area (at 9:00 p.m., in her pajamas) holding the two boxes she planned to use as the "text" for the Hands-Down Conversation, she began to think about how the students might decide which box was bigger. She anticipated students might bring up these ideas:

Figure 8.2 Box A (right) and Box B (left) ready to be revealed to the first graders

- Box B is longer/taller. Box A is shorter.

- Box A is wider. Box B is skinnier.

- Which box is bigger may depend on what you are trying to put inside of it. Box A would likely fit more apples in it than Box B, but Box B would fit more umbrellas.

- Box A has a greater volume (students might describe this by saying something like it has "more space inside it").

- Students might wonder which box is heavier (even if we say the boxes are empty).

- Students may ask what we mean by "bigger."

4. Plan time for immersion in the text.

Before launching a Hands-Down Conversation, we slow down to allow students time to process the text. In math we often ask students our two favorite questions: What do you notice? What do you wonder? We allow time for "on-your-own thinking," time for talking with a partner, and sometimes time for processing as a whole group around these questions.

> The text immersion for the box debate was simple. Kassia and Kelsey would place the two boxes in the middle of the Hands-Down Conversation circle and invite students to notice. They planned to say, "Let's take a look at these two empty boxes, Box A and Box B. On your own (no hands, no voices), think about what you notice." They intentionally pointed out that the boxes were empty—they didn't want students to focus on guessing what might be inside the boxes. They also introduced the "names" of the boxes, Box A and Box B, so that the students would have common language when talking about the boxes with their partners and the whole class.

5. Plan a launch and facilitate conversation.

In her book *Good Questions: Great Ways to Differentiate Mathematics Instruction in the Standards-Based Classroom*, Marian Small writes about several strategies for creating open questions. She refers to one of these strategies as "using 'soft' words," that is, words that are somewhat imprecise, undefined, or ambiguous (2017, 9). In *Up for Debate! Exploring Math Through Argument*, Chris Luzniak expands on this idea, observing that "by opening up the question to opinions and interpretations, students are not only developing arguments but also increasing their engagement with the problem" (2019, 29). Examples of "soft" or debatable words are *big/bigger/biggest, small/smaller/smallest, better/best/worst, bad/good, fair/not fair*, and *close to.*

See Table 8.1 for tips on launching a Hands-Down Conversation that nurtures disagreement.

Remembering how the original question ("How could we measure this bucket?") left her wondering, "But who cares?!," Kassia chose a launch that she hoped would spark curiosity and invite debate: "Now let's talk about this idea: Box A is bigger or Box B is bigger."

Because *bigger* is an ambiguous term (Does it mean taller? longer? wider? heavier? greater volume?), this word invites disagreement. It begs us to ask the question: What does bigger mean? Unlike the bucket question, the forced choice in the box launch (Which box is bigger?) gives students a reason to listen to each other and compare their own ideas with others'.

Kassia and Kelsey wanted to invite students to think about this "bigger box" conversation right at the beginning of the measurement unit, before they got into the nitty-gritty of what and how to measure. They wanted the students to feel a need for tools and units instead of just handing them some Unifix cubes and saying, "Here, you can measure the length of the box with these."

You could argue that Kassia and Kelsey never answered the question "Why do these boxes matter?" There was no real-world application. But this conversation launch did not need one. Asking students to choose a side about a question with no single right answer created what Fuller, Rabin, and Harel would call an "intellectual need" to talk, an "intellectual need" to begin to figure out, "What does bigger mean?" (2011).

The Box Conversation in Action

Let's take a look at a small part of the Hands-Down Conversation in Kelsey's first-grade class. Before launching the Hands-Down Conversation, Kassia took a few moments to review the micro-lesson on supporting our ideas with reasoning (Lesson 5.2, Supporting with Reasoning, Part 1: The *Why* Behind Our Ideas). Therefore, she was listening for the ways in which students would try out that skill in this conversation, in addition to listening to children's ideas about the math content.

Kassia: We're going to have a Hands-Down Conversation where you speak into the silence and you say, "Box A is bigger" or "Box B is bigger," but you're really focusing on telling us your *why*. Who would like to start us off with our Hands-Down Conversation? *(Kassia notices Miguel waving an enthusiastic hand.)* Can you start us off, Miguel?

Miguel: I noticed Box A is bigger because that box is more bigger than a triangle.

Angel: I think Box B is more bigger because if you stand it up it would be more bigger than Box A.

Daquan: Box B is actually bigger cause if you stand it up it's bigger than Box A.

Faruk: Box A is bigger because it is like this *(gestures with hands, outlining a cube shaped box)*.

Madeline: I think Box A is bigger because the squares are bigger and the triangle is smaller.

Rosita: I think that Box A is bigger because if you have Box B sitting flat then Box A is bigger. And also if something's in there, which it's probably not, then you can tear it up in pieces and Box A can be bigger than Box B.

Figure 8.3 A student explains his thinking about the boxes.

Camila: I think Box A is bigger 'cause you can tell the size of it, and the Box B is kind of small because of the size of it.

Kassia: I'm going to stop you right here cause I'm hearing something, an idea, come up a lot. A lot of you said if you stand Box B up, something's different. A lot of you are having that same thought. Who can start us off talking about *that idea* and your *why*. Can you start us off?

Harper: I want to change my idea. None of them [the boxes] are bigger. None of them are bigger because if you stand Box B up, then it is bigger, but if you put it down then Box A is bigger. So it kind of tells me that none of them are bigger.

(Kassia notices Bhavite excitedly showing the connection sign while Harper is talking. She also heard Bhavite talk about this same idea in a Turn and Talk before the conversation started. Kassia knows from prior experiences that while Bhavite sometimes has a hard time getting into the conversation, she does enjoy sharing her ideas with the whole group.)

Kassia: Hang on one second. Bhavite, I saw you show the connection sign when Harper said, "I think there isn't one that's bigger." Can you say more about that? And, everyone else, listen to see if you can add on to her idea.

Bhavite: None of them are bigger because first when you put Box B lying down, I was thinking Box A is the big box, and then when you change Box B to standing up, it change my mind to Box B is more bigger.

Kassia: How can you add on to *that* idea?

Timmy: I think the box that says Box B is the longest one because when it's flat it would be smaller than this one [Box A], but when it's up like this then Box B would be bigger than this box [Box A].

Next Steps for Kelsey's Class

Throughout the entire box conversation, many of the ideas Kelsey and Kassia anticipated did indeed come up—students talked about the length and height of the boxes, the shape of the boxes, and even alluded to the volume (". . . if something's in there . . . you can tear it up in pieces and Box A can be bigger than Box B"). And, of course, students also surprised them. They had not anticipated that the orientation of Box B (lying down or standing up) would matter so much to students as they considered the question of which box was bigger, but in retrospect they could see why it did. They closed the conversation by asking the students to turn and talk again about their ideas, and in one partner conversation they listened to a student say, "Yeah, but like, what is big? Like a building? Like God?" What a perfect question for the class as they entered their measurement unit: What is big? Students were ready to consider the different attributes we measure and how we might go about doing that.

In listening to students' words, Kassia and Kelsey also noticed that most students used reasoning to support their ideas, with some reasoning being very specific and other reasoning fairly broad. They noticed that, while students' ideas connected to one another in a general way, the class might keep thinking about different ways to add on to each other's ideas.

And finally, before beginning the conversation, they wondered if, at the end of the conversation, the first graders would ask them which box was indeed bigger. Would they still turn to the teachers for the "real right answer"? Not a single one of them did. They seemed to understand that perhaps there wasn't a single truth in this case. Their experiences in Kelsey's first-grade classroom encouraged them to delight in questions that are messy and not easy to resolve.

Nurturing Disagreement in Literacy

We can use the same general planning process to get students debating different interpretations of a text in literacy, although there are some important differences in the way each step plays out. Let's take a look at how we use our "planning for disagreement" process and how the resulting conversation might sound.

1. Choose and understand an important content goal or big idea.

As students read, they are always integrating many different goals and strategies at once, but as teachers, we usually have a few particular comprehension strategies in mind that we want to focus on. These strategies might come from our curriculum, or from a resource like Fountas and Pinnell's *Literacy Continuum* (2017). The first step is to choose a goal that seems like a good "next step" for the majority of the students in front of us, based on the comprehension work they have displayed in previous conversations and/or writing about the books they read. When we are working to nurture disagreement, we also want to make sure we choose a weighty goal with ambiguity lurking within it, so it can provide a lot to debate. Try asking yourself, *Could this goal result in multiple ideas and answers, or is there really just one way to think about this?* For example, a goal like "Express opinions about characters and their behavior" will leave us with more to negotiate together than "Recall important details about characters after a story is read," because expressing opinions opens itself to individual interpretation and perspectives (Fountas and Pinnell 2017, 35).

Kelsey's first graders were just entering a nonfiction unit of study. Kelsey and Christy did not have much prior student work in the genre to reflect on, so they decided instead to use this experience as a "preassessment" that would help them inform next steps in the unit of study. With that in mind, they turned to the "Interactive Read Alouds and Literature Discussion in Nonfiction" section of the *Literacy Continuum* for first graders (Fountas and Pinnell 2017, 37–39). There are *many* goals listed for students to work on during interactive read-alouds in first grade; however, for the purposes of encouraging debate, Kelsey and Christy started with a goal that felt like big, broad comprehension work and that would elicit differing responses and perspectives: *Understand that a nonfiction text can have different meanings for different people.*

2. Select a "text" that allows you to engage in the content work.

In this step, gather a few texts that will provide opportunities for this comprehension work, are appropriate choices for your readers, and have some shades of gray or "nuance." We make our final selection by reading each text while looking for debate. This is a process of "spying on ourselves as readers" (Fay, Moritz, and Whaley 2017, 152) and carefully noting when we come across something in the text that relates to our curricular goal *and* that we could look at from multiple perspectives. One indication that a text might work well is when we find ourselves forming an opinion (and we can also imagine how someone else might have a different opinion on the same thing).

> For Kelsey's first graders, Kelsey and Christy wanted to choose a nonfiction text that would bring out multiple perspectives. They began by seeking out nonfiction picture books written with a narrative or persuasive structure, which tend to elicit opinions and emotion more easily than those with a more traditional nonfiction structure. Keeping in mind their current science unit, text structure, and level of vocabulary, they collected a text set, and then read each text "looking" for debate. One book emerged as a clear choice: *Chameleon, Chameleon* (2005), by Joy Cowley. This book uses simple but descriptive language and vivid photos to tell the short narrative of a chameleon who, upon finding no food in "his" tree, sets out "slowly, slowly, step by step" to find food (eventually, a caterpillar) and avoid becoming food himself along the way. As they read, they noticed a juicy kernel for potential debate around the chameleon's behavior. Some students might find it "unfair" that the chameleon eats the caterpillar at the end, but others would not feel that way. They decided *Chameleon, Chameleon* would meet their curricular goals and nurture disagreement.

3. Anticipate students' thinking and what understandings they will bring to the text.

As Kucer teaches us, we must keep in mind the context in which our students are interacting with the text, their varying perspectives, and their background knowledge (2005). We want to reflect on what our students are bringing to the text and imagine the kinds of things they will say or think as they take it in. This reflection allows us to put ourselves in our students' shoes and consider the variety of interpretations and perspectives that will exist in our class, which in turn helps us plan for the debate.

THE POWER OF THE INTERACTIVE READ-ALOUD

An interactive read-aloud differs from, but does not replace, the more traditional read-aloud, in which the teacher and students enjoy a text together without calculated stopping places, just as a parent and child might do at home. An interactive read-aloud is a strategic teaching tool in which the teacher carefully plans how and when the class community will stop to talk about the text in order to support comprehension goals. There are many wonderful resources available to guide us as we plan interactive read-alouds that will set our students up for debate-filled Hands-Down Conversations. Chapter 5 of Maria Nichols's *Comprehension Through Conversation* (2006) is one such place to turn to. Nichols gives a thorough explanation of how teachers can scaffold comprehension strategically and purposefully while reading aloud a book to students.

Christy and Kelsey knew the first graders had some background knowledge about what animals need for survival and had learned a little bit about the food chain. They also knew that the class had previously done a lot of comprehension work in fiction, analyzing character emotions and connecting and empathizing with those characters. They anticipated that students would argue with a mixture of scientific and emotional reasoning. They imagined that the text might leave students with an opinion of chameleons ranging from fierce and bad to interesting and "cool," depending on their perspective and interpretation of the text.

4. Plan time for immersion in the text.

Interactive read-alouds are one method to immerse students in a text before the Hands-Down Conversation. This is an opportunity to carefully select stopping points where we pause the reading and think aloud to boost comprehension or simply draw students' attention to important passages that might lead to robust debate. We often, but not always, ask students to turn and talk about their thinking at these stopping points to give them the opportunity to hear another perspective as they build meaning and understanding. It is important to note that we also frequently choose to read the text in a traditional manner (front to back without stopping) for general enjoyment and to increase comprehension either before or after the interactive read-aloud. We find that repeated readings usually result in more students joining the Hands-Down Conversation when we have it.

In planning the interactive read-aloud of *Chameleon, Chameleon*, Kelsey and Christy went back to those pages where they first noticed there would be something to debate: the page where "the chameleon sees a big caterpillar," and the following page, where the chameleon's tongue zaps out and grabs the caterpillar from its leaf in a dramatic slow-motion photo. Up to this point, the reader is really focused on the chameleon's safety and rooting for his survival as he moves through the jungle. But when he has "success" grabbing and devouring the caterpillar, Kelsey and Christy anticipated students might change their opinion or perception of him. This page became one important place for students to talk with their partners. Kelsey and Christy also planned a few other stopping points that would further build this debate.

Figure 8.4 A stopping point in the book where students debate whether the chameleon's actions are justified.

5. Plan a launch and facilitate conversation.

To get students talking about the debatable aspect we have highlighted in a text, we carefully choose words to craft a statement or question as a launch (see Table 8.1 for some types of launches that get us debating). We also plan a few follow-up moves we might like to make during the conversation in case we need to reengage students in the debate. For example, we might use one of the launches we considered but did not select, or we might repeat of one of the stopping points from the interactive read-aloud that would get students thinking about the other side of the debate. In some circumstances, when all students end up agreeing with each other, we might even play "devil's advocate" by stating the counterargument or perspective that no one has considered. This move encourages students to strengthen and refine their arguments (or consider another side).

> Keeping their comprehension goal in mind, Kelsey and Christy wanted the launch to get Kelsey's students talking about their different perspectives on the chameleon. Here are some launches they considered:
>
>   A. Let's talk about this idea: The chameleon is bad.
>
>   B. Who do you like, the chameleon or the caterpillar?
>
>   C. What are you thinking now about chameleons?
>
> They thought that question B, being a binary choice, might lead to a situation in which students shared their ideas without elaboration. Question C was more open and less supportive than question A, but in thinking about these particular students, question C seemed right. Kelsey and Christy anticipated that the students would be ready to share some ideas, and they wanted to see if the disagreement would emerge naturally without heavy teacher involvement. They decided to launch the conversation with Question C. However, during the interactive read-aloud, one student, Natalia, said to her partner, Miguel, in a Turn and Talk, "I can't believe the chameleon ate that caterpillar. It was going to be a butterfly!" Miguel verbalized the opposing side, saying, "It's okay. It's natural." After she heard this, Christy decided to scrap her planned launch and launch the conversation the next day with these student quotes instead.

The Chameleon Conversation in Action

Christy: Yesterday we read *Chameleon, Chameleon*, and I heard two different ideas emerging about the chameleon. Natalia said, "I can't believe the chameleon ate that caterpillar. It was going to be a butterfly!" But then Miguel disagreed. He said, "It's okay. It's natural."

Let's talk more about this. What are *you* thinking about the chameleon? Would anyone like to start us off? (*Hands go up, including Bhavite's.*) Bhavite, I know you've been working to get your voice in our conversations. How about you start, and then we will go from there, hands down.

Bhavite: The lizard was being natural. Insects and a lot of animals eat other animals.

David: It's natural for animals to eat other animals.

Madeline: I think it's normal for the chameleon to eat the caterpillar because animals need something to eat.

Rosita: I think the chameleon has to be careful with that dangerous animal we saw in the book because it can hurt the chameleon.

Timmy: I think the chameleon is eating the caterpillar because he doesn't know it is going to turn into a butterfly.

Angel: I agree with Timmy because the caterpillar wants to be a butterfly.

Peter: I think it's natural. It's sort of their diet, it's what they eat.

Daquan: I think it's bad because the chameleon—all it's been through, and now it eats its own prey?! All those other animals were gonna eat it like *their* prey and now after all it's been through, it would eat that caterpillar?

Miguel: But it's natural. They eat different kinds of animals.

Ahmed: Yeah, it's the food chain.

Christy: Can I interrupt for a minute? A lot of you are saying this is just how animals work, but Daquan is saying—let me see if I got this right, Daquan—the chameleon is *so* scared it was going to get eaten. It felt more and more frightened, and it went through all of that, and then it just ate the caterpillar anyway?

Daquan: Yeah, after all it had been through.

Christy: After all it had been through, it was so scared that IT was going to be eaten, and then it went and ate the caterpillar. That is interesting. Turn and talk about that with your partner.

(*Students turn and talk. They are animated and passionate in their partner conversations about this topic. When they return to the whole group, everyone is leaning forward, charged and ready to go. Christy asks Edna, a typically quieter voice, to begin again.*)

Christy: Edna's going to continue our Hands-Down Conversation.

Edna: I think when it chews it, it won't turn into a butterfly. That's bad.

(Several students try to talk over each other next. They are really excited, and some are repeating themselves in an effort to get their voices into the conversation. Christy notices this and decides to use this teachable moment to see whether students can try to adjust this behavior themselves. She also knows this will require some further dialogue work, so it will probably continue to be a little messy right now because the students are so invested in the conversation!)

Christy: Let's wait just a moment. Instead of making your voice louder and louder, if you talk at the same time as someone else, find the eyes of the person who is also trying to talk and try saying, "You can go." And think about whose voices haven't been heard. Jocelyn was trying to get her voice in, so she might be someone who could go next.

Jocelyn: I am thinking of the journey of the chameleon not having food. It's a scared journey. It's going through and scared of a lot of things. And everything that might hurt it.

(Several students try to talk at once again. Someone says "Shhh." Peter notices Timmy trying to talk.)

Peter: We should let Timmy go.

Timmy: So, um, why the chameleon eats the caterpillar is he doesn't know that if he eats it that it won't turn into a butterfly. Because he does not know that.

Madeline: I think he *deserves* that caterpillar because he went a long way to eat that caterpillar and he has no food at his house and he has the colors to blend into the tree.

Harper: I think that after all of this he just goes and eats that tiny little caterpillar, I just [shakes her head] . . . I just agree with Daquan.

Christy: Let's stop our conversation there. We have even more to think about now. I'm thinking a lot about what Timmy said. He said, "The chameleon didn't know the caterpillar would turn into a butterfly. The chameleon didn't understand that." And I wonder, if the chameleon didn't know that, does it make it okay? Or are some of us still upset?

(Some students shake their heads, and several murmurs are heard.)

Christy: As you are studying other animals, let's think more about that—how some animals eat other animals and is that okay? Do we like some animals better than we like other animals because of that? Hmmm. So, would anyone like our final word today? Maybe someone who didn't speak?

(Jose raises his hand and Christy nods in his direction.)

Jose: Miguel said it's natural for animals to eat other animals and he, he . . . that's right. If they don't eat, they will die.

Next Steps for Kelsey's Class

After the conversation, Kelsey and Christy debriefed, thinking about both the students' discourse and their comprehension of the text. They were excited to note how many students supported their ideas with evidence, unprompted, both from within the text, and from their background knowledge, because that was the most recent dialogue move they had been focusing on. After the math conversation, they had noted it could be interesting to work more on connective language. However, a more immediate need arose in the reading conversation—the need to negotiate those instances when several students start talking at once. They had to address this need first so that everyone's voice could be heard. This would be a good next step for a dialogue micro-lesson.

In terms of comprehension, Christy and Kelsey set their sights on some of the bigger ideas that were emerging during the conversation. They thought students would be motivated to keep exploring this idea of "who eats whom" in science as they studied animals and read additional nonfiction texts in this science content area. Then the students could start making connections across these texts and experiences and have a Hands-Down Conversation on the significance of food chains. In addition, after reading some other texts, Christy and Kelsey could try analyzing how nonfiction authors position readers to "like" some animals more than others.

These are some of the types of conversations we explore more in Chapters 9 and 10.

Disagreement as a Way of Thinking

At the heart of conversations that nurture disagreement is the idea that considering different perspectives and bringing a skeptical lens to an idea is a productive way of building understanding. As students become more familiar with argumentation as a way of thinking across literacy and math, we find that they become more generous in the ways that they listen to each other, consider each other's ideas, and revise their own ideas.

Planning to Disagree

- Choose and understand an important content goal or big idea.

- Select a "text" that allows you to engage in the content work.

- Anticipate students' thinking and what understandings they will bring to the text.

- Plan time for immersion in the text.

- Plan a launch and facilitate conversation.

Chapter

9

Developing Theories Together

When we strive to uncover children's theories, we see how
they are constructed and as a result we can more carefully
construct our teaching.

—Karen Gallas, *Talking Their Way into Science: Hearing
Children's Questions and Theories, Responding with Curriculum*

As math was wrapping up for the day, Leani, a second grader in Ms. Bryan's class, piped up confidently, "You can't split odd numbers in half. That's a rule. You just can't. Like if I have seven stickers, that's an odd number. I can keep three and give three to my brother, but what about that extra one? You can only split even numbers in half." As the class listened to Leani's idea, some students nodded along. Some looked skeptical. A couple looked longingly out the window, eager to get outside to recess.

After letting the silence linger for a few moments, Ms. Bryan said, "That's an interesting idea, Leani. We will keep thinking about this idea together as a class. I'm going to write it down here on a piece of chart paper and put it on our Conjecture Wall. You're thinking this idea *might* be true: 'You can't split odd numbers in half. You can only split even numbers in half.' Did I get that right?" Leani nods. Ms. Bryan gestures to the rest of the class invitingly. "I'm looking forward to hearing what other people think about this idea."

Several weeks later, Ms. Bryan's class was working on equal share problems. Caleb and Andrea worked together on the problem: *Two friends want to share nine crackers equally. How many crackers should each friend get?* As the class gathered to share their ideas, Andrea waved her paper in the air and pointed excitedly at the conjecture about odd and even numbers that was posted on the wall. "This is like odd and even numbers. Except with crackers you can share an odd number in half. Nine crackers in half is four and a half."

One morning, Ms. Jackson's kindergarten class read the book *Peter's Chair* (Keats 1967) and discussed this idea: "Peter is a 'bad brother.'" During the conversation, many of the kindergarten students brought up their own experiences with the challenges of sibling relationships—fights, jealousy, and sharing woes. As the conversation wrapped up, Samira (who had a new baby sister) said, "My baby takes my stuff and chews it and drools on it. And Peter's sister took his crib and his chair. So I think baby brothers and sisters mess stuff up and so *that's* the problem. It's much harder to be bigger." Several students nodded in agreement.

As Ms. Jackson brought the conversation to a close, she left the class with this to consider: "You have all shared such interesting thinking about what it is like to be a sister or brother. I'm thinking about Samira's idea that it's harder to be the big sibling because little brothers and sisters take things and wreck things. Hmm. That's a theory some of us are playing around with. I'm wondering if we could think some more about that." Ms. Jackson wrote, *Maybe it's harder to be the big sister/brother* on a sentence strip and put it on their class Wonder Wall.

Later that week, Ms. Jackson's kindergartners continued their investigation by reading about the sibling relationship between Max and Ruby in *Bunny Cakes* (Wells 1997). Afterward, the students set out to express their thoughts about brothers and sisters through drawing and writing, and Ms. Jackson crouched down to confer with Racquel as she worked. "So, Racquel, what are you thinking about brothers and sisters right now?" Racquel spoke quietly, all the while continuing her drawing, "See, here I'm trying to do my Legos. But my little sister, Janelle, is messing it up. I'm mad."

Ms. Jackson responded, connecting back to the text, "Oh, like when Ruby, in *Bunny Cakes*, was trying to make her cake and Max kept spilling the ingredients?"

"Mmm-hmm," replied Racquel, "but Janelle's not allowed to play with Legos. She will eat them. So I told her no, and then she is left out." She pointed to her drawing again, looking at Ms. Jackson. "See, we both have a frowny face? 'Cause it's hard for *everyone*." Racquel had just offered an idea that revised the class's previous conjecture. *Maybe* the sibling relationship is really all about your perspective. With Racquel's permission, Ms. Jackson jotted down the new idea under their previous conjecture and started thinking about how to further explore the developing theory with the class.

Table 9.1 A Process for Developing Theories

	In Reading . . .	In Math . . .
Notice patterns	"Peter's little sister was getting all his old stuff, but it was still special to him. He really didn't want her to take his chair." "My little brother takes things from me and ruins them."	"I can split even numbers in half equally. I can share four, ten, twelve, or any even number of stickers equally between myself and my brother." "I can't split odd numbers in half equally. If I have three, seven, or thirteen stickers and I try to share them equally with my brother, there's always an 'extra' one leftover."
Develop conjectures	"Brother/sister problems really start with the younger one. It's much harder to be the big one."	"You can always split even numbers in half." "You can never split odd numbers in half."
Test out and revise conjectures	"It *is* hard to be the older sister when your younger sister messes up your work and takes your things. But we notice that then the little sister feels left out when she can't join in the big sister's activities."	"Hmm, but when we share nine crackers between two people, each person gets four and a half crackers."
Begin to form a theory	"So maybe *this* idea is true: Depending on your perspective, it can be harder to be the little sibling or it can be harder to be the big sibling."	"So, maybe *this* idea is true: You can always split even numbers in half equally and get whole things (or numbers). You can split odd numbers in half, but you'll have a fraction."

What Does It Mean to "Develop a Theory"?

From the time we are born, humans work to make sense of our environments by noticing patterns and developing theories about how the world works. Arthur Hyde writes that "humans are pattern-seeking, meaning-making creatures. We have experiences. We encounter people, events, phenomena, circumstances, thoughts, ideas, symbols, music, art, emotions. And what do we do with these things? We classify, organize, sort, group, pull apart, look at little pieces, grab a whole handful of pieces and put them back together" (2006, 44).

Babies start developing theories almost from the moment they are born. They notice patterns and begin to develop theories about their world. *Every time I cry, these parent people come pick me up.* Toddlers are expert theory-makers and testers. *When I whine in the grocery store, Grandma gives me a lollipop. But wait . . . that doesn't seem to work with Mom and Dad.* And preschoolers are perhaps the most delightful in the ways they craft theories about how the world works. *Every time it rains at night, mushrooms appear in the school garden the next day. Tiny mushroom seeds must be coming down in the raindrops.*

Building Theories Across Literacy and Math

In school, we can build on children's natural sense-making by orienting them to the ways that readers and mathematicians think and work, and by inviting them to engage in these practices. And while the practices of readers and mathematicians are often thought of as separate, there is actually considerable crossover in how readers and mathematicians develop theories. We notice patterns. We come up with theories (*What does ___ really mean? How does it work? Why does it work? Is this always true?*). We test and revise our theories. We throw out theories and make new ones.

In some contexts, the word *theory* has a very specific definition. A scientific theory, for example, is an idea that is accepted as true by the scientific community after repeated study through observation or experimentation. In our work with elementary school students, however, we are primarily interested in a much more informal and in-process understanding of *theory*. The opening

KEEPING TRACK OF OUR THEORIES

Because theories often take time to develop and to percolate throughout the students in the classroom, we like to find ways to make the students' emerging theories publicly visible in the classroom. In math, teachers may consider having a Conjecture Wall where they write down students' developing ideas and theories. Vivian Vasquez writes about creating an "Audit Trail" (or "Learning Wall") throughout the year as a public record of how the collective knowledge and understanding of the class shifts and develops over time (2003). Making theories public not only shows students that we value their in-process thinking, but also allows us to revisit the theories as we bump up against these ideas again and again.

vignettes from this chapter show how students might develop a theory over time with both reading and math content.

You may notice in Table 9.1: A Process for Developing Theories that we differentiate between the words *conjecture* and *theory*. We use the word *conjecture* with our students as well, to describe those tentative hunches or ideas about what *might* be true. Conjectures often develop when we start to notice patterns or regularity. We notice what stays the same, what changes, and how it changes.

We can think of the moment when we develop a conjecture the same way Stephanie Harvey describes the reading comprehension skill of synthesizing: "When we synthesize information, we take individual pieces of information and combine them with our prior knowledge. We begin to see a pattern emerge, and we form a new picture or idea" (2000, 143). But when we create a theory, we take this thinking a step further. We pull in additional texts and consider multiple perspectives until we collectively develop reasoning for *why*, *how*, and *when* something is true. We move from specific cases in which something is true to a more generalized understanding. Then we might refer to *that* generalized understanding as a theory. Whatever language we use to describe it, the most important idea about theory-making is that we offer students opportunities to notice patterns and begin to reason about them in ways that move from specific examples to generalizations.

What Does Theory-Making Sound Like in Math and Literacy?

When we listen to our student readers and mathematicians, we notice several contexts in which they intuitively develop theories. We find the theory-making contexts that follow helpful both in thinking about how students may already be developing theories about math and literacy and in helping us, as teachers, consider what types of questions we can ask to encourage theory-building in those contexts.

Theory-Making Context	What It Might Sound Like in Literacy	What It Might Sound Like in Math
Within a Single Text: Sometimes we develop a theory about how a single image, problem, text, or situation works. This theory helps us understand that particular text. Theories within a text are often expressed as tentative conjectures that can be further developed across multiple texts.	What theories are we developing about this character? What do we think life would be like in the setting (time/place) of this book? Why? How is your understanding of ____ developing from reading this section? What do we think might be the significance of ____ (*a symbol, object*, etc.) in this book? Why might this author have ____ (*chosen to make the main character a girl, ended the story at that particular moment*)?	How do we think this pattern might continue? How do you know? What stays the same? What changes? Why? What will definitely happen in this problem? What will definitely not happen? Why? Why do you think the person who collected this data chose to ____ (*collect data every month, ask this question, survey only first graders*)?
Across Texts: After working with several texts around a similar theme, idea, or pattern, we start to develop a more generalized understanding of what/how/why/when something is true.	After reading all of these texts, what do we think now about ____ (*themes such as friendship, beauty, relationships, conflict*, etc.)? How do words usually work when ____ (*we have a silent e, we have two vowels together*, etc.)? Why? When do they not work that way? What are we thinking about the impact of ____ on our lives (*nonfiction topics such as the invention of the light bulb, global warming, the Civil War*)?	What are you noticing that these patterns/problems/graphs/measurements have in common? What is the same/different about ____ (*counting by fourths vs. counting by eighths; representing data in a bar graph vs. a pie chart; measuring the length of an object using inches vs. centimeters*)?

Theory-Making Context	What It Might Sound Like in Literacy	What It Might Sound Like in Math
Across Texts: *(continued)*	Why do we think many authors/illustrators choose to ____ (*use flashbacks, dress the "evil" character in all black, include a character that learns a lesson*)?	What pattern do you see with these problems? Why/how does it work when you ____ (*multiply any number times ten; add one to each number in a subtraction problem; multiply two fractions less than one*)? After ____, what are you starting to think might be true about ____? (*After measuring the length of different objects in our classroom using cubes and popsicle sticks, what are you starting to think might be true about using different measuring units?*) What might the people who made these three graphs (*about a similar topic*) have been trying to point out or convince us of?
To Develop a Definition: We do this work as we try to make sense of what something *is*, especially when it is not an easily understood thing and the lines around it are blurry.	What makes a ____ (*genre*) book different from other genres? How is ____ different from ____ (*two related but different nonfiction topics*)? After reading all these books about ____ (*a difficult-to-define concept like "beauty" or "equality"*), what do we think it really means?	What makes a ____ a ____? (*What makes a square a square?*) What is always true about ____? What is sometimes true about ____? What is never true about ____? If that's a ____, is this also a ____? (*If that's a square, is this also a square?*)

Planning for Theory Making

The process of planning for theory-making mirrors the process of planning to nurture disagreement (Chapter 8). However, while the steps are similar, the way we approach each step differs depending on the type of conversation we are hoping to inspire. Theory-making builds on and extends the work of debate, and, therefore, much of what you considered in Chapter 8 will be useful here as well.

1. **Choose and understand an important content goal or big idea you want students to explore.** Consider what work might be good "next steps" for your students based on their current understandings. Then consider the authentic processes readers and mathematicians engage in as they do work around these ideas.

2. **Select a text or texts that allow students to notice patterns related to this goal or big idea.** Remember that we define *text* widely. A text may be a book, a poem, an image, a quote from a student, a graph, or a problem.

3. **Anticipate students' thinking and what understandings they will bring to the text.** What patterns might they notice? What theories might they develop as a result of this pattern-noticing?

4. **Plan time for immersion in the text.** You will want to give students some time to digest, play with, notice, or develop a connection with the text before you start building theories. Immersion is a time for noticing patterns and identifying some pieces of the puzzle. This time could be brief, such as providing some wait time to consider the text before a conversation begins. Or it could be more extensive, such as reading a book to students a few times over a week or inviting students to work on a math problem in pairs before coming to the conversation.

5. **Plan a launch and facilitate conversation.** The Hands-Down Conversation provides a chance to mine the collective thinking of the room about a topic. Depending on where you are in the theory-making process, you may have a Hands-Down Conversation to get emerging conjectures out "on the table" or to refine a theory that is already under construction.

6. **Offer multiple opportunities to revise ideas and theories over time.** After getting an idea about students' emerging conjectures, facilitate opportunities to grapple with the topic. Consider what counterexamples or additional perspectives you want to expose students to through tasks, texts, and hands-on experiences. Then come back and plan additional conversations (in pairs, clubs, and/or the whole group) to refine and develop your theories. It can be tempting, as a teacher, to jump in and "fix" children's understandings after a first conversation. It is ultimately more productive, however, to resist this urge and instead allow students space to grapple with important ideas.

Figure 9.1 Fifth-grade teachers Yolanda Corado Cendejas and Sanya Chopra plan for Hands-Down Conversations in their classrooms.

In the next part of this chapter, we enter the fifth-grade classrooms of Sanya Chopra and Yolanda Corado Cendejas. Sanya and Yolanda have been teammates for several years and frequently plan together, bouncing ideas off one another and supporting each other through the myriad of celebrations and challenges they encounter as classroom teachers. Upon entering their classrooms, you might have to take a moment to locate the teachers, as they are usually heavily engaged listening to students' ideas. They are both interested in developing communities of empowered speakers and listeners and building a community of trust. They make an effort to create environments in which students are comfortable sharing ideas with each other.

This "Week at a Glance" shows how we planned for Sanya's and Yolanda's fifth graders to develop ideas across the week in literacy and math. While we planned for similar experiences in both classrooms, in this chapter we highlight the ideas of Sanya's students in math class and Yolanda's students in reading class.

Week at a Glance: Developing Theories in Sanya and Yolanda's Classrooms

Monday	Tuesday	Wednesday	Thursday	Friday
Micro-lesson on Revising Ideas (Lesson 6.6)	Math: a.m.: Immersion (time to write and draw) about "sixths are bigger than fifths" p.m.: Hands-Down Conversation about "sixths are bigger than fifths"		Reading: Interactive read-aloud of *A Picnic in October*	Reading: Hands-Down Conversation about *A Picnic in October*

Let's take a look at the planning process we used to support fifth graders in developing theories.

Planning for Theory-Making in Literacy

1. Choose and understand an important content goal or big idea.

To select a comprehension goal or strategy to focus on, we start by considering what kind of theory-building work our students are already doing. This information may come from analyzing transcripts from previous Hands-Down Conversations, reflecting on small-group conversations or reading conferences, or reading what students have written about their reading. We seek out evidence that the students are looking for patterns or thinking beyond the text at hand and consider how we might extend the work they are already doing. After examining our students' work, we use our curriculum guide or a resource like Fountas and Pinnell's *Literacy Continuum* (2017) to select a goal that is an appropriate next step for the students in front of us *and* gets at the process of "putting together the pieces" to form a theory or new insight.

ASSESSMENT DRIVES INSTRUCTION

For more information on using formative assessments such as conversation transcripts and reading conferences to inform your instruction, check out Jennifer Serravallo's suggestions in *Teaching Readers in Small Groups: Differentiated Instruction for Building Strategic, Independent Readers* (2010).

Sanya's and Yolanda's fifth graders were working in a reading and writing unit of study on the genre *memoir*. As part of their unit, they had read several memoirs together and had done some definitional theory-building around what makes memoir different from other genres. Most students were able to explain that a memoir is reflective in nature and reveals the author's perspective on a previous time in her life. When Christy observed students in Turn and Talks after reading aloud a memoir, she noticed that many of them were making personal connections to the text and speaking about literal understandings, but not yet building theories about bigger themes or messages. The teachers had also mentioned that many students were writing memoirs that were primarily a list of memories or a straightforward retelling of an event, but not yet taking that reflective stance to identify and communicate a relatable message or theme in their writing. In thinking about how to nudge the students to consider theme both as readers and writers, Christy turned to the "Interactive Read-Alouds and Literature Discussion in Fiction" section of the *Literacy Continuum* for fifth grade (Fountas and Pinnell 2017, 69–72). Within the section subtitled "Messages and Themes," two goals caught Christy's eye: "Think across texts to derive larger messages, themes, or ideas" and "Notice and understand themes reflecting important human challenges and social issues" (2017, 70). Christy thought some work around these goals might be a good next step for the fifth graders.

WINDOWS AND MIRRORS

Rudine Sims Bishop writes about the importance of providing students with books that serve as both windows and mirrors. "Books are sometimes windows, offering views of worlds that may be real or imagined, familiar or strange" (1990, ix). On the other hand, books can be mirrors, offering a reflection, "and in that reflection we can see our own lives and experiences as part of the larger human experience" (ix). When supporting our students to build theories on a theme, we want to affirm and honor the diversity of ideas in our classroom as well as enhance it with perspectives that may not be present. Consider how you can combine texts that mirror your students' life experiences and understandings with texts that provide windows into additional perspectives.

2. Select a text or texts that allow students to notice patterns related to this goal or big idea.

The work of building a theory in reading starts with immersing students in texts that spark thought around an idea or concept. When we are working to build a theory across texts, we might plan ahead and gather several texts on a topic that we want students to explore. Or we might notice a theory emerging after we've had a debate-centered Hands-Down Conversation and think, "We need to get more texts that help students investigate that bigger idea and solidify their understanding."

Sanya's and Yolanda's classes had already read several picture book memoirs together, including *Bigmama's*, by Donald Crews (1991) and *When I Was Young in the Mountains*, by Cynthia Rylant (1993). They were also currently reading the novel *Front Desk*, by Kelly Yang (2018). Christy wanted to choose an additional text that would highlight the reflective nature of a memoir and also get students developing a theory about one of life's "important human challenges and social issues." Ideally the challenge would be highly relatable for them and relevant to writing their own memoirs. As Christy browsed a collection of possible texts, she came across A *Picnic in October*, by Eve Bunting (1999). In this book, Tony, a boy around ten or twelve years old, tells the story of how his family makes him go on a picnic each October to the Statue of Liberty to commemorate his grandparents' immigration from Italy many years ago. He is embarrassed by the tradition and finds it "dumb," until near the end of the text, when his perspective shifts a little and some understanding emerges. Christy knew that the book wasn't a memoir, since it was not written about the actual author's life, but it was written in a memoir-esque style of looking back and reflecting on a tradition. *And* it was focused on an important and challenging theme of the adolescent experience. Adolescents are at an age when they want to feel like everyone else, and the differences between their own families and others' can feel embarrassing and painful. This same theme was touched upon in *Front Desk*, and Christy knew that some of the students were wrestling with it in their own memoirs. Christy wondered whether the fifth graders could start building, as a class, some theories about this part of the human experience.

3. Anticipate students' thinking and what understandings they will bring to the text.

In the early stages of theory-building, you can anticipate what conjectures your students might develop based on a combination of the information in front of them and their previous experiences. You can imagine potential responses by trying to put yourself in the students' shoes and considering how students at their age and developmental stage often think about the world. You might ask yourself, "How do *I* think this works?" and "How might my *students* think this works?" In other instances, you and your students may have already started building conjectures about this topic, and you may even have recorded some of their ideas. In that case, you can anticipate how their current understanding will impact their interpretation of this new text.

> Christy knew Yolanda's and Sanya's students were at a prime age for noticing their families' differences and judging them, and she anticipated they would make plenty of personal connections. But what sorts of theories might they start to construct around this experience? Christy noticed that in *A Picnic in October*, Tony changes his perspective on the event and begins to appreciate his family's tradition a little bit. Christy was curious how students would view or explain this change. She first considered what theories *she* held about the topic. How *does* our perspective on our family change over time? Is there a pattern in how that perspective shifts? Then Christy anticipated what the students in front of her might think, and projected some possibilities: *Maybe* the students would theorize that we don't realize our families are different when we are little because we don't know how other families work, but then we notice these differences when we are older and start to talk to our friends or visit other friends' houses. *Maybe* the students would conjecture that our perspective shifts again when we are older. Anticipating students' thinking informed Christy's plan for immersion in the text.

4. Plan time for immersion in the text.

An interactive read-aloud is a useful way to give students time and support as they immerse themselves in the text and start developing theories. When planning any interactive read-aloud, we carefully select stopping points that will guide students to think more deeply about our focus. If our focus is building a theory about a larger message or theme, we select places to stop where that theme bubbles up in a text, and we highlight it, either by "thinking aloud" (more supportive) or asking the students to do some thinking and talking together (less supportive). For more on interactive read-alouds, see the text box in Chapter 8 titled "The Power of the Interactive Read-Aloud."

> When planning the interactive read-aloud of *A Picnic in October*, Christy knew she wanted to focus on how the narrator's perspective of his family shifted over time, to set the students up to consider why and how this shifting perspective works in life. Each of the places Christy chose to stop while reading supported this focus. For example, at the point where Tony is watching his family blow kisses at the Statue of Liberty, he scornfully reflects, "I sincerely hope no one is watching" (Bunting 1999, 23). At this point, Christy planned to stop and say, "This is rough, how he's feeling about his family right now. Turn and talk about this feeling." Later, when he changed his perspective, Christy planned to reveal her own thinking, saying, "There's a change right here, when he chokes up, looking up at the Statue of Liberty. He is realizing something about all of this . . . and his family. I'm wondering what made his perspective change." These stopping points highlight the theme and lay the groundwork for students to begin developing conjectures about the reasons and ways we change how we feel about our families over time.

5. Plan a launch and facilitate conversation.

To support our students in building theories, tentative language in our launch is especially important. We want to open the door to multiple possibilities yet set the students on a path to talk about something big. It is a challenging balancing act. As teachers, we have already done some thinking about possible theories ourselves, and have anticipated some conjectures students may bring up, so we have to be careful to not just lead students to guess what we are thinking. To protect against this, we start by presenting the topic broadly and doing some listening. We can always come in and narrow the focus later with a facilitation move, if needed. One way to launch the conversation is to simply state the broader theme and ask our students to start talking about that idea. For example, we might say, "The book *Bunny Cakes* made us think a lot about how brothers and sisters get along. Let's talk about that." Once our students are familiar with the idea of making conjectures and building theories, we could try a launch like "What theories are you developing about _____ after reading these books?" or "One of our previous conjectures about this topic was _____. What are we thinking now?"

Christy knew the fifth graders were just beginning to theorize on the topic of shifting perspectives on our families, so she decided to start by having a broad conversation about the theme. She was aware that she needed to carefully word her launch to focus the students on the theme while not leading them to any preplanned conclusions. So Christy thought she would try saying something like this: "Sometimes we are embarrassed by our own families. But we didn't always feel that way. Our perspective on our own family changes over time. Let's have a Hands-Down Conversation about that." Christy also planned a few prompts she might use during the conversation to keep it going:

- What do you think caused Tony to change his perspective on his family in *A Picnic in October?*

- Why do you feel differently about your family now than when you were a little kid?

- Who has changed, you or your family?

- Do you think your perspectives will change again as you get older?

- Why do you think authors write about times that are embarrassing?

The Family Conversation in Action: Building Theories About Changing Perspectives

Let's listen in to an excerpt of the Hands-Down Conversation that took place the day after Christy's interactive read-aloud of *A Picnic in October* in Yolanda's class and see what kinds of conjectures emerged.

Christy: Yesterday, when I listened to your Turn and Talks during *A Picnic in October*, I noticed a lot of you talking about how embarrassed Tony was about his family, and some of the times when you have felt embarrassed about your own families. But he didn't always feel that way. Neither did you! Our perspective on our families changes over time. Let's have a Hands-Down Conversation about that.

Jean: Okay, like my mom is so loud, sometimes she sings or whatever when we are in public, or yells, and she is *so* embarrassing.

(Several students nod and groan.)

Trevor: I got lost once and my mom was yelling my name in Target. OMG. It was so bad. I closed my eyes so I couldn't see if people were looking at me—like that kid (*Trevor gestures toward the book*) didn't want anyone watching his weird family, right?

(There is laughter, and then a pause.)

Michelle: Some of my parents' rules are so embarrassing—like I can't do what other kids can do.

(Some nodding, and a moment of silence follows.)

Liya: Umm, I think I have another idea? I think this whole thing is actually about different cultures. When I was a little kid my mom always made me wear dresses because she's from Ethiopia, right? And now I tell her I don't want to. But she still wants me to, and we have fights about it, 'cause she says I look like a boy.

Marco: But what's that have to do with what we are talking about?

Farique: 'Cause, it affects who you *are*. Your culture.

Debra: Yeah, our cultures, they make us different. And it feels weird, you know? My mom too, in her country, all the girls wear dresses. And I had to when I was little. But now I'm like, "Mom, in America girls wear pants or whatever."

Adam: In my family, every birthday we sing "Happy Birthday" in Arabic, and most of our friends speak Arabic, but then one time my school friend came, and I was so embarrassed we were singing in Arabic.

Flora: At our birthdays, my mom always pushes our face in the cake, it's just what we always do, you know? And I get embarrassed about it even though it is kinda funny.

Jean: What?! Why do you do that?

Flora: It's just . . . um . . .

Alejandro: Yeah, in Mexico, we do that too, it's just . . . common.

Christy: I hear many of you are talking about how things we observe our families doing now are embarrassing, even though we used to think they felt okay when we were little, right? I think it's important to point out that Liya has made a conjecture. There's a theory developing among us, which is this: *Maybe* the reason we sometimes feel embarrassed of our families now is because our family culture and traditions are different from some of our friends' family traditions. Is that what you were saying, Liya?

(Liya nods.)

Adam: Yeah, I think she's right. When your friends are from the same country, it isn't as embarrassing. And in that book *(he gestures toward* A Picnic in October*)* the boy felt weird 'cause his grandparents were from Italy and doing stuff that was different.

6. Offer opportunities to revise ideas and theories over time.

This step takes place after a conjecture is made (perhaps in a Hands-Down Conversation) and allows the class to continue working toward the development of a more robust and balanced theory. It is important to provide students with experiences, images, or texts that will be contradictory or disruptive to what they have come to believe. When students have to accommodate this new information, it helps them refine and revise their theories. Here are some options you may want to do following a Hands-Down Conversation in which students have begun to develop a theory in literacy:

- Write down their conjecture(s) in a public space to keep a record of their thinking.

- Seek out another book or text that presents an alternative perspective.

- Have different groups of students read/explore different texts that share a theme or topic and come together as a class to compare and contrast their findings.

As Christy reflected on the conversation with Yolanda's students, she was surprised by the conjecture that had begun to emerge, because it wasn't what she had anticipated. It made Christy pause. As a white teacher, born in the United States, Christy hadn't focused in on the experience of being an adolescent *and* an immigrant as she personally made conjectures about "why our perspectives on our families change." But Christy realized, after listening to her students, that more time was needed to explore this perspective and this voice. Christy planned to seek out more texts that would help the class engage in this work.

In addition, Christy thought it could broaden the class's developing theory to further explore an idea that some students voiced at the beginning of the conversation: the idea that feeling embarrassed by our families is also a cross-cultural adolescent experience. How could the class combine *both* perspectives and observations into a theory that would explain adolescents' shifting perspectives on their families? The conjecture the students had developed was a valuable step toward the goal of understanding "themes reflecting important human challenges and social issues." But the students would keep thinking on this theme together.

Next Steps in Dialogue for Yolanda's Class

Yolanda's students demonstrated a lot of dialogic strengths in their conversation. Christy noticed that a good variety of students entered the whole-group conversation, although the Turn and Talks that took place during the interactive read-aloud were also important opportunities for some of the quieter voices to express their ideas. The students managed to share the floor without conflict, and there was definitely evidence of listening and linking ideas. There was evidence they were keeping the conversation on track, such as when they asked each other questions and checked in to ensure all comments were relevant. Liya made a lovely move when she signaled to the group that she was ready to introduce a new idea. One possible next step for dialogue with this group might be to use Lesson 7.5, Taking the Conversation to a New Place, as an opportunity to highlight Liya's talk move and discuss how helpful that behavior was for moving their conversation toward developing a conjecture. Another idea would be to do some work around Lesson 7.6, Summarizing, and see if the students could take more of the ownership for that work, because Christy was still doing most of the summarizing during this conversation.

Planning for Theory-Making in Math:

1. Choose and understand an important content goal or big idea.

Understanding the content is the first step for planning any kind of math instruction. And while it is important to understand the math content from the grade level we teach, it is also critical to understand how content ideas grow from grade to grade. Understanding the content of prior grade levels is particularly important when we consider the ways students may develop theories. We can ask ourselves: "What kinds of understandings will students bring to a task or conversation? What partial understandings might we build on?"

> As they began to plan a unit on fraction computation, Kassia and Sanya decided to revisit ideas related to developing fraction number sense, a goal that stretches across the elementary grades and beyond. While fifth graders are expected to apply their fraction number sense to computation with fractions, it is important to continue offering opportunities for students to revise and add to their theories about how fractions work. Here are some of the fraction ideas that Kassia and Sanya, as teachers, revisited:
>
> - Fractions are numbers that can be placed on a number line.
>
> - If the numerator and denominator are equal, the fraction represents one. All whole numbers can be represented as fractions.
>
> - If the numerator is greater than the denominator, the fraction is greater than one. If the numerator is less than the denominator, the fraction is less than one.
>
> - "Fractions representing parts of wholes can be compared only if the whole is known in each case or assumed to be the number one" (Small 2019, 219).
>
> - For any given whole, the smaller the denominator, the bigger the piece. The bigger the denominator, the smaller the piece.

2. Select a text or texts that allow students to notice patterns related to this goal or big idea.

As in literacy, the work of developing a theory in math begins by immersing students in "texts" that allow them to notice patterns and encounter ideas multiple times. As Tracy Johnston Zager explains in *Becoming the Math Teacher You Wish You'd Had*, "The first step in mathematical reasoning is to sniff out interesting patterns in numbers, shapes, operations, relationships, and so on. Once we've noticed and identified the patterns, we can play with them, test them out in different conditions, see when they hold and when they break, and figure out what structures they reveal" (2017, 247). As students bump into patterns and mathematical ideas again and again, they begin to form ideas about how and why things work. We also want to present "texts" that expand students' understanding of the mathematics by disrupting a pattern that students have noticed or challenging a conjecture that they have put forward.

> As they thought about the fraction work Sanya's fifth graders had engaged in thus far in the school year and in years past, Kassia and Sanya noticed that most students had internalized the idea that the smaller the denominator, the bigger the piece, and the bigger the denominator, the smaller the piece. They applied this understanding when comparing fractions and when checking to see if an answer was reasonable when computing with fractions. However, they also noticed that at times some students lost track of the whole in their fraction work. Was it one-quarter of a cookie? Or one-quarter of the batch of twenty-four cookies? Was $\frac{1}{20}$ a reasonable answer for $5 \times \frac{1}{4}$? Kassia and Sanya decided to choose a problem that would challenge the notion that a smaller denominator always meant a bigger piece and allow students to bump into the idea that the whole matters when we're working with fractions. They chose the "Always, Sometimes, or Never" statement "Sixths are bigger than fifths." They suspected that while work around this statement might begin as a debate, the conversation would quickly shift toward theory-making.

"ALWAYS, SOMETIMES, OR NEVER" TASKS

For more on "Always, Sometimes, or Never," see the Google document of resources curated by Tracy Johnston Zager at tinyurl.com/K6ASN. This google document includes a variety of "Always, Sometimes, or Never" statements organized by content area. It also includes links to education blogs explaining the various ways teachers use this kind of task.

3. Anticipate students' thinking and what understandings they will bring to the text.

As we anticipate our students' thinking, either by reviewing student work from a prior task or by reflecting on our students' words and actions, we can choose to understand their ideas generously. Karen Gallas writes that "misconceptions are not always hastily put together. They are the result of observation, imagination, and logic . . ." (1995, 100). With this insight in mind, we can choose to presume that students' ideas reflect understanding and sense-making (even when we see or hear incorrect answers!), and we can choose to be curious about what students *do* know and how they will bring their understandings to new texts.

While Sanya and Kassia had some ideas about how students *might* respond to the "Always, Sometimes, or Never" statement "Sixths are bigger than fifths," they were curious to see what students would actually do when given time to write and draw about this idea in their journals. Giving the students the question ahead of the conversation allowed Sanya and Kassia, as teachers, to better prepare for ideas that might come up in the conversation.

As Sanya and Kassia looked over the students' responses to the statement "Sixths are bigger than fifths," they noticed a number of things:

- Many students argued that fifths are always bigger than sixths because "the smaller the denominator, the larger the piece." Some drew representations of $\frac{1}{6}$ and $\frac{1}{5}$ to illustrate this point.

- Some students converted the fractions to decimals in order to compare them. While this shows understanding that fractions can be renamed as decimals, the process of calculating one divided by six and one divided by five is arduous. Other students used a procedure to find a common denominator ($\frac{1}{5} = \frac{6}{30}$ and $\frac{1}{6} = \frac{5}{30}$ so $\frac{1}{5} > \frac{1}{6}$) in order to compare the fractions. Looking at this student work made Sanya and Kassia wonder whether these students had other strategies for comparing the fractions and, if so, why they did not use them with this problem.

- A few students wrote that sixths *could* be bigger than fifths if you had a lot of sixths and fewer fifths. One student drew a representation of $\frac{5}{6}$ next to a representation of $\frac{1}{5}$ to illustrate this point.

- None of the students mentioned that sixths could be bigger than fifths if the wholes were different. Sanya and Kassia weren't sure whether to be surprised by this or not. While it is true that, when we compare fractions, we assume the whole to be one unless otherwise stated, Sanya and Kassia thought some students might look for other ways to make the statement "Sixths are bigger than fifths" sometimes true. Because they hoped to bring out the idea that the whole matters when working with fractions, they knew they would have to consider how to introduce this idea into the Hands-Down Conversation.

4. Plan time for immersion in the text.

While the immersion in the text may happen just prior to the Hands-Down Conversation, there are times when it makes sense for the immersion and the Hands-Down Conversation to happen on two separate occasions, just as in reading. This is especially true when the text is more complex and students will need time on their own and in pairs to grapple with the ideas, write and draw, and talk with each other. In theory-making Hands-Down Conversations, we are often building on prior work and prior immersions in texts and bringing the ideas from those experiences to the Hands-Down Conversation circle after several interactions with a concept.

> With Sanya's fifth graders, Kassia and Sanya decided to immerse students in the "Always, Sometimes, or Never" statement by giving them time to write and draw in their journals. Providing this type of immersion seemed particularly important for a question about which students might want to draw a representation. Kassia and Sanya also wanted to use students' work to help them anticipate the ideas students would bring to the Hands-Down Conversation and choose which ideas they might use as a launch for their conversation.

5. Plan a launch and facilitate conversation.

As we build conjectures and claims in math, we are usually considering what is true (or not true), when something is true (or not true), and why and how that something is true (or not true). Here are a few common launches to a theory-making Hands-Down Conversation in math:

- Some of us are starting to think _____ might be true. Let's think more about that idea. Is it true? Is it always true?

- It seems that we all agree that _____. But *why* does that work? *Why* will that always work?

- Delores is saying that we will never see a _____ in this pattern. It's not possible. How can we be sure? How can you prove this?

- Yesterday we thought _____ was true. We tried it with a bunch of numbers, and it worked. But today Zair told us that he found a number that doesn't work! Let's talk about what we're thinking about our conjecture now. Is it changing? Is it staying the same?

Before launching the Hands-Down Conversation, Kassia and Sanya wanted to give students a sense of the ideas they had seen in the student journal responses. They wanted to give students time to digest each other's ideas, and they also wanted students to know that there was disagreement and a lot of lingering uncertainty around the statement 'Sixths are bigger than fifths.' They showed two student journal responses (with the permission of the students who created them) and asked students to turn and talk about what they noticed and understood about their classmates' ideas.

Then they launched the conversation in this way: "When you worked in your journals, a lot of you were really convinced of your ideas. You had some solid reasoning. Now that you've talked to a partner, maybe your idea has stayed the same and maybe it's changed some. In this Hands-Down Conversation, our challenge will be to stay open to revising our ideas about the 'Sixths are bigger than fifths' statement. Who can start us off talking about where they are in their thinking now?"

The "Sixths Are Bigger Than Fifths" Conversation in Action

Let's take a look at how a part of this Hands-Down Conversation went in Sanya's classroom.

Briana: *(pointing at Pier's work, Figure 9.2)* I wrote about it like Pier. You can think about the denominator as people. The less people there are, the more of the cake you get. The more people there are, the less cake you get.

Everett: Like we cut up all those fractions in third grade to see that one-half is the biggest, then one-third is a little smaller. Then one-fourth, and that keeps going. Because you're cutting the paper in more pieces.

Maya: *(pointing at Katy's work, Figure 9.3)* But I'm thinking like Katy. What if you have five-sixths and only one-sixth or two-sixths? Even three-sixths is just a half.

Jasper: Yeah, what about if it's an improper fraction? Like you could have eight-sixths, which is more than one, and only one-fifth or even five-fifths. Eight-sixths is still gonna be more because it's more than one.

(Several more students chime in, continuing to make similar arguments. Kassia and Sanya think it is important to give some time for this conversation, because the ideas being debated are important, but they also want to introduce a new but related idea to the class. After a few more minutes of discussion, Kassia asks if she can bring up an idea for the students to consider.)

Kassia: I'm going to draw something up here on the chart paper. Here's a BIG sheet cake *(draws big rectangle)* and here's a really itty-bitty tiny sheet cake (*draws tiny rectangle*). Would you rather have one-sixth of the big cake or one-fifth of the tiny cake? Turn and talk to your partner.

(*Kassia listens in to one Turn and Talk partnership, Abram and Olivia.*)

Abram: Definitely one-sixth of the big cake. That could be a lot of cake. Think of cutting a whole big cake into only six pieces and you're going to eat one of those pieces. Usually you wouldn't share a cake with only six people total. But look at that tiny cake. That's like a nothing cake. One-fifth of that would be like a bite.

Olivia: Yeah, but I'd need to know what kind of cake. Maybe it's lemon cake and I hate lemon cake. I wouldn't want a sixth of that big cake.

Abram: So you'd want the fifth of the tiny cake if it was lemon cause that's the smaller one.

Olivia: (*Rolling her eyes*) I guess, but really I don't want any lemon cake at all.

(*As the Turn and Talk ends, the students turn back to the whole-group conversation.*)

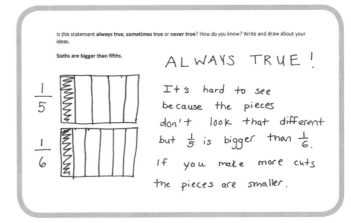

Figure 9.2 Sanya's class began the Hands-Down Conversation by discussing two pieces of student work. The image above is a re-creation of Pier's work.

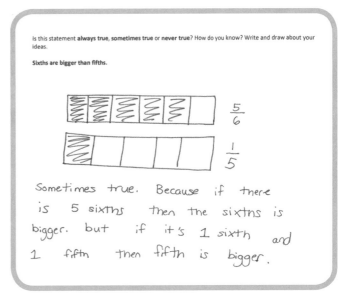

Figure 9.3 A re-creation of Katy's work

Pier: This was like a trick, kind of. Like we know fifths are usually bigger than sixths, like one-fifth and one-sixth. But you have to think about what you have. Like the whole thing. Fifths are only bigger than sixths if you're talking about two big cakes or two little cakes. If you have two different cakes, it might be different.

Luisa: Sometimes you have to say, "One-sixth of what?" or "One-fifth of what?"

Briana: But like, one-fifth is still bigger, right? Like you'd still write one-fifth is greater than one-sixth (*drawing the "greater than" symbol in the air*)?

Listening to Sanya's students talk about why fifths are bigger than sixths confirmed what Kassia and Sanya noticed in other conversations and in written work. These students had noticed patterns and developed the theory that "the bigger the denominator, the smaller the piece, and the smaller the denominator, the bigger the piece." They were convinced of this idea. They had noticed it in the equal share problems, in the fraction games they had played, and in the manipulatives they had worked with. As the conversation continued, it became clear that for some students in this group, there was no ambiguity around this idea. Without some further nudging, they were not going to start discussing the idea that the whole matters. As Kassia listened, she wondered how to introduce this idea without taking over the conversation, without just telling them, "Hey, if the wholes are different, sixths might not be smaller than fifths." Kassia decided instead to offer them the "Would you rather . . . ?" question. As she asked the question, she wondered, "Am I leading too much? Should we just stop the conversation now and then I can think more about designing a task to help them grapple with this idea?" Teaching is made up of thousands of in-the-moment decisions, often occurring simultaneously. On this day, in this moment, Kassia decided to offer the "Would you rather . . . ?" question.

6. Offer multiple opportunities to revise ideas and theories over time.

It is tempting to want each conversation to end in a tidy way, with all children constructing parallel and complete understandings. This just isn't how math (or most learning!) works. There are several ways to conclude a Hands-Down Conversation in which students have been working to develop theories:

- Record students' emerging theories for revisiting later. You may write down their ideas in your own notes or record a theory publicly for children to continue to grapple with after the conversation.

- Ask students to write about their new thinking. What are they thinking about the question/topic now? Why?

- Plan follow-up tasks for students to push their thinking around the content.

The single "Always, Sometimes, or Never" task that Sanya's fifth graders journaled about offered a wealth of insight into how these students were thinking about comparing fractions. Not all of those ideas made their way into the conversation that day, but the students' responses prompted the teachers to reflect on how they might continue to build students' fraction number sense and make connections between that number sense and the fraction computation they worked on in fifth grade. Kassia and Sanya wondered how the fifth graders might connect the idea "the whole matters" to their work with multiplying fractions. For example, if the students encountered the multiplication problems $\frac{1}{4} \times 8$ and $\frac{1}{8} \times 12$, would they have a sense of which product would be larger?

Next Steps in Dialogue for Sanya's Class

Sanya and Kassia noticed evidence that students were revising their ideas, as they had discussed in a micro-lesson earlier that week (see "Week at a Glance"). Even though most students did not use explicit sentence stems like "I'm changing my thinking" or "I'd like to revise my idea," they had their own ways of talking about how their ideas were changing, and Sanya and Kassia hoped to highlight some of these ways in a follow-up micro-lesson.

Sanya and Kassia also noticed that it was a little quiet in the whole-class conversation but much more lively in the Turn and Talk partnerships. This reminded them that, as teachers, we should offer many opportunities for talking and listening. The ideas shared in the whole-class Hands-Down Conversation are not the only thinking that matters. It is important to pull up beside partners and listen. It is important to "listen" to the student work we collect. It is important to find ways to listen to students who do not talk in whole-class settings. How can we highlight and position students' ideas, even when students do not share them in the whole-class setting? How can we make sure that the Hands-Down Conversation community is about more than what is said in the whole group?

Developing Theories As a Way of Thinking

We position our students as thinkers and researchers of their world when we take time to talk about, revise, and develop theories together. Our students become more reflective about what "truth" is, and more comfortable persevering to understand something that doesn't have a quick answer or solution. These habits of mind will serve them well and benefit us all as they grow into the adults of the future.

Here are some additional resources on mathematical reasoning and on making argumentation central to the elementary math classroom:

- *Thinking Mathematically: Integrating Arithmetic and Algebra in Elementary School,* by Thomas P. Carpenter, Megan Loef Franke, and Linda Levi (2003)

- *Connecting Arithmetic to Algebra: Strategies for Building Algebraic Thinking in the Elementary Grades,* by Susan Jo Russell, Deborah Schifter, and Virginia Bastable (2011)

- *But Why Does It Work? Mathematical Argument in the Elementary Classroom,* by Susan Jo Russell, Deborah Schifter, Reva Kasman, Virginia Bastable, and Traci Higgins (2017)

- *Becoming the Math Teacher You Wish You'd Had: Ideas and Strategies from Vibrant Classrooms,* by Tracy Johnston Zager (2017)

Planning to Develop Theories Together

- Choose and understand an important content goal or big idea.

- Select a "text" that allows you to engage in the content work.

- Anticipate students' thinking and what understandings they will bring to the text.

- Plan time for immersion in the text.

- Plan a launch and facilitate conversation.

- Offer multiple opportunities to revise ideas and theories over time.

10

Engaging with the World

If you are neutral in situations of injustice, you have chosen the side of the oppressor. If an elephant has its foot on the tail of a mouse and you say that you are neutral, the mouse will not appreciate your neutrality.

—Desmond Tutu

In August 2019, 680 people suspected of being undocumented immigrant workers were arrested and detained in Mississippi by US Immigration and Customs Enforcement (ICE) agents. "The state's US Attorney for its Southern District labeled the operation as the 'largest single-state immigration enforcement operation' in United States history" (*All Sides* 2019). News outlets around the country reported on the raid, although the ways in which they wrote about the event differed significantly. A headline from *BuzzFeed News* read, "Families 'Are Scared to Death' After a Massive ICE Operation Swept Up Hundreds of People" (Aleaziz 2019). A headline from *Breitbart News* read, "ICE Arrests 680 Illegal Aliens in Largest Single-State Raid in U.S. History" (Binder 2019).

The *BuzzFeed News* article focused on information gained from members of the immigrant community affected by the raids. It quoted Luis Cartagena, a local pastor who said, "It [the raid] looked like an invasion in a war . . . People are terrified. They are scared to death" (Aleaziz 2019). The article ended by sharing the perspective of Dianne, the fiancée of one of the detained workers. "'He was trying to make a better life for his children,' she said. 'You see these kids hurting and crying, knowing their parents aren't coming home soon. I've seen that all day. People are freaking out'" (Aleaziz 2019).

The *Breitbart* article, on the other hand, focused exclusively on quotes from US attorney Mike Hurst ("We are first and foremost a nation of laws . . . Without the enforcement of law, there is no justice") and ICE officials ("These are not victimless crimes. Illegal immigrants create vulnerabilities in the marketplace") (Binder 2019).

At some point in our lives, many of us probably viewed the news—whether in the form of newspapers, nightly television reports, or websites—as representing "the facts" or "the truth." However, our lived experiences have probably led us to question the notion of objective news. So what are we to do? How do we interpret and understand the information we consume and decide what to do about it?

Vivian Vasquez, an education professor and critical literacy scholar, imparts advice on becoming media literate, saying, "For most of us, our ideologies are invisible to us. Step one is to be conscious that we are hearing things a certain way. Step two is to ask ourselves *why* we hear things that way. That level of self-reflection and self-analysis is important to understand how to hear others more clearly" (Vasquez 2017). Then, she advises, we must learn how to take in information with a critical eye and to ask ourselves a series of questions as we engage with any story:

- Who is the source and what do I know about them?

- Could the story have been told differently?

- Whose perspective may be missing?

- Who benefits and who is disadvantaged by a particular telling of the story?

We can use these questions to analyze articles like the ones about the ICE operation. What are the sources of these two articles? What perspectives do the authors bring to their reporting? Whose story is told and whose is missing? And what does all of this mean for how we make sense of the events happening in our world?

As teachers, we have a powerful responsibility to help our students make sense of the world around them. Our students have been taking in information from a wide variety of sources since birth, and each new generation of students has a previously unparalleled exposure to media, messages, and information. Every single one of these messages is created by an individual or group that has its own beliefs, biases, and agendas. And as much as we would like to believe that there are certain impartial sources we can all depend on for the truth, we must understand and teach our children that *no* text is neutral. This kind of critical analysis goes beyond news sources to include all the texts that surround us. As mentioned in previous chapters, we broadly define *text* as any form of recorded communication (visual, numerical, graphic, etc.). And "*all* texts are created from a particular perspective with the intention of conveying particular messages" (emphasis added) (Vasquez 2017, 3).

USING MATH TO ENGAGE WITH THE WORLD: THE LIBRARY INVENTORY

Many teachers have little experience teaching students to use math to engage with the world outside of the classroom. Few textbooks advocate this kind of work, and most teachers did not experience this kind of lesson in their own math classes as students. So it is not surprising that many of us feel some discomfort when doing this work in mathematics. However, once we begin to view math as a tool for critically analyzing the world, we will see opportunities for this work all around us.

At our school, second-grade classes engaged in conversations about identity, race, and racism in which they read and discussed picture books on these topics and painted self-portraits using paints they mixed to match their own skin color. As a part of this ongoing work, some classes inventoried books from their classroom libraries, collecting data on the race of characters represented in picture books. They then analyzed this data and made plans to take action by seeking out more books with main characters who are people of color.

Here are some other questions students might investigate through the lens of mathematics as part of a library inventory:

- What kinds of families and homes are represented in the books in our classroom and school libraries? Students may be interested in sharing about their own families and whether they feel families like theirs are represented in the library books. Note that personal sharing should be completely voluntary—not all children want to talk about their family or home with the class, and that should be respected.

- Who are the authors of the books in our classroom or school libraries? Is gender and racial diversity represented in our library? Are books about people of color written by authors who are people of color or only by white authors? For more on this topic, see the #ownvoices hashtag on Twitter (Yorio 2018).

- Whose perspectives are represented in the books we read? Bob Peterson writes about analyzing books students might read in their social studies curriculum. "I have students analyze children's books about Christopher Columbus, tabulating whose views are represented. For instance, how many times do Columbus and his men present their perspective and how many times do the Taíno Indians present theirs?" (2013, 14).

- What do you wonder about our library? What kinds of books would you like to see in our library? How can we figure out if these books are in our library already or if we need more? You may consider engaging students with David Huyck and Sarah Park Dahlen's infographic "Diversity in Children's Books 2018" (2019) and comparing the books in your library with the data they present. (https://readingspark.wordpress.com/2019/06/19/picture-this-diversity-in-childrens-books-2018-infographic/)

Engaging with the World in Both Literacy and Math

A first step toward becoming savvy text consumers is for children to fully understand that every text has an author and is influenced by that author's perspective, biases, and experiences. An author of a written text makes both conscious *and* unconscious moves, such as their word choice, their use of graphics or data, and the weight they place on different parts of the text. Children can learn to analyze these decisions to determine both the overt and implicit messages a text conveys and to verbalize their own beliefs about those messages. Additionally, we can empower our students to make informed decisions about how they may take action or "talk back" to the text once they have analyzed it.

Among literacy folks, this branch of instruction is commonly referred to as critical literacy. But while critical literacy work is often taken up by teachers of reading and writing, there are many opportunities for teachers of mathematics to engage students in this work as well. One way we can do this is by analyzing texts that are mathematical in nature, such as data and graphs. David J. Whitin and Phyllis E. Whitin refer to this kind of analysis as "critical numeracy," in which "readers dig beneath the surface of data to better evaluate their usefulness and to understand how numbers are constructed by authors to portray a certain version of reality" (2011, front matter). A different way to integrate mathematics with critical literacy is to bring a mathematical lens to a text that, at first glance, may not seem particularly mathematical in nature. In this case, we use math as one way of analyzing the text and considering the perspectives represented within it. We find it powerful to teach children critical literacy skills side-by-side in their math and reading classes, to better prepare students to be critical consumers of information in their world.

Honing Our Own Skills

As we engage children in the work of critical literacy and numeracy, it is helpful to continue to refine our own ability to examine texts as well. One way to practice this skill is by looking around your own school building and analyzing the texts you find: the way the dress code policy is written in your school handbook, the mural that is painted in your school lobby, and the way test-score data is reported and presented on your district web page. These are all texts that are constructed by individuals (or groups of individuals). They communicate both an overt, intended message *and* implicit information about the authors' beliefs and values. Let's practice using a critical literacy lens to examine this school-based text, for example:

KUPSTON ELEMENTARY SCHOOL
Holiday Charity Breakfast and Silent Auction

Come connect with other parents and support our Kupston students!

When? 8:30–9:30 a.m., Tuesday, December 16

Why? Some families in our school are in need of Christmas presents and warm clothes for the winter.

How? Tickets cost $25 and all money will be donated to students in need! Buy tickets between December 8–15 at the school office during drop-off or pickup.

Fun silent auction items include

- Dinner for two at Joe's Italian Restaurant
- Mani/Pedi at Nail Spa on Main Street
- Blow dry and style at Hair Bar Blow Outs
- And much more!

Please sign up online to bring a breakfast item to share.

TEACHER TIP: BOOKMARKING SENSITIVE SITUATIONS

When we engage in critical literacy and numeracy with our students, our conversations can sometimes move into emotional territory (either for ourselves or for students). In his book *Not Light, But Fire: How to Lead Meaningful Race Conversations in the Classroom*, Matthew Kay encourages us to lean into the discomfort, but to do so with preparedness. "Many of us entered the classroom with a *classroom management* mandate to keep the peace at all costs. If we are not careful, such a mandate can dupe us into forgetting that great ideas are volatile. Race ideas, doubly so. So if we wish to create a dialogic curriculum that engages race, it stands to reason that our students' opinions will eventually clash. We should be ready to thrive in these moments" (2018, 49). However, sometimes we will find ourselves in a situation in which we don't feel prepared to thrive. We do not stubbornly press forward in these instances, possibly undoing some of the work we have done to build the community and trust among our students. Instead, we can put a bookmark in a conversation. When we do that, we first say something that honors the significance of the topic: "I'm hearing how passionate our classroom community feels about _____." Then, we take a pause, during which we can do one or more of the following: (1) provide time for written reflection to take the pulse of what our students are thinking and feeling; (2) reflect on how the conversation is personally impacting us, perhaps by talking to a friend or writing; (3) gather some additional resources that might add missing information or perspectives to the conversation; and (4) evaluate what format might be best for us to return to the conversation (whole-group, small-group, or one-on-one). We indicate to our students during this pause that we are not abandoning the issue, but we want to regroup: "I want to take some time to think more about this issue and gather some resources for us, so we can all learn more about _____ together. Let's pause our conversation just for now."

Try asking yourself some of these questions about this text (or any text) to help you uncover messages beneath the surface.

- Whose voices are represented and whose are missing in this text?

- What views are represented in this text? What views are not represented?

- Which experiences are privileged and which are marginalized in this text?

- What did the author want me to believe after reading this text?

- What are the ways this text could be rewritten to reposition the reader?

(adapted from Harste 2014, 95)

Small but Mighty

As Vivian Vasquez, Hillary Janks, and Barbara Comber remind us in their article "Critical Literacy as a Way of Being and Doing," critical literacy and numeracy go beyond examining and analyzing a text. It is really about "making sense of the sociopolitical systems through which we live our lives and questioning those systems" (2019, 307). Therefore, when we engage in this work, we invite students to discuss topics that have traditionally been taboo in school, such as gender, class, race, ability, and ethnicity. These topics may sound like work that only high school students should do. They may even sound like something that doesn't belong in school at all. *What will my principal say? How will the parents react? What if I say something wrong?* This discomfort is understandable, but it doesn't mean that we should avoid important issues.

For example, we know that talking about race in (and out of) school is particularly uncomfortable for many people. After a read-aloud of the book *The Colors of Us*, by Karen Katz (2002), a picture book about skin color, one distressed second grader blurted out to Christy, "We can't talk about people's skin color! That's racist!" Many children, like this second grader, have already gotten the message that talking about skin color or race is inappropriate, that talking about race is in and of itself a racist act. And it is true that traditionally, conversations about issues such as race have been considered to be off-limits at school. However, we argue that our elementary-aged students are already thinking through these issues *and* bringing them into the classroom. If we listen carefully to the comments our students are making to each other—on the playground, in the lunchroom, or under their breath in our classrooms—we can get a glimpse into the social issues they are working through and thinking about. The table "Listening Below the Surface" outlines some kinds of comments you might have heard from students and suggests what issues they might *really* be talking about.

Table 10.1

Listening Below the Surface

What students might be saying	What they might *really* be talking about
"Your name is weird!" "She can't speak English; don't ask her." "Ew, what is that food?"	Culture
"You wear that sweatshirt every day!" "We went to Italy for vacation. Where did you go?" "My dad said I don't have money for the book fair."	Class
"This game is for boys only." "Pink is for girls." "Why are you playing with her? Is she your *girlfriend*?"	Gender

continues

What students might be saying	What they might *really* be talking about
"This is so easy; why can't you do it?" "Why do I always have to go with that other teacher?" "I'm the best/fastest at this!"	Ability
"You have to use a brown crayon to draw yourself, not the peach one." "Do you even need sunscreen?" "You can't be that character because you're not white."	Race
"Why do you have two moms?" "Why does your grandpa always pick you up?" "You don't look like your dad."	Families

(adapted from Fairfax County Public Schools: Pacing and Planning Guide, Unit 6: Critical Literacy, Grade 2)

If we, as teachers, decide not to discuss these issues with our students at school, we do not make them go away. Instead, we just push them underground where children will do their best to figure things out based on what they observe and what they hear. In refusing to deal with issues head on, we perpetuate the systems that are already in place, privileging certain individuals and groups over others. We must consider the "value of giving up the eggshell walk that permits power differentials and the dominant discourse to go unchallenged in many classrooms" (Copenhaven-Johnson, Bowman, and Johnson 2007, 243). Children are already working through these issues, and they are doing it during the school day, whether we condone it or not. We can choose to supply them with tools to investigate these issues in a way that allows them to think critically about what they observe, and, hopefully, work for change in the world. We firmly believe there is a place for this work in every classroom. Therefore, in this chapter, as in Chapters 8 and 9, we outline a planning process for how we encourage students to engage with the world using Hands-Down Conversations in both math and literacy classes.

Planning to Engage with the World

The planning process for engaging students with the world is similar to the processes we use for nurturing debate (Chapter 8) and building theories (Chapter 9). However, there are important differences in how we approach each step and how this process begins and ends.

1. **Choose an issue.** Decide what issue might be important for you and your students to spend time critically analyzing. This issue may come from something you notice in your classroom or from greater community or world issues.

2. **Identify content goals.** Consider how you can explore this issue through the lens of your content goals in math and/or literacy. Sometimes you can explore an issue in an integrated fashion through math and literacy, and other times the issue lends itself better to one content area or the other.

3. **Select a "text" or "texts" that allow students to explore the issue, and anticipate students' thinking.** The "text" may be a data representation, a visual image, a book, or a print advertisement. You also might collect a set of texts that introduce differing perspectives and allow your class to do comparative work. When selecting texts, consider your students' perspectives and experiences, and anticipate how they may react to the text(s).

4. **Plan time for immersion in the text(s).** Start by giving students time to understand the author's intended message, considering the choices and decisions the author made. Consider how you can nudge students toward critical analysis, seeking out implicit meanings and uncovering the author's perspective/biases.

5. **Plan a launch and facilitate conversation.** Hands-Down Conversations provide an opportunity for students to dig deeper into critical analysis of the text or text set. Students develop and revise their own ideas about a text or issue as a result of listening to and interacting with differing perspectives on the same text.

6. **Invite students to take action.** Provide students with an opportunity to reflect on their developing thoughts on the issue and decide what they want to do as a result. "So, now what?" is a question we often ask students at this point in the process. Sometimes the action is simply asserting our beliefs (*I think pink is a color that everyone can wear, not just girls*), and other times taking action might be writing a letter, email, or tweet to someone, or communicating our learning with other students or community members.

Figure 10.1 Second-grade teacher Pagan Bragdon listens to a student talk about her weekend.

In this chapter, we explore the process of planning a Hands-Down Conversation to engage with the world in Pagan Bragdon's second-grade class. Pagan is a passionate teacher who works hard to develop strong relationships with her students. If you stop by Pagan's classroom as the school day begins, you will often see her engaged one-on-one with students in her class, sometimes listening intently to a story from home or just greeting a child who has come over to her for a quick hug. Pagan is focused on fostering her students' individual and collective identities, highlighting and celebrating the diversity in her classroom, and helping each child be aware and proud of their unique strengths. This "Week at a Glance" illustrates how an integrated investigation played out in math and reading across two weeks.

As you follow our story in Pagan's class, you can reflect on how you might experiment with this planning process in your classroom.

Week at a Glance: Engaging with the World in Pagan's Classroom

Week One

Monday	Tuesday	Wednesday	Thursday	Friday
Reading: Interactive read-aloud of *Emily's Art*	Reading: Interactive read-aloud of *Three Cheers for Tacky*		Reading: Immersion in the Under Armour sneaker ad and Hands-Down Conversation	Math: Immersion in the Target website and Hands-Down Conversation

Week Two

Monday	Tuesday	Wednesday	Thursday	Friday
	Math: Collecting data from Target website based on students' questions and making graphs to display that information. Hands-Down Conversation to analyze graphs and reflect on the text's messages. Students compose tweet to Target.	Written reflection and "The Beliefs" Hands-Down Conversation	Share Target's reply to their tweet with students.	Redesign the Sneaker Project and share.

Engaging with the World in Literacy and Math

1. Choose an issue.

Vasquez, Janks, and Comber remind us that the most important element of choosing an issue to investigate with our students is finding one that is relevant to them. "Using the topics, issues, and questions that they raise should be central to creating an inclusive critical curriculum" (2019, 306). Here are three methods you might use to identify these issues.

- *Listen to students during down time:* As outlined in the table "Listening Below the Surface," one of the best ways to know what issues students are grappling with is by listening to them talk with each other. When you notice a certain issue coming up again and again in social conversation, you may want to consider investigating this topic as a class. For example, in Christy's kindergarten classroom several years ago, she had three times as many boys as girls. Most five- and six-year-olds spend time talking about gender, but this year, the lines students were drawing between girls and boys were particularly rigid. Christy knew that they needed to spend some time as a class exploring gender and deconstructing the "rules" concerning girls and boys so the class could move toward building a more cohesive community.

- *Look for opportunities within your assigned curriculum:* Sometimes an issue will bubble up based on content you have introduced to the class, usually as part of your assigned curriculum. For example, when first graders in one teacher's class read about Martin Luther King Jr. as part of their social studies curriculum, the teacher was unsure how to react to student questions such as "What about if you were from Pakistan back then? I'm brown, not black. So then what?" Rather than brushing past these types of questions and moving on, you can lean into the discomfort, and take it as a sign that this is an issue worthy of further critical investigation. Other times, in planning for a unit of study, you may decide that particular content lends itself well to an exploration of an issue. For example, third-grade teacher Ilana Greenstein connected her fraction unit to an investigation of wealth distribution in the United States (Greenstein 2019).

- *Keep your eyes and ears open for broader social and community issues:* Another way you might identify an issue is by being aware of what is going on in your students' neighborhoods, communities, and the world at large. Keeping a finger on the pulse of local and national issues will give you a window into what might be important to students' families and what is on your students' minds. For example, when a fifth-grade teacher knew that the issue of immigrant rights was weighing heavily on her students' minds, she decided to bring the news into the classroom. She also made a point of checking in personally with students who may have had more direct experience with this issue to make sure the discussions did not retraumatize them.

As we choose issues and prepare for discussion, it is critical that we continually reexamine and evaluate our own biases and the limitations of our understanding around a given topic. Here are some sources we turn to for developing our own understanding:

- Teaching Tolerance's Social Justice Standards (https://www.tolerance.org /frameworks/social-justice-standards). Teaching Tolerance provides standards and resources for teachers engaging in work around the domains of identity, diversity, justice, and action.

- Rethinking Schools (www.rethinkingschools.org). Rethinking Schools is a publisher of books and a magazine focusing on equity issues in schools.

When Christy and Kassia first sat down with Pagan to chat about their work together, Pagan spent some time reflecting on the kinds of things the students had been talking about lately. "What's the number one issue in your class these days?" Christy asked. Pagan knew right away. She had recently noticed an increase in comments among her students about ability. One student had just started leaving the classroom daily to attend a self-contained special education classroom during reading and writing workshop, and other students had been asking questions about this change. On the soccer field at recess, a couple of students had been jockeying for power and position, each claiming to be "the best" soccer player in the class, leaving most of the other children feeling frustrated and angry. And finally, a handful of students' parents had been notified recently their child would attend the gifted center in third grade, and there were several underground comments flying back and forth among the students about who would be going and who wouldn't, and what it all meant: "You won't see me next year because I'm going to a smart-kid class."

The second graders in Pagan's classroom were navigating some important issues. Christy and Pagan might have been tempted to try to squash these conversations because they, as teachers, felt uncomfortable or because they were eager to move on to more "academic" content. They might have been inclined to respond to comments like those from Pagan's students by saying, "We don't need to talk about this in school," or "Everyone is special and important. Let's all just be kind to each other." And while these teacher responses might be well intentioned, the consequences of comments that sweep children's authentic and sometimes raw questions under the rug can be damaging.

Despite the fact that they, as teachers, were uncertain about how to respond to students' comments, they also knew ability/competition was the right issue to tackle, and they decided to do so in an integrated project through both math and literacy lenses. A primary goal for the investigation was that the students would explore their personal beliefs about ability and begin to recognize the impact that various social systems around us have on those beliefs.

Engaging with the World Through Literacy

2. Identify content goals.

In literacy, there are a host of subskills that work together to allow us to critically analyze a text. Many of these skills are categorized as "thinking *about* the text" by reading experts such as Fountas and Pinnell. Here are just a few:

- Understand the role of an author and illustrator.

- Be aware of the various writing techniques an author employs and consider how they impact your reading of a text, including illustrations, elements of genre, organizational tools, language patterns, and vocabulary.

- Notice when authors are trying to teach a lesson or persuade readers.

- Form opinions about a text or author and support opinions with evidence.

(Adapted from Fountas and Pinnell 2017, 42–47)

While we do not ask students to use these skills in isolation, we may, at times, choose to focus more heavily on building our students' ability in one particular area. To determine a focus, we use the same process as we did in Chapters 8 and 9: First, we examine our curriculum or a resource such as Fountas and Pinnell's *Literacy Continuum* (2017) to see what skills are most age-appropriate for our students. Second, we analyze the data we have collected on our students, including recent Hands-Down Conversations, data from reading conferences, and notes students have jotted while reading (for upper-elementary students), to see which skills they are controlling, and what would be the best next steps.

When choosing a focus for Pagan's second graders, Christy and Pagan recognized that a great deal of the second-grade curriculum had been focused on determining author's purpose and message. It was late in the school year when they started this project, and Pagan knew (from data collected informally during small-group reading lessons and recent formal reading assessments) that most of her students were proficient with this skill. Students were also able to express opinions about a text, such as describing a favorite part or explaining why they liked or disliked the text. However, Christy and Pagan thought they might be able to stretch the students to begin critiquing author and illustrator actions in ways that went a little deeper. As outlined in the *Literacy Continuum*, second graders are expected to "talk critically about what a writer does to make a topic interesting or important" (Fountas and Pinnell 2017, 494). They decided this would be a good focus, based on expectations for second grade and the proficiencies that the students were already demonstrating.

3. Select a "text" or "texts" that allow students to explore the issue, and then anticipate students' thinking.

We must search widely when choosing texts to dissect a particular issue with our students. We want children to understand that we are bombarded by messages and ideas everywhere, and we all have a responsibility to analyze these messages and decide how to respond. "It is especially important that everyday texts be an integral part of our language arts program, as this is where literacy is occurring in the lives of our students" (Harste 2014, 93). No type of text is off the table—cereal boxes, awards, blogs, song lyrics, historical markers, and so on. As teachers, we sometimes find ourselves reading within just a few genres with our students and even sticking with our few favorite titles, because they feel comfortable. But by limiting our text set, we end up limiting our students' ability to comprehend and critique a wide variety of texts, especially those that require visual literacy (such as figuring out where one's eye should look first in a nonlinear text). Stretching our own imaginations and comfort zones when we select texts will serve our students well as they learn to read the world around them.

In addition to looking for different genres during our text search, we also want to search widely for different perspectives and messages. One way to do this is to ask ourselves, "What is the dominant perspective on this issue?" and then seek out texts that communicate alternative perspectives. Another option may be to seek out an example of the dominant or privileged perspective as well as some examples of more marginalized perspectives for students to compare. Similarly, with regard to media literacy, Vasquez (2017) recommends comparing what our favorite or familiar media outlet and a less comfortable media outlet say about the same story.

> For Pagan's class, Christy wanted to collect a mixture of picture books and "everyday" texts and make sure that multiple perspectives and beliefs about ability/competition were presented within those texts. She began her search by collecting some fictional picture books on the topic of competition. Interestingly, most of the books seemed to communicate variations on the same message: "It's okay if you're not the best at something; we all have different abilities." Christy imagined that this was a familiar message that students had heard from teachers and/or parents in the past. She thought it would be worthwhile to unpack this message with students and then compare it with the contrasting messages about competition we get from other sources. Christy selected the picture books *Emily's Art,* by Peter Catalanotto (2001), and *Three Cheers for Tacky,* by Helen Lester (1996).
>
> Christy then continued her search online by browsing advertisements for sports apparel and accessories, anticipating that these texts would probably carry a different message about competition than the picture books had. She came across a series of Under Armour ads for

sneakers with the slogan "Do you hear footsteps, or are they hearing yours?" The ads featured successful athletes modeling Under Armour footwear, or at least implying that they wear it. Christy anticipated the students would notice that the ad communicated a message that speed, competition, and winning were in fact very important, in sharp contrast to the picture books. Christy chose one of these advertisements to add to her text set for the class to investigate together.

4. Plan time for immersion in the text(s).

When investigating a text from a critical stance, we start by teaching students to notice the author's craft and techniques and work to "figure out" some of the author's intended messages. Vasquez describes this process as first reading *with* a text, before reading *against* it (Vasquez 2017). A key question driving our work when we read *with* a text is "What does the author want me to think?" If we are using a book as the text, we can do this exploration with an interactive read-aloud (as discussed in Chapters 8 and 9), carefully selecting stopping points where we can examine a particular author move or technique and analyze how it impacts the message. If we are examining visual images or a format such as a flyer, advertisement, or poster, we can help students fully take in the elements of a text using a routine like "See, Think, Wonder" (Project Zero 2015). This routine asks students to slow down their looking—first taking in exactly what they *see*, then conjecturing about what they *think* those things might represent or mean, and finally discussing what they *wonder*.

> In Pagan's classroom, Christy and Pagan planned interactive read-alouds with *Emily's Art* and *Three Cheers for Tacky* that focused on understanding the author's message and examining some of the techniques the author used to communicate that message. They planned for the interactive read-alouds to take place over the course of several days. (See "Week at a Glance: Engaging with the World in Pagan's Classroom" on page 191 for the two-week timeline of this project.) During and after each read-aloud, the students engaged in Turn and Talks to discuss their personal interpretations of the message and begin to explore how it matched or didn't match with their own beliefs.
>
> After reading the books with the class, Christy immersed the students in comprehending the Under Armour advertisement, using the "See, Think, Wonder" routine. Using one color of sticky notes, Christy recorded the things students noticed first (one comment on each sticky note); no conjectures or value judgements were allowed yet. Comments included "a sneaker with stripes," "a man running," and "green smoke." Then students returned to the things they noticed and talked with their partners about their thoughts on each one. Christy used a different color

sticky note next to the first ones to record the conjectures. Next to "a man running," for example, another sticky note was added with the idea "I think he's probably a famous fast runner." The students had a good deal of discussion about the meaning of the slogan ("Do you hear footsteps or are they hearing yours?") during this part of the routine. At one point, a student stood up and asked another child to act out running in a race with him to depict how you would hear footsteps behind you if someone was catching up to you. Lastly, students shared some "wonders," which Christy recorded on a third color sticky note. Here are some examples: "Does Under Armour put their logo on everything they make?" "Do they have girls in their ads or just boys?" This entire routine was done with the students raising their hands and seated in a group facing forward in the meeting area to view the ad, which was projected on the SMART Board. Christy chose to use hand-raising for this conversation because she wanted to guide the structure of this routine (redirecting students if they started to share what they "wondered" before it was time, for example). She also wanted to carefully capture and record each child's thinking and give it equal "airtime."

5. Plan a launch and facilitate conversation.

After students have had time to investigate a text, a Hands-Down Conversation is a useful tool to facilitate collaborative critical analysis. The format of the Hands-Down Conversation allows students to openly explore how the text has impacted different readers in the room. We sometimes choose other techniques to support student critical analysis before the Hands-Down Conversation, such as individual writing/drawing about a text or discussing the text in partnerships. At other times, we may decide to reread the text together with this new critical lens, or just revisit our previously selected stopping points and model our own thinking and critique out loud before we have a conversation. You will know how much support you want to put into place based on the complexity of the text and your students' familiarity with this kind of work.

To launch a Hands-Down Conversation that will support students in analyzing a text, you might start by asking students either to walk in the author's shoes ("What might this author want us to think/do?") or to walk in their own shoes ("What does this text make you think or want to do?") For more ways to launch this type of conversation, consider using the questions in the section called "Honing Our Own Skills," page 186.

In Pagan's room, she and Christy decided to analyze the Under Armour ad using a Hands-Down Conversation for two main reasons. First of all, it was one of the first times the students had done work unpacking this type of visual text. Secondly, although the message in the Under Armour ad was one that children surely had been exposed to, it was also a message that was rarely discussed openly in a school environment. Christy and Pagan wanted to make it clear to students that it was okay to talk about this message in school (the idea that competition and being the best *is* an important value), because it does have a strong impact on the way many people think and act. Part of what the students seemed to be grappling with in their social comments and conversation was the dissonance between these messages and the differing beliefs and values among the students. They needed to get it all out in the open. To launch the conversation, Christy decided to start with the question "What does this ad make you think or want to do?" Christy also anticipated she might need to probe a little further during the conversation to ask students to connect their thinking about ability and "being the best" with the ad.

The Sneaker Ad Conversation in Action

Christy: Okay, now that we have really investigated this sneaker ad, we are going to have a Hands-Down Conversation about it. Go ahead and move with your talk partner to the outside of the rug. (*Students move quickly and familiarly to find a seat around the perimeter of the carpet next to their Turn and Talk partners. Christy takes a seat just behind the circle with paper and pencil.*) Great. You're ready. So, can we all talk together and see if we can figure this ad out even more? Let's start with this: What does this ad make you want to do?

Yanni: Well, it makes me want to buy these sneakers!

Georgia: Yeah, they are really trying to convince you to buy them.

Tanner: I think the sneakers are probably comfortable and fast.

Adam: And you can win, probably.

(*There is a lull in the conversation.*)

Christy: I wonder what messages Under Armour is trying to send us about "winning" or being "the best?"

Audrey: That man [in the ad] is probably the best, so they put him in there so everyone else will think that they can be the best.

Yanni: They [Under Armour] use these ads because they want to be the best.

Jennie: But it doesn't matter if you're best.

Skye: I connect with Yanni. They put the best people in the ads so people want to buy the shoe.

Georgia: And they put that fire and smoke in there to trick people into thinking that shoe will make you run so fast you're on fire.

Nadia: That's just a computer trick.

Patrick: I saw a Lego ad once that said it was easy to build the kit, but it actually wasn't, so ads can really be not true.

Mary: So, I don't think those shoes are actually better. Or best. It's a trick, really. Anyway, I agree with Jennie, you don't have to be the best.

Adam: I guess the shoes don't make you best, because you actually have to practice, but you *could* win if you practice with the shoes on.

In this snippet of Hands-Down Conversation, Pagan's students were working through some important ideas. They were thinking through how authors (and companies) make decisions to put certain things in their ads in an attempt to convince consumers of something. ("They put the best people in the ads so people want to buy the shoe," and "That's just a computer trick.") The students were also beginning to figure out how a text like the Under Armour ad impacts them, as consumers. The next steps were for the students to further consider what they themselves believe, which they were just beginning to touch on in this conversation. Jennie, for example, was asserting that "it doesn't matter if you're best," and Adam was still pretty interested in winning, and whether these shoes would help with that or not!

Our project did not stop here. In math class, the students continued to unpack the messages about ability that are all around them.

Engaging with the World Through Math

2. Identify content goals.

We may think that children have to learn a prerequisite amount of math before using it as a tool for critical analysis. Perhaps, we think, when students are older they can use algebra to analyze the living wage or the Pythagorean Theorem to design a wheelchair ramp. Both are excellent topics for older students that are discussed in *Rethinking Mathematics: Teaching Social Justice by the Numbers* (Gutstein and Peterson 2013). However, if we truly believe that elementary school children can engage in the practices of mathematicians, we must also trust that they can use their understanding of mathematics to analyze the world. When Kassia's daughter was a preschooler she reported that she was going to "count the number of white people and brown people in our family." As a four-year-old she could already use her understanding of mathematics and race to try to better understand her own family and other people's families. When planning for the intersection of math and social issues, we can trust children to make sense of their world.

Furthermore, we agree with Gutstein and Peterson that "students can recognize the power of mathematics as an essential analytical tool to understand and potentially change the world, rather than merely regarding math as a collection of disconnected rules to be rotely memorized and regurgitated" (2013, 2). Therefore, it is not enough that we make connections to social issues through math; we must also be intentional in planning for the math content and not offer students a watered-down version of the mathematics.

As Pagan's class was immersed in a unit on data, Kassia and Pagan decided that the ongoing ability investigation was the perfect opportunity for the second graders to collect and analyze data that was meaningful to *their* lives, something that textbooks often skip over in favor of asking students to poll each other about their favorite ice cream flavor year after year. In reviewing the big ideas for data collection and analysis, Kassia and Pagan used Marian Small's *Understanding the Math We Teach and How to Teach It* (2019) to help focus their data work on several big ideas.

- "Most data collection activities are based on the prior sorting of information into categories" (529).

- "To collect data, you must create appropriate questions and think about how to best gather the data" (529).

- "Graphs are powerful displays since visual displays quickly reveal information about data" (530).

It is important to note that these big ideas about data are often oversimplified for elementary school students, especially those in the primary grades. When collecting and analyzing data with young students, we rarely let them grapple with the messiness of real-life data, instead preselecting neat categories and questions around which students should collect and analyze data. The real process of engaging with data involves lots of mucking around and revising, and Kassia and Pagan wanted the second graders to experience this as well.

3. Select a "text" or "texts" that allow students to explore the issue, and anticipate students' thinking.

Advertisements, catalogues, and children's books are often ideal texts for elementary students to analyze mathematically both because the information contained in these texts is relevant and engaging and because the sample size of information is manageable. Just as with every "text" selection in math, it is important for the teacher to anticipate how students might approach the work. When selecting a source of data, we, as teachers, should take some time to notice patterns in the data, consider potential questions we might ask about the data, and think about possible ways to organize the data.

> Building on the work Christy and Pagan did around the Under Armour advertisement, Kassia looked for a way the second graders could use a mathematical lens to analyze data and the messages that corporations send us about ability through the texts they create. She chose the kids' sneaker section of the Target website as a text for two reasons. First, Target was a familiar store and brand for most of the second graders. Shopping for shoes in a store or online was also a familiar experience for most students and likely one that they had not yet critically analyzed. Second, because Target organizes its website into 'girls' sneakers' and 'boys' sneakers' sections, Kassia knew students would be able to analyze messages about gender as they relate to ability. As she browsed through the website herself, Kassia anticipated what the second graders might notice about the boys' and girls' sections, how they might sort the shoes within these sections into categories, and what questions they might ask about the data.

4. Plan time for immersion in the text(s).

When children (and adults!) first engage with a text, many read it with a noncritical lens. As with a literacy-focused text, we often read "with" a text before reading "against" it (Vasquez 2017). Children browsing a holiday toy catalogue, for example, are likely to spend time reading about what items are available this season and picking out toys they would like to receive. It is important to allow children an opportunity to notice and wonder about the text, even if what they notice and wonder about does not align with the reasons we chose the text. Our goal is not to simply lead children down a well-manicured path toward the conclusion we hope they will come to, but rather to allow them space to grapple with a text in all its complexities.

> On the first day Kassia visited Pagan's classroom, she began by allowing time for students to take a deep dive into noticing and wondering about the Target website's sneaker section: "Many of you have experience buying shoes with your family. Maybe you've even shopped at Target or on the Target website. We have printed off two parts of Target's website—the section called "boys' sneakers" and the section called "girls' sneakers." Ms. Bragdon and I are so curious to hear what you notice as you look at these pages."
>
> Pairs of students went off to different spots in the classroom and began to flip excitedly through the printed versions of the website. Kassia and Pagan invited students to write on the printed website pages by saying, "Maybe there will be something you want to write down or figure

Figure 10.2 Two second graders consult a poster-size printout of Target's "girls' sneakers" and "boys' sneakers" sections and jot down their noticings.

out as you're talking with your partner so that you can share it with the class when we come back together." As Pagan and Kassia listened in to students' talk, they first heard many students connecting what they saw to their own lived experiences:

"Oooh, my brother has these shoes!"

"I want these glitter shoes so much, but my mom says they're not good for wearing to school so I can't get them."

"Hey, did you see those shoes with the smiling avocado?!"

"Look how much these cost! They're the most expensive on the whole page!"

Without any more prompting than "You can write on this paper," some students began to count different kinds of shoes or circle things they saw as going together (e.g., all the shoes with Velcro or all the light-up shoes). One group counted the number of girls' sneakers and the number of boys' sneakers. Another group counted the number of girls' sneakers with laces and the number of boys' sneakers with laces. Others were interested in quantifying the light-up sneakers, sneakers with Velcro, and sneakers with characters on them. The students were using mathematical noticings to sort the data into categories and ask questions about the data that were meaningful to them.

5. Plan a launch and facilitate conversation.

One of the best ways to get people (adults and children alike) talking is by asking them to discuss their own noticings and questions, rather than always beginning with our own teacher questions. In planning to critically analyze a text through the lens of mathematics, you can begin by asking students to share their own noticings and wonderings. Students may begin to analyze the perspectives communicated through the text on their own, or you might prompt them with one of the questions outlined in the section "Honing Our Own Skills" on page 186.

Pagan and Kassia expected that Target's sneaker selection would provide a lot of conversation material for the second graders. While they planned to give students time to talk with partners as they browsed the website pages, they also expected that talking in a Hands-Down Conversation would be productive. They planned to say something like, "You've all noticed that Target has two sections on its kids' sneaker website: 'girls' sneakers' and 'boys' sneakers.' And you've noticed that the sneakers in those sections are different. Let's talk about what you're noticing about the shoes in the 'girls' sneakers' section and the 'boys' sneakers' section." They then planned several possibilities for a mid-conversation prompt. Here are two examples:

- What messages might Target be sending us with this website?
- What does Target want us to believe or think we already believe? What do you believe?

Throughout the conversation, Kassia and Pagan planned to observe how students used the data to support their claims and to consider how they might support students in further work with the data after this initial conversation.

The Target Sneakers Conversation in Action

Jennie: Girls' shoes are really colorful; the boys' aren't as colorful.

Skye: And girls' shoes have more fancy decorations.

Audrey: Target is telling us that dark colors are for boys and light colors are for girls.

Patrick: There's an avocado shoe in the girls' sections only. There's no avocado shoe for boys!

Tanner: That's not fair! You can like colors if you are a boy!

Breanne: There are some gray shoes for girls, but not a lot.

Audrey: Boys shoes are almost totally black and white.

Eva: But maybe that's because girls *like* light colors. Like I want pink sneakers like these ones I'm wearing. I don't want gray sneakers.

Leon: Colors don't matter; it only matters that they fit.

Jennie: But Target might not have even designed these shoes. They're just selling them.

Yanni: I guess if you want different colors you have to go to a different store. Target wouldn't want to lose business so maybe they need to sell different shoes.

Kaleb: I noticed that the number of boys' shoes is thirty-five and the number of girls' shoes is twenty-six.

Maria: So there are nine less shoes for girls because thirty-five minus nine equals twenty-six.

Tanner: Boys have an odd number of shoes and girls have an even number of shoes. And there are sixty-one total because thirty plus twenty equals fifty, fifty plus five equals fifty-five, and fifty-five plus six equals sixty-one.

Kassia: You've noticed so much about Target's sneaker website. And it sounds like some of you are starting to think about the messages that Target is sending with its "boys' sneakers" and "girls' sneakers" sections. Let's talk more about these messages. What are they? And what do you think about these messages?

Georgia: They want us girls to wear high-tops or pink shoes. There's more of those shoes for girls than for boys. But girls don't have as much lace shoes for running.

Leon: Hey, Target is trying to tell us what to wear!

Nathan: But sometimes I wear light colors, and I'm a boy.

Nadia: And I like black. It matches anything!

Leon: And sometimes girls can wear boys' shoes and a boy might want a colorful shoe.

Jennie: My sister got boys' shoes.

Audrey: No, there are no boys' shoes. They split it for no reason. That's their identity. If boys don't like black, brown, or white, maybe that's their identity. It just matters that they like it or not.

(The conversation among the second graders continued for several minutes around the topic of whether there are "girl colors" and "boy colors" and whether Target should put "all the girl and boy sneakers together in one big website." As the conversation began to wrap up, Pagan and Kassia wanted to remind the second graders of the other noticings they had gathered during the partner exploration.)

Kassia: Many of you did some counting of different kinds of shoes today. Kaleb and Yessica had the question "How many total girls' sneakers and boys' sneakers are there on Target's website?" And so they counted each section's sneakers and wrote that down. I'm wondering what other questions you might want to investigate tomorrow? What other questions could we collect data on?

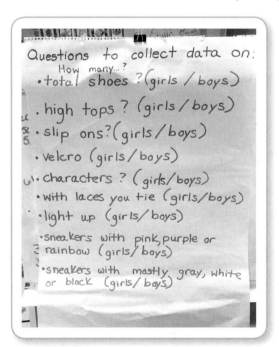

Figure 10.3 Pagan's second graders brainstormed a list of questions to guide their data collection.

(After a Turn and Talk with their partners, consulting their printed copies of the Target website as well as the color, poster-size version on the board, the students had an extensive list of questions they would collect data on the next day they worked together (Figure 10.3).)

6. Invite students to take action.

It is important that we not stop at teaching our students to critique texts, but that we also empower our students to take action. Harste reminds us that "our goal needs to be to create agents rather than consumers of texts" (2014, 100). We must communicate to students that we can "talk back" to texts in a variety of ways. Sometimes talk back simply means that we gain some clarity around a text's messages and express what we think about them. Other times, we can give students an authentic opportunity to take action and engage with the world. One example of action is encouraging students to redesign a text and transform it into one that communicates a message more closely aligned with the students' ideals and beliefs.

In Pagan's class, we ended up with one spontaneous opportunity for action, and one that we had planned ahead of time. After the second day of investigation in math class, during which students collected data around the questions they had developed a couple of days prior (Figure 10.3), groups of students created graphs to share with peers.

After a gallery walk in which students noticed and wondered about each other's graphs "Boys have double the number of light-up shoes!" (Figure 10.4) and 'Target thinks girls want high-top shoes' (Figure 10.5), Kassia asked the students, "So, what would you want to say to Target?" After recording some of their ideas on the whiteboard, Kassia invited the students to compose a tweet to Target and told them she would share their graphs with the company.

When we shared Target's tweet, one second grader raised her hand and said, "Next we could look at the 'girls' toys' and 'boys' toys' sections of their website!"

We also planned an activity for students to engage in a redesign process that would allow them to communicate their developing beliefs about ability. We told the students that this was an opportunity to "talk back" to the two sneaker companies (Target and Under Armour) we had discussed by designing their own sneakers and

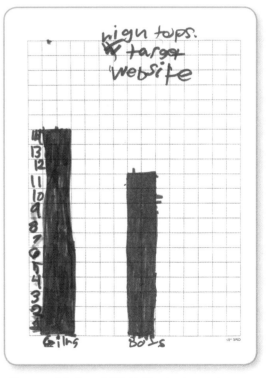

Figures 10.4 and 10.5 Students made graphs based on the data they collected from Target's website.

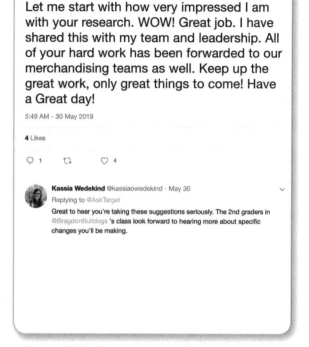

Figure 10.6 One of the second graders' tweets to Target

Figure 10.7 Two days later, Target tweeted a reply to the students.

an advertisement for them. Before launching into the sneaker ad redesign, we offered Pagan's students a chance to grapple with their own beliefs about the ability issue in a Hands-Down Conversation. We anticipated that some students might have revised or more clearly understood their own ideas on ability as a result of our investigation.

The Beliefs Conversation

To prepare for the conversation, Christy asked Pagan's students to spend a little time drawing and writing to reflect on their current beliefs: "So we've spent some time thinking about the messages you hear from ads, books, teachers, and friends about 'being the best.' We are learning that those messages are *other* people's opinions. And you get to make up your own mind. Take some time to write or draw about what you believe right now about 'being the best.' We will come together to talk about it in a few minutes." Students then gathered in a circle on the carpet with the half-pieces of paper on which they reflected.

Christy: You have your reflections with you, and you can use them if they are helpful while we talk. Let's have a Hands-Down Conversation now about this: What do *you* believe about being the best?

Nadia: I believe no one is perfect. More than one person can be the best, depending on the day, or what they do—like soccer, or reading, or helping people.

Leon: Well I think one person can be the best—"the best" basically means just one.

Audrey: But you could keep trying, and then maybe you could become the best one day.

Maria: Two people can be the best at the same thing. Or you could be best at different things.

Skye: I think people have different opinions—some people think being the best is not important but others do.

Patrick: What do you mean by that? I don't get what you mean.

Skye: Like some people have different opinions. I guess we don't all think the same way.

Yanni: Yeah, Skye is right—she means some people disagree because they have a different opinion about what is important.

Christy: I think Skye is helping us understand that there is more than one opinion here, right, Skye? (*Skye nods.*) Some of you think that being the best is just for one person. But some of you are saying, "No, it really doesn't have to be one person. More than one person can be the best at different things." So here's what I'm wondering. What do we do when *you* believe one thing, and then you get a message that is different? Like if you believe being the fastest is not all that important, but then you see an ad that says, "Buy these sneakers and be the fastest," or a friend says, "I'm the fastest," how do you deal with that when you have a different belief?

Breanne: Well, then you're kinda down. 'Cause if someone says to you, "I'm the best," it means "I'm better than you."

Nadia: It's confusing—like maybe they think they are the best at something, and you don't really care about that sport or whatever, but now you feel like you have to care.

Patrick: Maybe you could just try to get better and say to yourself, "It doesn't matter."

Yanni: Yeah, I agree with Patrick, or you could think, "I'm the best at something else I'm good at, and this thing doesn't matter."

Tanner: Or just say, "Who cares?"

Christy: So you're beginning to think about how we all have different opinions and perspectives, and it can be challenging to stand up for what we believe in, right? One way you express what you believe is to get your message out in the world. You can take action. So tomorrow, we are going to try that. We are going to think about those Target sneakers, and that Under Armour ad, and design your own sneaker ad to show what you believe about being the best. You can be thinking about that tonight. If you were in charge, what kind of sneaker would you make, and how would you make an ad to communicate what you believe about being the best?

The Sneaker Redesign Project—A Culmination

In the student-redesigned sneaker advertisements we are able to see evidence of how these students are now clearly and confidently expressing their beliefs about winning, competition, and ability.

Take Audrey, for example, the student who designed the ad for the shoe she named "Rowshi" (Figure 10.8). In describing her ad, Audrey said she wanted to be clear that she had created a mostly black shoe because "girls look cool in dark colors too." In the math Hands-Down Conversation about Target, we remember her dismay that "Target is telling us that dark colors are for boys and light colors are for girls." Audrey's belief that girls should have equal access to dark colors (which she previously held, but which was solidified through the project) comes through in her ad. She thought that the name "Rowshi" sounded fast and strong, and it would show people that girls can be those things. Her choice of the slogan "Never give up, just keep trying your best" was an interesting reflection of how this project had influenced her. Audrey was one of the soccer players who had most aggressively been proclaiming her status as "the best" on the playground over the previous few

Figure 10.8 Audrey's redesigned shoe advertisement

Figure 10.9 Leon's redesigned shoe advertisement

months. However, she did a lot of listening to her classmates and heard some new ideas and perspectives over the course of this exploration. Her slogan represents the resulting shift in her thinking.

Leon, the student who designed the shoe called "Winner Winner Chicken Dinner" (Figure 10.9), expressed a contrasting belief—that winning (not just doing his personal best) is his goal. The Hands-Down Conversations and shoe redesign project provided a forum for him to express this belief in a productive and respectful manner with his classmates ("Well, I think one person can be the best— 'the best' basically means just one").

Lastly, Skye's ad for the "Rainbow Gamer" shoe (Figure 10.10) communicates a third perspective. Her picture depicts a boy deciding to go shopping in the girls' shoe section of the store, with the slogan "Be what you want." This two-week exploration

Figure 10.10 Skye's redesigned shoe advertisement

allowed Skye to really grapple with the varying opinions in the class ("I guess we don't all think the same way,") and consider how the individual can make their own choices—about everything from their shoe color to their beliefs. In each of these students' shoe ads, we see evidence of how exploring the issue of ability/ competition through critical literacy and numeracy impacted the individual students' thinking about the issue.

While we know that societal issues are not resolved through single experiences, this investigation had the potential to have a community-wide impact. By addressing this issue together, the class developed a common language and comfort level discussing ability. The comments that had been passing back and forth no longer needed to be whispered but instead could be discussed in the open. Students were better equipped to discuss their opinions and feelings on this matter, even if they differed from their classmates.

Next Steps for Pagan's Class in Literacy

This project went beyond having social impact for the students. Students' literacy skills grew as well throughout this two-week learning experience. Our original focus for the project was that students would begin to "talk critically about what a writer does to make a topic interesting or important" (Fountas and Pinnell 2017, 494). We saw evidence of this goal in some critical talk about the author's decisions during the Under Armour ad Hands-Down Conversation, such as when one student observed, "They put that fire and smoke in there to trick people into thinking that shoe will make you run so fast you're on fire." The sneaker redesign ads also demonstrate students' beginning understanding of how they, as authors, can communicate their own beliefs in their work. Leon was one student who was surprised by the revelation that companies are influencing us. ("Hey, Target is trying to tell us what to wear!"). His slogan in the sneaker ad, "Buy this and you will win" (Figure 10.9), demonstrates his developing understanding that an author makes choices to convey beliefs and persuade. Next steps for Pagan's students are to continue this kind of critical looking and talking about texts, as this was an initial experience for them. Their emerging understandings about advertisements make ads a good text type to continue examining, with the plan to eventually transfer their developing skills to other types of texts as well.

Next Steps for Pagan's Class in Math

The Target sneaker investigation was one small step toward the larger goal of viewing mathematics more broadly and as a tool for analyzing the world. This goal is particularly important for the content area of data, since being critical consumers of data is increasingly important in our ever-changing world.

One unexpected issue that came up in our conversations about the Target sneaker data was that of developing categories and "deciding what gets counted" (Whitin and Whitin 2011, 41). One group of students developed the conjecture that Target thought boys were better at sports than girls because "there are more lace shoes for boys than girls and you need laces to run fast." Pagan and Kassia encouraged the group to go back into the data to see if this conjecture was supported by evidence. As the group began to count the number of sneakers with laces in the boys' and girls' sections, a debate arose around what "counted" as "lace shoes." Some kids argued that "lace shoes" are only "lace shoes" if the laces are functional and used to tighten and tie the shoe. Other students viewed "lace shoes" more expansively, also counting slip-on and Velcro-fastened sneakers with decorative laces that did not tie.

In this debate, the students had stumbled upon a critical issue in statistics, an issue Whitin and Whitin describe in *Learning to Read the Numbers*: "Children . . . [were] learning that there are limitations to their purported results because of the definitions they choose to use. In short, everything hinges on the definitions and categories" (2011, 42). Adults working with data must also grapple with the issue of definitions and categories when collecting and analyzing information on issues such as homelessness and unemployment, for example. (Who counts as "homeless"? What does it mean to be "employed"?) The ways we develop definitions are not neutral and reflect our biases and the messages we wish to communicate through the data.

As Pagan's students continue to work with data in second grade and beyond, they will explore other ways that people communicate messages through data. For example, while all of the second graders chose to represent their Target data using bar graphs (they had recently learned about bar graphs as part of the data unit of study), they should continue to explore how different representations of data might be used to communicate different messages.

Next Steps in Pagan's Class for Dialogue

Pagan's class experienced four Hands-Down Conversations and several opportunities to collaborate with partners during the two weeks of this exploration. During that time, the students demonstrated multiple strengths in the ways they talked and listened to one another. We saw evidence of many of the dialogue moves outlined in Chapters 4, 5, and 6. Students were taking turns, sharing the airspace, and staying on topic. (And when off-topic comments did come up, as they do in conversations with children and adults alike, they did not cause the conversation to lose momentum.) There was ample evidence of listening, and students' comments were often connected to each other. Some students asked clarifying questions and compared their ideas ("I agree with _____" or "I connect with _____").

During this project, Christy and Kassia were particularly curious about how students would revise their ideas. There seemed to be evidence of changes in thinking. However, none of the students talked explicitly about the process of how and why they revised their ideas. Perhaps Christy and Kassia could have better supported students in this work by providing more specific questions for reflection ("How did your thinking change? Why?"). We also think a good next step in dialogue might be to teach some ways to express a shift in thinking (Micro-lesson 6.6, Revising an Idea). While it can feel a little scary to admit when we are revising our thinking, we hope that over time students will feel safe talking about the ways their ideas and beliefs are evolving.

Engaging with the World as a Way of Thinking

When we invite students to grapple with the issues of our society, we prepare them to be active, thoughtful, and engaged citizens of the world. Elementary school is not too early for us to teach our students that they have a responsibility to analyze texts critically, an ability to form their own beliefs about the world, and the power to act on those beliefs.

Planning to Engage with the World

- Choose an issue
- Identify content goals.
- Select a "text" or "texts" that allow students to explore the issue, and anticipate students' thinking.
- Plan time for immersion in the text(s).
- Plan a launch and facilitate conversation.
- Invite students to take action.

PARTING THOUGHTS

When we first started thinking about classroom discourse together many years ago, we thought a lot about our role as teachers and our talk. What should we say to students? What practice should we provide? What talk prompts should we use? But over time, our focus has shifted. We have found that the best teaching and learning moments come from the times when we focus less on what *our* next teaching move will be and instead focus more on truly listening to our students. We have learned that the most productive way to nurture student discourse is to trust that our students are capable and are already making sense of their world. Our work, as teachers, is more about uncovering what students are already thinking about and building on these ideas rather than transferring any knowledge or skills we have.

Hands-Down Conversations are a tool for nurturing this kind of discourse community. We believe that our students are ready to speak out.

Speak out with clarity and confidence.

Speak out with respect for those around them.

Speak out to express their beliefs.

Speak out to improve their world.

and

Speak out while continually listening and learning from others.

When we trust in our students and stand by their sides to celebrate and support their conversational growth, we prepare them for a future that is unmediated by teachers. We prepare them for a world in which they will put their hands down and speak out.

If You Notice... Try...

A Complete List of Dialogue Micro-lessons

If you notice . . .	You might try . . .
You're ready to get started!	**Lesson 4.1** What's a Hands-Down Conversation?
Some students are jumping into the conversation too quickly, and you know everyone needs processing time.	**Lesson 4.2** Wait Time
You're ready to introduce Turn and Talk partnerships.	**Lesson 4.3** Turn and Talk, Part 1: Getting Started
Students are ready to get to know their Turn and Talk partners better and learn more about intentional listening.	**Lesson 4.4** Turn and Talk, Part 2: Getting to Know My Talk Partner
When students turn and talk, it's mostly a "share" time in which each person says one thing and then they are "done," without really listening to the other.	**Lesson 4.5** Turn and Talk, Part 3: I'm a Strong Listener

If you notice . . .	You might try . . .
Students have had some practice with Turn and Talk partners and are ready to transfer these skills to small-group conversations.	**Lesson 4.6** Conversation Clubs
Students are mumbling or talking so quietly that other children can't hear them.	**Lesson 4.7** We Talk So Everyone Can Hear Us
The Hands-Down Conversation feels unbalanced in terms of participation.	**Lesson 4.8** Too Many Voices at the Same Time OR **Lesson 4.9** Chirping Crickets
You have a few students who dominate the whole conversation and/or a few students who rarely talk.	**Lesson 4.10** Self-Monitoring Voices
Your students have been working on various talk and listening moves (like those taught in Lessons 4.1–4.10), and you want to encourage individual growth and reflection.	**Lesson 4.11** Setting and Reflecting on Goals with Partners

If you notice . . .	You might try . . .
Students are sharing ideas and opinions that may be unrelated or tangentially related to the topic of conversation.	**Lesson 5.1** Keeping the Conversation Focused
Students are sharing opinions and ideas, and might be trying to explain their reasoning, but it isn't very clear yet.	**Lesson 5.2** Supporting with Reasoning, Part 1: The *Why* Behind Our Ideas
Students are supporting their ideas with reasoning and are beginning to consider what kinds of evidence best supports their ideas.	**Lesson 5.3** Supporting with Reasoning, Part 2: Digging Deeper into the *Why*
Students are sharing ideas without monitoring how their partner(s) are understanding their ideas.	**Lesson 5.4** Am I Being Clear?

If you notice . . .	You might try . . .
Students are using talk moves and demonstrating listening "behaviors," and are ready to refine their listening moves. One clue that students are ready for this work is when they repeat the ideas of others in a conversation.	**Lesson 6.1** Paraphrasing: Listening *So Closely* and Saying an Idea in Your Own Words **Lesson 6.2** Cloudy or Clear: Asking Clarifying Questions
Students are most interested in their own ideas and haven't yet discovered the power and excitement that come with listening to understand what others think. Perhaps only a few students in the room are considered "listen-worthy" by their peers.	**Lesson 6.3** Looking Inside Our Brains: Curiosity About Other Ideas
Students are expressing their own isolated (and perhaps somewhat unrelated) ideas in conversations and are ready to learn more about connecting their ideas.	**Lesson 6.4** Same or Different? OR **Lesson 6.5** Adding On, Part 1: Linking Ideas OR **Lesson 6.6** Revising an Idea

If you notice . . .	You might try . . .
Students are agreeing and disagreeing with each other but often see it as a binary, all-or-nothing choice.	**Lesson 7.1** Analyzing an Idea
When students disagree with an idea, they state their own idea without giving evidence or a justification for their disagreement.	**Lesson 7.2** Refuting a Claim
Students are beginning to connect their ideas to other ideas in the conversation. They might be saying, "I'd like to add on . . . ," but the relationship between their comment and the previous one is unclear, or it's a restatement.	**Lesson 7.3** Adding On, Part 2: Growing Ideas
The conversation "doesn't go anywhere" or keeps circling back to the same few ideas over and over.	**Lesson 7.4** Staying Together: Taking a Conversation Journey
Students may be clunky or abrupt in the way they bring up a new point, leaving other listeners confused about where the conversation is going.	**Lesson 7.5** Taking the Conversation to a New Place

If you notice . . .	You might try . . .
Students are ready to take on even more ownership of the direction of the conversation.	**Lesson 7.6** Summarizing
You, as a teacher, are noticing many interesting things about your class's dialogue. You're ready to write your own dialogue micro-lessons.	**Lesson 7.7** The "Last Lesson": Writing Your Own Talk Micro-lessons

Conversation Map Template

Sample Social and Classroom Community Topics

As you get started with Hands-Down Conversations, you may want to integrate social and classroom community topics into Morning Meeting or when you have a few extra minutes at the end of the day. These kinds of conversations are lighter academically, but they help students continue to develop as talkers and listeners while building community. We try to choose topics that everyone can weigh in on and that have no "right" answer.

- Inside recess is better or outside recess is better.

- If you could live the life of any book character we have read about this year, who would you choose?

- Line leader is a more important class job than class librarian.

- We should have chocolate milk every day as a choice in our cafeteria. Yes or no?

- Would our school be better if kids could wear wheelie shoes?

- Snakes are dangerous or snakes are not dangerous.

- Would you rather have the power to fly or be invisible?

- How would you change our class playground to make it truly awesome?

- The worst kind of pizza is _____.

- It would be better if it was winter all the time than if it was summer all the time.

- Video games are bad for kids. What do you think?

- Agree or disagree: It is never okay to break a school rule.

- Would you rather be five years older or five years younger?

- Sharks are the scariest animals.

Aleaziz, Hamed. 2019. "Families 'Are Scared to Death' After a Massive ICE Operation Swept Up Hundreds of People." *BuzzFeed News*, August 7. https://www.buzzfeednews.com/article/hamedaleaziz/ice-raid-operation-mississippi-workplace-families.

All Sides. 2019. "680 Unauthorized Workers Arrested in Mississippi." August 8. https://www.allsides.com/story/ice-arrests-680-unauthorized-workers-mississippi.

Barlow, Angela T., and Michael R. McCrory. 2011. "3 Strategies for Promoting Math Disagreements." *Teaching Children Mathematics* 17 (9): 530–539.

Binder, John. 2019. "ICE Arrests 680 Illegal Aliens in Largest Single-State Raid in U.S. History." *Breitbart News*, August 7. https://www.breitbart.com/politics/2019/08/07/ice-arrests-680-illegal-aliens-in-largest-single-state-raid-in-u-s-history/.

Bishop, Rudine Sims. 1990. "Mirrors, Windows and Sliding Glass Doors." *Perspectives: Choosing and Using Books for the Classroom* 6 (3): ix–xi.

Boaler, Jo. 2017. "Math Class Doesn't Work. Here's the Solution." *Time*, October 5. http://time.com/4970465/how-to-improve-math-class/.

Boyd, Maureen, and Lee Galda. 2011. *Real Talk in Elementary Classrooms: Effective Oral Language Practice*. New York: Guilford.

Calkins, Lucy. 2000. *The Art of Teaching Reading*. New York: Pearson.

Carperter, Thomas P., Megan Loef Franke, and Linda Levi. 2003. *Thinking Mathematically: Integrating Arithmetic and Algebra in Elementary School*. Portsmouth, NH: Heinemann.

Cazden, Courtney. 2001. *Classroom Discourse: The Language of Teaching and Learning*. Portsmouth, NH: Heinemann.

Chapin, Suzanne H., Catherine O'Connor, and Nancy Canavan Anderson. 2013. *Classroom Discussions in Math: A Teacher's Guide for Using Talk Moves, Grades K–6*. Sausalito, CA: Math Solutions.

Copenhaver-Johnson Jeane F., Joy T. Bowman, and Angela C. Johnson. 2007. "Santa Stories: Children's Inquiry About Race During Picturebook Read-Alouds." *Language Arts* 84 (3): 234–244.

Danielson, Christopher. 2016a. "Wait! What Are We Counting? On Ambiguity and Units." *Teaching Children Mathematics Blog*. October 7. https://www.nctm.org/Publications/Teaching-Children-Mathematics/Blog/Wait!-What-are-we-counting_-On-Ambiguity-and-Units.

———. 2016b. *Which One Doesn't Belong?* Portland, ME: Stenhouse.

Ehrenworth, Mary. 2017. "Why Argue?" *Educational Leadership* 74 (5): 35–40.

Emdin, Christopher. 2016. *For White Folks Who Teach in the Hood . . . and the Rest of Y'All Too: Reality Pedagogy and Urban Education*. Boston: Beacon.

Erikson Institute Early Math Collaborative. 2019. "Big Ideas." https://earlymath.erikson.edu/why-early-math-everyday-math/big-ideas-learning-early-mathematics/.

Fairfax County Public Schools. 2018. "Unit 6: Critical Literacy, Grade 2." Fairfax County Public Schools Planning and Pacing Guide.

Fay, Kathleen, Chrisie Moritz, and Suzanne Whaley. 2017. *Powerful Book Introductions: Leading with Meaning for Deeper Thinking*. Portland, ME: Stenhouse.

Fearnley-Whittingstall, Hugh. 2007. *The River Cottage Meat Book*. Emeryville, CA: Ten Speed Press.

Fisher, Douglas, Nancy Frey, and Carol Rothenberg. 2008. *Content-Area Conversations: How to Plan Discussion-Based Lessons for Diverse Language Learners*. Alexandria, VA: ASCD.

Fountas, Irene, and Gay Su Pinnell. 2017. *The Fountas & Pinnell Literacy Continuum*. Portsmouth, NH: Heinemann.

Franke, Megan L., Elham Kazemi, and Angela Chan Turrou. 2018. *Choral Counting & Counting Collections: Transforming the PreK–5 Math Classroom*. Portsmouth, NH: Stenhouse.

Freire, Paulo. 2018. *Pedagogy of the Oppressed, 4th ed*. New York: Bloomsbury Academic.

————. 2005. *Teachers as Cultural Workers: Letters to Those Who Dare Teach, Expanded Edition*. Cambridge, MA: Westview.

Fuller, Evan, Jeffrey M. Rabin, and Guershon Harel. 2011. "Intellectual Need and Problem-Free Activity in the Mathematics Classroom." *International Journal for Studies in Mathematics Education* 4 (1): 80–114.

Gallas, Karen. 1995. *Talking Their Way into Science: Hearing Children's Questions and Theories, Responding with Curriculum*. New York: Teachers College Press.

Greenstein, Ilana. 2019. "Macaroni Social Justice." *Rethinking Schools Magazine* 33 (4). https://www.rethinkingschools.org/articles/macaroni-social-justice.

Guan Eng Ho, Debbie. 2005. "Why Do Teachers Ask the Questions They Ask?" *RELC Journal* 36 (3): 297–310.

Gutstein, Eric (Rico), and Bob Peterson, eds. 2013. *Rethinking Mathematics: Teaching Social Justice by the Numbers*. 2nd ed. Milwaukee, WI: Rethinking Schools.

Harste, Jerome C. 2014. "The Art of Learning to Be Critically Literate." *Language Arts* 92(2): 90–102.

Harvey, Stephanie. 2000. *Strategies That Work: Teaching Comprehension to Enhance Understanding*. Portland, ME: Stenhouse.

Heffernan, Margaret. 2012. "Dare to Disagree." TED Global. https://www.ted.com/talks/margaret_heffernan_dare_to_disagree.

Huyck, David, and Sarah Park Dahlen. 2019. "Diversity in Children's Books 2018" (http://sarahpark.com/) blog, June 19. Created in consultation with Edith Campbell, Molly Beth Griffin, K. T. Horning, Debbie Reese, Ebony Elizabeth Thomas, and Madeline Tyner, with statistics compiled by the Cooperative Children's Book Center, School of Education, University of Wisconsin-Madison: http://ccbc.education.wisc.edu/books/pcstats.asp. Retrieved from https://readingspark.wordpress.com/2019/06/19/picture-this -diversity-in-childrens-books-2018-infographic/.

Hyde, Arthur. 2006. *Comprehending Math: Adapting Reading Strategies to Mathematics, K–6.* Portsmouth, NH: Heinemann.

Johnston, Peter H. 2012. *Opening Minds: Using Language to Change Lives.* Portland, ME: Stenhouse.

Kay, Matthew. 2018. *Not Light, but Fire: How to Lead Meaningful Race Conversations in the Classroom.* Portsmouth, NH: Stenhouse.

Kazemi, Elham, and Allison Hintz. 2014. *Intentional Talk: How to Structure and Lead Productive Mathematical Discussions.* Portland, ME: Stenhouse.

Kelly, Sean. 2008. "Race, Social Class, and Student Engagement in Middle School English Classrooms." *Social Science Research* 37 (2): 434–448.

Kohl, Herbert. 1995. *I Won't Learn from You: And Other Thoughts on Creative Maladjustment.* New York: The New Press.

Kohn, Alfie. 2013. "A Dozen Essential Guidelines for Educators." Blog. https://www.alfiekohn.org/blogs/dozen-essential-guidelines-educators/.

Kucer, Stephen. 2005. *Dimensions of Literacy: A Conceptual Base for Teaching Reading and Writing in School Settings.* 2nd ed. Mahwah, NJ: Lawrence Erlbaum.

Lingard, Bob, Debra Hayes, and Martin Mills. 2003. "Teachers and Productive Pedagogies: Contextualising, Conceptualising, Utilising." *Pedagogy, Culture and Society* 11 (3): 399–424.

Luzniak, Chris. 2019. *Up for Debate! Exploring Math Through Argument, Grades 6–12.* Portsmouth, NH: Stenhouse.

McAfee Brown, Robert. 1984. *Unexpected News: Reading the Bible with Third World Eyes.* Louisville, KY: Westminster John Knox Press.

Nichols, Maria. 2006. *Comprehension Through Conversation: The Power of Purposeful Talk in the Reading Workshop.* Portsmouth, NH: Heinemann.

Nystrand, Martin. 1997. *Opening Dialogue: Understanding the Dynamics of Language and Learning in the English Classroom.* New York: Teachers College Press.

O'Connor, Catherine, Sarah Michaels, Suzanne Chapin, and Allen G. Harbaugh. 2017. "The Silent and the Vocal: Participation and Learning in Whole-Class Discussion." *Learning and Instruction* 48:5–13.

Paley, Vivian. 1986. "On Listening to What Children Say." *Harvard Educational Review* 56 (2): 122–131.

Peterson, Bob. 2013. "Teaching Math Across the Curriculum." In *Rethinking Mathematics: Teaching Social Justice by the Numbers*, 2nd ed., ed. Eric (Rico) Gutstein and Bob Peterson. Milwaukee, WI: Rethinking Schools.

Peterson, Ralph and Maryann Eeds. 2007. *Grand Conversations: Literature Groups in Action*. New York: Scholastic Teaching Resources.

Project Zero. 2015. "See, Think, Wonder." Harvard Graduate School of Education. http://pz.harvard.edu/resources/see-think-wonder-at.

Pranikoff, Kara. 2017. *Teaching Talk: A Practical Guide to Fostering Student Thinking and Conversation*. Portsmouth, NH: Heinemann.

Raban, Bridie. 2001. "Talking to Think, Learn and Teach." In *Talking Classrooms: Shaping Children's Learning Through Oral Language*, ed. Patricia G. Smith. Newark, DE: International Reading Association.

Ray, Katie Wood, and Lisa B. Cleaveland. 2004. *About the Authors: Writing Workshop with Our Youngest Writers*. Portsmouth, NH: Heinemann.

Ringgold, Faith. 1990. *Tar Beach Two* [Silkscreen on Silk]. Philadelphia Museum of Art, Philadelphia, PA.

Russell, Susan Jo, Deborah Schifter, and Virginia Bastable. 2011. *Connecting Arithmetic to Algebra: Strategies for Building Algebraic Thinking in the Elementary Grades*. Portsmouth, NH: Heinemann.

Russell, Susan Jo, Deborah Schifter, Reva Kasman, Virginia Bastable, and Traci Higgins. 2017. *But Why Does It Work? Mathematical Argument in the Elementary Classroom*. Portsmouth, NH: Heinemann.

Serravallo, Jennifer. 2010. *Teaching Reading in Small Groups: Differentiated Instruction for Building Strategic, Independent Readers*. Portsmouth, NH: Heinemann.

Small, Marian. 2017. *Good Questions: Great Ways to Differentiate Mathematics Instruction in the Standards-Based Classroom*. New York: Teachers College Press.

———. 2019. *Understanding the Math We Teach and How to Teach It, K–8*. Portsmouth, NH: Stenhouse.

Smith, Margaret S., Elizabeth K. Hughes, Randi A. Engle, and Mary Kay Stein. 2009. "Orchestrating Discussions." *Mathematics Teaching in the Middle School* 14 (9): 548–556.

Teaching Channel. 2019. "Increasing Participation with Talk Moves." January 1, 2020. Video, 1.53. https://library.teachingchannel.org/landing-page?mediaid=zyvLAzcw&playerid=G5XelQfj

Teaching Tolerance. 2019. "Social Justice Standards: A Framework for Anti-Bias Education." Teaching Tolerance. https://www.tolerance.org/frameworks/social-justice-standards.

Thompson, Pat. 2002. *Schooling the Rustbelt Kids: Making the Difference in Changing Times*. Crows Nest NSW, Australia: Allen & Unwin.

Vasquez, Vivian. 2003. *Negotiating Critical Literacies with Young Children*. Mahwah, NJ: Lawrence Erlbaum.

———. 2017. "Take Fake News by the Reins." By Jay Sullivan. *Forbes Magazine*, June 22. https://www.forbes.com/sites/jaysullivan/2017/06/22/take-fake-news-by-the-reins.

Vasquez, Vivian, Hillary Janks, and Barbara Comber. 2019. "Critical Literacy as a Way of Being and Doing." *Language Arts* 96 (5): 300–311.

Wagenschein, Martin. 1970. *Ursprüngliches Verstehen und exaktes Denken*, I–II [*Original understanding and exact thinking*, vol. 1–2]. Translated by Christof Weber. Stuttgart, Germany: Klett Verlag, 1970.

Whitin, David J., and Phyllis E. Whitin. 2011. *Learning to Read the Numbers: Integrating Critical Literacy and Critical Numeracy in K–8 Classrooms*. New York: Routledge and the National Council of Teachers of English.

Yorio, Kara. 2018. "#OwnVoices Not Familiar to All." *School Library Journal*, October 24. https://www.slj.com/?detailStory=ownvoices-not-familiar-all.

Zager, Tracy Johnston. 2017. *Becoming the Math Teacher You Wish You'd Had: Ideas and Strategies from Vibrant Classrooms*. Portland, ME: Stenhouse.

Avi. 2003. *The Secret School*. Boston, MA: HMH Books for Young Readers.

Bildner, Phil. 2015. *Marvelous Cornelius: Hurricane Katrina and the Spirit of New Orleans*. San Francisco, CA: Chronicle Books.

Bunting, Eve. 1999. *A Picnic in October*. Boston, MA: HMH Books for Young Readers.

Catalanotto, Peter. 2001. *Emily's Art*. New York: Simon and Schuster.

Cowley, Joy. 2005. *Chameleon, Chameleon*. New York: Scholastic.

Craighead George, Jean. 2014. *Galapagos George*. New York: HarperCollins.

Crews, Donald. 1991. *Bigmama's*. New York: Greenwillow Books.

Graham, Bob. 2017. *How to Heal a Broken Wing*. Somerville, MA: Candlewick.

Himes, Rachel. 2017. *Princess and the Peas*. Watertown, MA: Charlesbridge.

Janeczko, Paul. 2001. *Dirty Laundry Pile*. New York: HarperCollins.

Katz, Karen. 2002. *The Colors of Us*. New York: Henry Holt.

Keats, Ezra Jack. 1967. *Peter's Chair*. New York: Puffin Books.

Khan, Rukhsana. 2010. *Big Red Lollipop*. New York: Viking.

Lee, Suzy. 2008. *Wave*. San Francisco, CA: Chronicle Books.

Lester, Helen. 1996. *Three Cheers for Tacky*. Boston, MA: HMH Books for Young Readers.

Medina, Meg. 2015. *Mango, Abuela, and Me*. Somerville, MA: Candlewick.

Rylant, Cynthia. 1993. *When I Was Young in the Mountains*. New York: Puffin Books.

Wells, Rosemary. 1997. *Bunny Cakes*. New York: Viking.

Williams, Vera B. 1982. *A Chair for My Mother*. New York: Greenwillow Books.

Wyeth, Sharon Dennis. 2002. *Something Beautiful*. New York: Random House Children's Books.

Yang, Kelly. 2018. *Front Desk*. New York: Arthur A. Levine Books.

A

academic achievement, 11
action, inviting students to take, 189, 205–206, 206f.
agency, 8, 137
agreements, 118–121, 128–129. *See also* disagreements
ambiguity
  disagreements in math and, 142
  guided practice following a micro-lesson and, 47
  planning for and launching a Hands-Down Conversation and, 23–24
  play and, 132–134
anchor charts, 48–49, 48f, 71.
  answer-performing hand-raising and, 8
  listening self of teachers during Hands-Down Conversations and, 34
  overview, 14
argument construction. *See also* debatable ideas; debates; disagreements; reasoning, supporting
  math learning and, 141–147, 143f, 146f
  overview, 137
  planning Hands-Down Conversations that nurture, 138–140, 140f

B

background knowledge, 89–91
balancing talking and listening in conversations, 70–73, 74–75. *See also* listening
Barlow, Angela, 137
Bastable, Virginia, 179

Becoming the Math Teacher You Wish You'd Had (Zager), 173, 179
Bigmama's (Crews), 166
Big Red Lollipop (Khan), 134
Bildner, Phil, 107
Bishop, Rudine Sims, 166
Bragdon, Pagan, 190, 190f, 193–211
Buckley, Mary Anne, 41–42
Bunny Cakes (Wells), 157, 168
Bunting, Eve, 166
But Why Does It Work? Mathematical Argument in the Elementary Classroom (Russell, Schifter, Kasman, Bastable, & Higgins), 179

C

Calkins, Lucy, 9
Carpenter, Thomas P., 179
Catalanotto, Peter, 195–196
Celebrate Struggle and Uncertainty facilitation move, 38t
celebrating struggle, 31f, 115–116, 115f
Cendejas, Yolanda Corado, 4, 105, 164
Chair for my Mother, A (Williams), 8
Chameleon, Chameleon (Cowley), 149, 151–154
Chapin, Suzanne, 16
Chopra, Sanya, 105, 164
Choral Counting & Counting Collections (eds. Franke, Kazemi, & Turrou), 79
Clarify facilitation move, 38t
  changes of teacher/facilitator role over time and, 31f, 115–116, 115f

clarifying information, 31f, 115–116, 115f
clarifying understanding, 64–65
  micro-lessons that address, 102–103
clarity in expressing thoughts and ideas, 78–83, 92–93.
Classroom Discussions in Math (Chapin, O'Connor, & Anderson), 9
Colors of Us, The (Katz), 187
Comber, Barbara, 186, 192
community, Hands-Down Conversation.
  balancing conversations with content and, 26–27, 26f
  overview, 5–6
  shifting to, 9–19, 10f, 12f
  turn and talks and, 62
compliance, 8
Comprehension Through Conversation (Nichols), 53, 114–115, 149
conjecture development. *See also* theory testing and development
  overview, 158t, 160
  theory-making in literacy and, 167, 168–171
  theory-making in math and, 175–176
conjecture testing and revision, 158t. *See also* conjecture development; theory testing and development
Conjecture Wall, 159
Connecting Arithmetic to Algebra (Russell, Schifter, & Bastable), 179
connection
  listening and linking ideas and, 94–99, 95f, 96f, 98f

connection, *cont.*
micro-lessons that address, 100–111
quiet students and, 16
content
balancing with conversations, 26–27, 26f
disagreements and, 138–140, 140f, 141–143, 148–149
engaging with the world and, 189, 194, 199–201
literacy learning and, 148–149, 165–167, 194
math learning and, 141–143, 172–173, 199–201
speaking and listening skills and, 27
theory testing and development and, 163, 165–167, 172–173
Conversation Club structure
balancing conversations with content and, 71
creating micro-lessons and, 130
guided practice following a micro-lesson and, 46–47, 47f
micro-lessons that address, 68–69
conversation maps
creating micro-lessons and, 130
teacher roles and, 33–34, 33f
template for, 219
Counting Collections, 78–79, 79f, 82
Cowley, Joy, 149
Crews, Donald, 166
"Critical Literacy as a Way of Being and Doing" (Vasquez, Janks, & Comber), 186
crosstalk, 57
curiosity
micro-lessons that address, 104–105
overview, 20–23, 22f
planning Hands-Down Conversations that nurture disagreement and, 139
play and, 132–134

D

Dahlen, Sarah Park, 184
Danielson, Christopher, 141–142
"Dare to Disagree" TED talk (Heffernan), 136
debatable ideas. *See also* argument construction; debates; disagreements
disagreements and, 138–139, 151–154
literacy learning and, 151–154
planning for and launching a Hands-Down Conversation and, 23–24, 24t, 138–139
debates, 106–107, 118–121. *See also* argument construction; debatable ideas; disagreements; reasoning, supporting
decision-making, 3, 23–24, 24t–25t
Dillane, Mary Beth, 13–14, 51
disagreements. *See also* argument construction; debatable ideas; debates; reasoning, supporting
listening self of teachers during Hands-Down Conversations and, 34–35
literacy learning and, 147–154, 150f
math learning and, 141–147, 143f, 146f
micro-lessons that address, 106–107, 118–121, 128–129
overview, 136, 137, 154
planning Hands-Down Conversations that nurture, 138–140, 140f, 155
speaking self of teachers and, 36
summarizing and, 128–129
distractions, 84–85
"Diversity in Children's Books 2018" (Dahlen), 184
"Dozen Essential Guidelines for Educators, A" (Kohn), 29

E

Eeds, Maryann, 9
Ehrenworth, Mary, 136

Emdin, Christopher, 17
Emily's Art (Catalanotto), 191, 195–196
English learners, 11
Erikson Institute Early Math Collaborative, 141–142
evidence to support ideas, 86–91

F

facilitation moves. *See also* micro-lessons
guided practice following a micro-lesson and, 46–47, 47f
speaking self of teachers during Hands-Down Conversations and, 36, 37t–39t
Focus (or Stay on Topic)
crosstalk and, 57
interruptions and, 57, 70–71, 74–75
micro-lessons that address, 84–85, 126–127
overview, 37t
shifting topics, 126
For White Folks Who Teach in the Hood . . . And the Rest of Y'all Too (Emdin), 17
Franke, Megan L., 79, 179
Freire, Paulo, 7, 10
Friend, Kelsey, 22f, 139, 140f
Front Desk (Yang), 166, 167

G

Galapagos George (George), 112–113
Gallas, Karen, 156, 173–174
George, Jean Craighead, 112
goal setting
disagreements and, 141
engaging with the world and, 189, 194, 199–200
literacy learning and, 165–167, 194
math learning and, 141, 199–200
micro-lessons that address, 76–77
theory testing and development and, 165–167

Good Questions (Small), 144
Graham, Bob, 51–52
Greenstein, Ilana, 192
growing ideas, 112–117, 115*f*, 118–
131. *See also* ideas, talking
about; linking ideas
guided practice following a micro-
lesson, 46–47, 47*f*

H

hand-raising, 8–9
Harbaugh, Allen G., 16
Harvey, Stephanie, 160
Heffernan, Margaret, 136
Higgins, Traci, 179
Himes, Rachel, 125
Hintz, Allison, 9
How Many? (Danielson), 141–142
How to Heal a Broken Wing
(Graham), 51–52
Huyck, David, 184

I

ideas, revising, 171
ideas-in-process, 14–15
information processing, 15–16
Initiate-Respond-Evaluate (IRE)
pattern of discourse, 8–9,
11–12
Intentional Talk (Kazemi & Hintz), 9
intentional talking and listening
communities, 9–10, 10*f*, 12*f*,
13*f*. *See also* community,
Hands-Down Conversation
interactive read-alouds, 167–168.
See also read-alouds
interruptions, 57, 70–71, 74–75

J

Janks, Hillary, 186, 192
Johnston, Peter, 21, 39
journals, talking about, 73
journey, conversations as, 124–127

K

Katz, Karen, 187
Kay, Matthew, 186

Kazemi, Elham, 9, 79
Keats, Ezra Jack, 24*t*
keeping a conversation going,
72–73, 84–85, 126–127.
See also silences during
conversations; starting
conversations
Kneale, George, 136
Kohn, Alfie, 29, 57
Kucer, Stephen, 137

L

language, 17
launching a Hands-Down
Conversation. *See also* Hands-
Down Conversations in
general
how to launch, 57, 119, 145, 151,
163, 168–169, 175–176, 189,
197–198, 202
overview, 23–24, 24*t*–25*t*,
134–135, 168–170, 175–176,
197–199, 202–208
single-word launches, 23–24, 25*t*
types of launch, 24–25, 138–139
Learning to Read the Numbers
(Whitin & Whitin), 210
lessons, 5–6, 27. *See also*
micro-lessons
Lester, Helen, 195–196
Levi, Linda, 179
linking ideas, 94–99, 95*f*, 96*f*, 98*f*,
100–111. *See also* growing
ideas; ideas, talking about
listening. *See also* balancing talking
and listening in conversations;
Paraphrase or Ask Clarifying
Questions facilitation move;
changes of teacher/facilitator role
over time and, 31*f*, 115–116,
115*f*
conversation maps and, 33–34,
33*f*
creating micro-lessons and, 130
engaging with the world and,
187*t*–188*t*, 192

guided practice following a
micro-lesson and, 46–47
linking ideas and, 94–99, 95*f*,
96*f*, 98*f*
listening self of teachers during
Hands-Down Conversations
and, 34–35
micro-lessons that address, 64–65
overview, 3
physical self of teachers during
Hands-Down Conversations
and, 30–31
planning for and launching a
Hands-Down Conversation
and, 23–24
quiet students and, 15–16
speaking and listening skills and,
27
teacher roles and, 13
Literacy Continuum (Fountas &
Pinnell), 148, 165–166, 194
Luzniak, Chris, 144

M

Mango, Abuela, and Me (Medina),
129
Marvelous Cornelius (Bildner), 107
McCrory, Michael, 137
meaning construction
argumentation and, 137
co-construction, 81
hand-raising and, 8
ideas-in-process and, 14–15
quiet students and, 16
Michaels, Sarah, 16
micro-lessons. *See also* facilitation
moves; lessons;
beginning with students, 50–55,
51*f*
creating, 130–131
decisions regarding which and
when to use, 42–43
facilitation moves and, 36,
37*t*–39*t*
list of, 213–218
overview, 5–6, 40–42, 44–45,
213–218

micro-lessons, *cont.*
  planning for Hands-Down conversations and, 134
  speaking and listening skills and, 27
  structure of, 44–49, 47f, 48f
  talking about ideas and, 78–83
Miner, Steve, 35
mistakes, 22–23
Mundy, Jess, 12

N

natural-sounding talk, 17
Nichols, Maria, 53, 114, 149
notetaking
  balancing talking and listening in conversations and, 75
  conversation maps and, 33–34, 33f
  creating micro-lessons and, 130
  overview, 30–31, 34, 57
  staying focused on the topic and, 85
  transcribing dialogue, 32, 32f, 130
Not Light, But Fire (Kay), 186

O

O'Connor, Catherine, 16
off-topic comments, 84–85, 126, 126–127
"On Listening to What the Children Say" (Paley), 20
open-mindedness, 137
opinions, 118–121. *See also* disagreements; ideas, talking about; theory testing and development
"Orchestrating Discussions" (Smith, Hughes, Engle, & Stein), 143
ownership, 3, 128–129

P

Paley, Vivian, 20
Paraphrase or Ask Clarifying Questions facilitation move, 38t, 64–65, 100, 100–101

participation in classroom discourse. *See also* student roles; talking in conversations; teacher roles; voices in conversations
  changes of over time, 31f, 115–116, 115f
  conversation maps and, 33–34, 33f
  micro-lessons that address, 58–59, 74–75
  overview, 11–12
patterns, noticing, 158t, 161–162. *See also* theory testing and development
Pedagogy of the Oppressed (Freire), 10
perspectives
  argumentation and, 137
  disagreements in literacy and, 149–150
  theory-making in literacy and, 167, 169–170
  theory-making in math and, 172, 173–174
Peter's Chair (Keats), 24t, 157, 158t
Peterson, Bob, 183–184
Peterson, Ralph, 9
Picnic in October, A (Bunting), 166, 169–170
play, 132–134
poverty, 11
previous experiences, 89–91
Princess and the Peas (Himes), 125

Q

questioning
  engaging with the world through math, 202–205, 204f, 205f
  play and, 132–134
quiet students
  micro-lessons that address, 68–69, 74–75
  shifting to a Hands-Down Conversation community and, 15–16
  turn and talks and, 105

R

Raban, Bridie, 81
read-alouds
  disagreements in literacy and, 149
  planning for and launching a Hands-Down Conversation and, 23–24
  theory-making in literacy and, 167–168
reasoning, supporting. *See also* argument construction; disagreements
  disagreements in math and, 145–147
  micro-lessons that address, 86–91, 120–121
  refuting a claim and, 120
reflection, 48, 130
reinforcing micro-lessons, 48. *See also* anchor charts; reflection
resistance, 16
Rethinking Mathematics (Gutstein & Peterson), 199–200
Rethinking Schools, 193
revising ideas
  micro-lessons that address, 110–111
  theory-making in literacy and, 171
  theory-making in math and, 178–179
Ringgold, Faith, 127
risk-taking, intellectual, 137
River Cottage Meat Book, The (Fearnley-Whittingstall), 49
Rogers, Ellen, 104
Russell, Susan Jo, 179
Rylant, Cynthia, 166

S

Same or Different routine, 69, 106–107
Schifter, Deborah, 179
Secret School, The (Avi), 87, 91
sentence frames and sentence starters, 17–18

Serravallo, Jennifer, 9, 68, 165
Sheeran, Ed, 7
shifting topics, 126–127
"signpost" language, 126–127. See also journey, conversations as
silences during conversations, 58–59, 72–73, 74–75. See also balancing talking and listening in conversations; participation in classroom discourse; starting conversations
"Silent and the Vocal, The" (O'Connor, Michaels, Chapin, & Harbaugh), 16
silent students
  micro-lessons that address, 68–69, 74–75
  shifting to a Hands-Down Conversation community and, 15–16
  turn and talks and, 105
Small, Marian, 142, 144, 200
small-group conversations, 68–69
socioeconomic status, 11
Something Beautiful (Wyeth), 4–5, 25t
staying focused on the topic, 84–85, 126–127
Stewart, Alice, 136
struggle, celebrating. See celebrating struggle
student quotes, 23–24, 25t
student roles. See also voices in conversations;
  balancing conversations with content and, 26–27, 26f
  changes of over time, 31f, 115–116, 115f
  disagreements in literacy and, 149–150
  disagreements in math and, 143–144
  listening self of teachers during Hands-Down Conversations and, 34–35

physical self of teachers during Hands-Down Conversations and, 30–34, 32f, 33f
quiet students, 15–16
shifting to a Hands-Down Conversation community and, 10–19, 10f, 12f, 13f
speaking self of teachers during Hands-Down Conversations and, 36, 37t–39t
theory-making in literacy and, 167
theory-making in math and, 172, 173–174
Summarize facilitation move
  changes of teacher/facilitator role over time and, 31f, 115–116, 115f
  micro-lessons that address, 128–129
  overview, 39t
synthesizing, 31f, 115–116, 115f

T

thoughts and ideas; ideas, talking about; listening; voices in conversations;
  guided practice following a micro-lesson and, 46–47, 47f
  physical self of teachers during Hands-Down Conversations and, 30–31
  shifting to a Hands-Down Conversation community and, 10–19, 10f, 12f, 13f
  speaking and listening skills and, 27
  speaking self of teachers during Hands-Down Conversations and, 36, 37t–39t
  wait time before, 58–59
Talking Their Way into Science (Gallas), 156
talk partners, 61. See also Turn and Talk facilitation move
Tar Beach 2 (Ringgold), 127

teacher roles. See also voices in conversations;
  balancing conversations with content and, 26–27, 26f
  changes of over time, 31f, 115–116, 115f
  curious stance and, 21–23
  decisions regarding, 29–30
  engaging with the world and, 185–186
  listening self and, 34–35
  physical self and, 30–34, 32f, 33f
  reflecting on, 39
  shifting to a Hands-Down Conversation community and, 10–19, 10f, 12f, 13f
  speaking self and, 36, 37t–39t
teacher's voice, 3–4
Teachers as Cultural Workers (Freire), 7
Teaching Readers in Small Groups (Serravallo), 165
Teaching Tolerance, 193
text selection and immersion
  disagreements and, 138, 141–143, 144, 148–149, 150, 150f
  engaging with the world and, 189, 195–197, 200–202
  literacy learning and, 148–149, 150, 150f, 167–168, 195–197
  math learning and, 141–143, 144, 175, 200–202
  planning for and launching a Hands-Down Conversation and, 138
  theory testing and development and, 161–162, 163, 167–168, 175, 180
theory testing and development
  keeping track of theories, 159
  literacy learning and, 165–172
  math learning and, 172–179, 177f, 179–180
  micro-lessons that address, 118–131
Thinking Mathematically (Carpenter, Franke, & Levi), 179

Thompson, Pat, 18
Three Cheers for Tacky (Lester), 191, 195, 195–196
transcribing dialogue, 32, 32f, 130. *See also* notetaking
Turn and Talk facilitation move
  creating micro-lessons and, 130
  guided practice following a micro-lesson and, 46–47, 47f
  micro-lessons that address, 60–65
  overview, 37t
turn-taking in conversations, 70–71, 74–75
Turrou, Angela Chan, 79
Tutu, Desmond, 181

U

uncertainty
  becoming comfortable with, 22–23
  planning Hands-Down Conversations that nurture disagreement and, 138

Understanding the Math We Teach and How to Teach It, K–8 (Small), 142, 200
Up for Debate! Exploring Math Through Argument (Luzniak), 144

V

"Vacuum Cleaner's Revenge, The" (Janeczko), 85
Vasquez, Vivian, 159, 182, 186, 192, 195–196, 201
voices in conversations. *See also* student roles; talking in conversations; teacher roles
  micro-lessons that address, 68–71, 74–75
  overview, 3–4
  quiet students and, 15–16
  shifting to a Hands-Down Conversation community and, 10–19, 10f, 12f

W

Wagenschein, Martin, 15
What/Why/How structure, 46
When I Was Young in the Mountains (Rylant), 166
Which One Doesn't Belong? (Danielson), 141–142
"Which One Doesn't Belong?" routines, 13–14, 13f
Whitin, David J., 184
Whitin, Phyllis E., 184
Williams, Vera B., 8
working theories, 23–24, 25t. *See also* theory testing and development
Wyeth, Sharon Dennis, 4, 25t
Y
Yang, Kelly, 166

Z

Zager, Tracy Johnston, 49, 173, 179